COLLINS

SPORTSWATCHER'S**GUIDE**

First published for Marks and Spencer 1993
by HarperCollins*Publishers* London

This edition published in 1994 by
CollinsWillow
an imprint of HarperCollins*Publishers*
London

ISBN 0 00 218467 2

Designed by Bev Speight
Illustrations by Lynda Payne

Cover photographs by Allsport

Printed and bound in Hong Kong

COLLINS

SPORTS WATCHER'S

GUIDE

PAUL WADE
Foreword by Sebastian Coe

CollinsWillow
An Imprint of HarperCollinsPublishers

Sportswatching provides easy reference to each sport, so that you can consult the book quickly and easily as you watch a new sport for the first time, or when you have a question about a sport you are watching for the hundredth time!

Each sport is listed in alphabetical order in the table of contents. Several sports are listed under popular names – Soccer, for instance, is also listed under Football, but each refers to the same pages in the book.

A few entries do not appear in alphabetical order in the book itself. For instance, Powerlifting is a weightlifting technique, so it follows right after its 'parent' sport. Similarly, Pool and Billiards are found under Snooker.

Although most sports are played by both men and women, we often refer to 'he' or 'him' in the text. This is for brevity rather than bias.

In this book you will find out:

- where the sport takes place

- the equipment the players use

- how they win

- what the basic rules are

- what skills are required by top-class performers

- what tactics are required by top-class performers

- the words that TV commentators use to describe the sport.

Football (Rugby League)	152	Racing (Horse)	100
Football (Rugby Union)	158	Rallying	142
Golf	82	Relays (Athletics)	10
Greyhound Racing	87	Rhythmic Gymnastics	95
Gridiron Football	68	Rowing	148
Gymnastics	90	Rugby League	152
Hammer Throwing	15	Rugby Union	158
Heptathlon	11	Running	8
High Jump	14	Sailing	164
Hockey (Field)	96	Shot Put	15
Hockey (Ice)	106	Show Jumping	60
Horse Racing	100	Skating	111
Hurdling (Athletics)	16	Skiing	170
Hurdling (Horse Racing)	100	Ski Jumping	178
Indycar Racing	140	Snooker	180
Javelin	15	Soccer	74
Judo	121	Speed Skating	116
Karate	124	Speed Skiing	175
Karting	145	Speedway	130
Kayaking	41	Sprinting	10
Ice Hockey	106	Squash	186
Ice Skating	111	Steeplechase (Athletics)	16
Lawn Bowls	31	Steeplechase (Horse Racing)	100
Long Distance Running	13	Sumo	125
Long Jump	14	Swimming	188
Luge	118	Synchronized Swimming	192
Marathon	13	Table Tennis	196
Martial Arts	120	Taekwondo	124
Middle Distance Running	12	Tennis	200
Monster Truck Racing	144	Tenpin Bowling	31
Motocross	130	Three-day Event	60
Motorcycling	126	Track and Field Athletics	8
Motor Racing	132	Triathlon	206
Motor Rallying	142	Triple Jump	14
Mountain Biking	56	Truck Racing	145
National Hunt Racing	100	Volleyball	207
Netball	146	Walking	13
Nordic Skiing	176	Water Polo	194
Pentathlon	11	Waterskiing	210
Pole Vault	14	Weightlifting	214
Pool	185	Wrestling	220
Powerlifting	218	Yachting	164

Olympic medallists: Nicola Fairbrother (top left), Linford Christie (top right), Chris Boardman (bottom left) and Steve Redgrave (bottom right).

FOREWORD

Sportswatching is the ideal companion for both newcomers to a sport and veteran fans. There is little doubt that the growth in the coverage of sport on television encourages more youngsters to try new sports. Even parents and grandparents are inspired to participate and take on new challenges when they see the party-like atmosphere of, for example, the London Marathon.

Every sport has its own set of rules and skills, tactics and jargon. *Sportswatching* helps you to understand the background against which today's stars perform. Youngsters learn by example, so sports stars have to be well-behaved as well as successful. At the same time, their best strokes, throws, kicks or jumps are imitated by thousands.

Once inspired, the best youngsters need to progress from local events to county events, then national and even international events. That costs money. Luckily, the Sports Aid Foundation can help. Some of the heroes and heroines in this book were given grants early in their careers. Nicola Fairbrother and Linford Christie, Chris Boardman and Steve Redgrave went on to win Olympic fame. Many others did not, but still did their best and enjoyed the competition and friendship that sport offers to all of us, at whatever level we participate.

Sebastian Coe, OBE MP
Vice Chairman and Trustee
Sports Aid Foundation

The first Olympic champion was a cook called Korebos back in 776BC . . . a far cry from the pressure of modern-day athletics with its electronic timing and scoreboards.

ATHLETICS

TRACK EVENTS DECIDE THE FASTEST HUMAN OVER A SET DISTANCE,
WHILE FIELD EVENTS TEST COMPETITORS' ABILITY TO THROW AND JUMP THE
FURTHEST OR THE HIGHEST. SOME 25 DIFFERENT EVENTS TEST
MEN AND WOMEN TO THEIR LIMITS

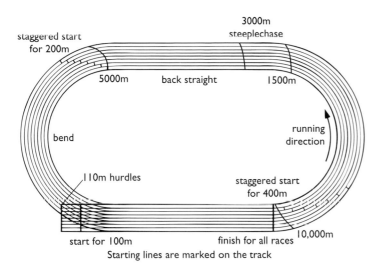

staggered start for 200m

3000m steeplechase

5000m   back straight   1500m

bend

running direction

110m hurdles

staggered start for 400m

start for 100m   finish for all races   10,000m

Starting lines are marked on the track

The standard track is a circuit of 400m (about 440yd) long; with the exception of the mile, world records are only recognized over metric distances. Most new tracks, and certainly all those used for international competition, have an artificial surface. This is usually a rubberized compound that can be used in any climate.

Races are run anti-clockwise, so the inner curve is always to the left of the runner. The exceptions are the short sprint and hurdle races over 100 and 110m, where the straight in front of the main stand is used. The same finishing line is always kept.

Eight lanes, to separate competitors, are marked out on the track. Other marks include those for staggered starts. In races which begin on a bend, like the 200 and 400m, it may look as if some athletes have been given an advantage, starting ahead of their rivals. But to counteract the effect of running wide round a bend, the starting lines in each lane are staggered, and each athlete is starting at an identical distance from the finish.

For the sprint events, starting blocks are fixed to the track. The foot plates are angled and adjustable.

Sprints (100m, 200m, 400m) and Relays (4 x 100m, 4 x 400m)

For the sprint events, starting blocks are fixed to the track. The foot plates are angled and adjustable according to the physique and preferred starting position of the individual athlete. An electrical built-in false start detector indicates whether any athlete's foot has left the blocks fractionally before the gun sounded. Electrical timing is started automatically by a connection to the starter's pistol, and results can be read off from the photo-finish picture to the nearest one-hundredth of a second.

Identifying numbers are allocated at a competition and must always be visible and are usually pinned on the chest and back. Although several runners (notably Africans) have competed successfully barefoot, most athletes wear some sort of special spiked shoe. These vary from event to event and according to individual preference. Spikes can be a maximum of 9mm (about 3/8in) long with up to 11 spikes permitted, all 4mm in diameter. By contrast, in the throwing event or long distance running events, a flat rubber soled shoe is worn.

In the sprint events the winner is the athlete whose torso (not head, arm or leg) crosses the line first. In the relays the winner is the team that finishes first, as long as all three baton change-overs during the race have been accomplished within the permitted zones, each 20m (22yd) long. In sprints and relays a photograph often decides placings in top events.

All sprint races are run in lanes, and the only exception to this is on the last three stages of the 4 x 400m relay, where the teams can break (leave their lanes) for the inside lane on the back straight of the second runner's lap. Otherwise, they cannot set foot in anyone else's running lane during a sprint race.

The races must begin from a stationary start, with the officials satisfied that all competitors are absolutely still before the starting pistol is fired. If an athlete is judged to have moved before the pistol sounds, the starter fires a second shot to signify it was a false start, and the runners have to stop and return to the assembly line. Any runner charged with causing two false starts is automatically disqualified.

The starter for the sprint races gives two commands: the first is 'on your marks' at which the competitors move up to the starting line and settle themselves comfortably in their starting blocks, resting on one knee, with their fingers behind, but not on, the line itself. The second command is 'set!', when the resting knee and hips are lifted and most of the body weight is moved forward onto the arms. Uncomfortable it may be, but after two or three seconds the gun sounds.

For the sprint and hurdle events up to 200m, as well as the long and triple jumps, the speed of the wind is measured by a special gauge. If the following wind is blowing at more than 2m (6ft 6in) per second, then any record time or distance cannot be

ratified as it would be considered wind-assisted.

To reach top speed in a 100m race (about 45kmph [28mph] for men, 40kmph [25mph] for women) from a motionless start takes around 40m (44yd), but even that speed can be held for only 15–20m (16–22yd) before the runner imperceptibly begins to slow again. However, the successful sprinter maintains relaxed form at top speed and in the closing stages tries to avoid tightening up the shoulders, jaw, neck and arms, which would lead to tension and lack of efficiency. Relaxation, under even the tightest competitive situation, is vital, and the correct use of a dip finish can win a close race.

The dip is a deliberate lean forward with the chest a metre or so from the finish in an exaggerated effort to get the torso across the line first.

Decathlon, Heptathlon

These multi-event competitions are two-day mini-tournaments to find the best all-round track and field athlete. Each individual performance in the events earns the athlete a certain number of points. For example, in the men's decathlon, a 100m run in 11.25 seconds earns 806 points, a time of 11.26 seconds earns 804 points, and so on. It is the total number of points from these 10 events which really matters, not the individual placing of the athlete in any of them. Similarly, the women compete in seven events, the heptathlon.

The breakdown of events is as follows:

DECATHLON

1st day – *100m; long jump; shot put; high jump; 400m*

2nd day – *110m hurdles; discus; pole vault; javelin; 1500m*

HEPTATHLON

1st day – *100m hurdles; high jump; shot put; 200m*

2nd day – *long jump; javelin; 800m*

LINFORD CHRISTIE The sight of 32-year-old Linford Christie, wrapped in the British flag, was etched into the minds of television viewers around the world in August 1992. The 1.89m (6ft 2in) tall Londoner confirmed his world class by winning the Olympic 100m in Barcelona in 9.96 seconds. A late starter 'because I was lazy', the Jamaican-born sprinter's stairway to success began with the 1986 European title. He added more European and Commonwealth gold medals as well as two silvers (100m and sprint relay) in the 1988 Seoul Olympics. Remarkably consistent on big occasions, he set a European record of 9.87 seconds when he won the 1993 World Championships.

FASTEST MEN ON EARTH

The fastest 100m race in history took place in Tokyo at the 1991 World Championships. Six men broke the 10 seconds barrier in the final. Carl Lewis (USA) set a new world record of 9.86 seconds; Leroy Burrell (USA) 9.88, Dennis Mitchell (USA) 9.91, Linford Christie (GB) 9.92, Frankie Fredericks (Namibia) 9.95, and Ray Stewart (Jamaica) 9.96 followed him home. Subsequent press reports allege that the track was harder (and therefore faster) than rules allow. The records, however, stand.

A burst of pace off the final bend is often where middle distance races are won and lost.

Middle Distance Events

Middle distance running races are those situated in the no man's land between the sprints and the long distance races: the 800m and 1500m, or mile.

The events are straightforward races, run anti-clockwise on the track. Intermediate times are called by an official timekeeper at the end of each lap, and before the last lap a bell is rung.

The first bend of the 800m is run in lanes to avoid collision at the start, but at the beginning of the back straight, competitors can break for the inside lane.

Although deliberate physical contact or obstruction is forbidden, the sheer speed at which top class athletes are travelling, with each trying to get into the right position, means that the occasional elbow clash or push is inevitable. In an 800m race, for example, the competitors are often running only a few seconds slower than in a 400m race, where they have lane divisions. At 1500m, the pace is relatively slower.

The pacemaker is whoever takes the lead early in the race, dictating how fast the rest of the field will be running. The preferred tactical position is to be just behind the right shoulder of the leader, as it is easier to follow than to lead. So why should anyone want to lead? The answer is that sometimes no one does! Instead, particularly in a 1500m or 1 mile race, the field will almost jog around the first lap with no one wanting to take on the pacemaking role. Anything slower than 60–61 seconds for the first lap of an international 1500m race suggests this reluctance, and the race will instead become a battle of nerves to see who will succumb to the urge to pick up the pace first.

In certain races, usually special invitation events, or races where one or more competitor is hoping to run a record time, a pacemaker or 'rabbit' may be included in the field with the specific task of setting a good speed for the opening lap or two. He then often drops out. Although pacemaking is officially frowned upon, it is difficult to prove the difference between deliberate planned pacemaking and an athlete's individual decision to run the opening laps very fast. Many world records, including Sir Roger Bannister's breaking of the four-minute mile barrier in 1954, have been accomplished with the help of pacemaking.

Once in a while, the pacemaker takes everyone by surprise, moving out into a long lead . . . and then hanging on to win. In the main, however, races for championships are decided in the last 300m (328yd) when the runners make a break for home. Even then, clever runners keep final reserves of energy for the 50m (55yd) sprint to the line, taking the leaders by surprise.

It is wise to drink fluids during a marathon.

Long Distance Events

The long distance events for men are the 5000m (3 miles) and 10,000m (6 miles); for women, the 3000m (2 miles) and 10,000m. Both men and women run the marathon over 42.195km (26 miles 385yd).

Long distance runners have often been innovators in athletics kit, because of the extreme nature of their event. Vests are cut to the minimum, with white preferred as it reflects the sun. Lightweight, brief-cut shorts reduce the chances of leg chafing, as will some dabs of petroleum jelly. Shoes are as light as possible without risking foot injury.

The most common sight in marathons now is the mesh vest, which allows air to flow more freely to the body for cooling purposes on a hot day.

The long distance events are fought out largely on stamina, with each competitor trying to run at a pace which – over the length of the race – will wear down his rivals. The eventual winner of a distance track race up to 10,000m (6 miles) is rarely out of the leading group throughout the race; moreover, international runners are now so fit that the result is sometimes only decided in the final lap at a pace just slightly below sprinting speed. Unless the pace being set is suicidally fast, no athlete with hopes of victory will normally let the leaders get away from him. So watch for the smooth-moving, relaxed runner amongst the leading group. His breathing will not be laboured, and if any gap opens, he will be the first to close it.

In the marathon, because of its relatively greater length, it is possible for a runner to move up through the field and win. The testing time comes between 28 and 36km (18 and 22 miles), the point at which many runners suddenly hit 'the wall'. This is the time when all the glycogen, an energy source in the muscles, has been exhausted, and the body starts to draw instead on its fat reserves for fuel, which can be a painful and tiring experience after two hours of running. There is no such thing as a world record in the marathon as every course is different. Commentators tend to talk about 'world best' times instead.

WALKING

Race walking takes place both on the track and the road, but the major international competition distances are 20km (12½ miles) and 50km (31 miles) on the road, which are Olympic events. The 50km is 8km (5 miles) further than the marathon, so it is the longest race on the Olympic programme. Race walking for women is over 5 and 10km (3 and 6 miles). Rules say that 'walking is a progression by steps so taken that unbroken contact with the ground is maintained'. In other words, the toe of the rear foot must not break contact with the ground until the heel of the advancing foot has touched down. This line between maintaining contact and breaking it can be a very fine one, and judges are appointed to watch the competitors' feet at various stages of a race to ensure that contact is being maintained.

The race walker's hip action, which may appear somewhat eccentric at first sight, has a definite purpose. The wiggle is a deliberate rotating of the hips to bring about a longer stride than is possible in ordinary walking.

The Jumps

HIGH JUMP

Competitors can choose their opening height and can also forego an attempt at any height. But once they have had three successive failures, they are eliminated. The take-off has to be from one foot only, and the run-up can be made from any angle on the semi-circular approach area known as the fan. In case of a tie, placings are decided on the basis of fewer failures. The Fosbury Flop involves a head-first clearance, crossing the bar on the back, and landing on the neck and shoulders. It was first used successfully by 1968 Olympic champion Dick Fosbury.

THE LONG & TRIPLE JUMP

The judges examine the take-off board very closely after an athlete has taken a long or triple jump, looking at the layer of plasticine next to the edge of the board to see whether any spike marks have been made. If so, a red flag is raised and the jump is void. In the long and triple jumps, competitors have a maximum of six trials. Only a one-footed take-off is allowed, with the distance jumped measured from the edge of the take-off board nearest to the sandpit. The jumper aims to get on the board, and as close to the edge as possible on each jump without going right over it.

Just before landing, the jumper shoots out both feet in front of him to gain some extra distance, but he must not overbalance and fall back, as the measurement is taken from the mark made nearest to the take-off board. If he puts a hand back to steady himself, for instance, his hand mark, and not his feet marks, will be measured.

A good jumper must sprint flat-out with head up, not looking for the board. Once in the air some jumpers try to put in a stride in mid-air (hitchkick) while others hang momentarily before swinging their arms and legs forward violently before landing.

For the triple jump (formerly known as the hop, step and jump), the competitor takes off on one foot, lands on the same foot (the hop), takes a long step to land on the other foot (the step) – still on the runway – and then lands on both feet in the sand pit for the jump.

POLE VAULT

This is often described as 'gymnastics on the end of a pole' because the athlete uses a fibreglass pole to lever himself up to and over a metal crossbar. He lets go of the pole at the moment of clearance, and lands on a specially-made landing bed. Only men take part in this event. The runway is usually 45m (50yd) long with a box sunk into the ground for the pole. This is the only event where athletes are allowed to use their own equipment. Once any vaulter has had three consecutive failures, he is eliminated from the event.

If the pole falls forwards and knocks the bar off it would count as a failure, but it is allowed to fall into the pit.

A strip of plasticine or putty shows at once if a jumper's foot was over the board.

The Throws

JAVELIN

Every competitor is allowed six throws taken from a runway 20–25m (22–27yd) long, and the competitor has to release the implement and come to a halt before reaching the white scratch line marking the end of the runway. He must not cross the line, or touch the ground in front of it, otherwise the throw is ruled a foul. The javelin has to land point first, making a mark in the turf even if it does not stick in, to be declared valid and measured. If it lands flat and makes no mark, the throw is void.

The thrower pulls back the throwing arm four strides before the moment of delivery, and on the final stride brings it through fast for the actual throw, while at the same time trying to flight it; trajectory which is too high or too low will cause it to fall short.

SHOT, DISCUS, HAMMER

The shot is spherical and made of solid metal. The discus is made of wood with a metal rim, a bit like a tiny flying saucer. The hammer consists of three parts: a spherical metal head, a length of wire connected to the head by means of a swivel, and a grip (or handle) connected to the wire by a loop. Gloves for the protection of the hammer thrower's hands are permitted, but not for the discus or shot.

The shot, discus and hammer are all thrown from circles, concrete slabs in the ground. The shot is held under the chin and has to be 'put' rather than thrown by straightening the arm.

In the discus a $1^3/4$ turn technique is normally used, with the thrower gripping the discus in the spreadeagled fingers of one hand. In the shot and discus, throwers must not tape their fingers together to get a better grip, they have to show an official their hands before each throw. In general, hammer throwers, gripping the hammer handle with both hands, swing it around twice to get it moving, then turn three times in the circle to accelerate the hammer and then finally release it.

For good technique in the shot put, watch for a full extension at the waist in delivery, and a long follow-through with the putting hand after delivery. In the discus, watch for a long and loose throwing arm; the further away the discus is from the body during the turn, the faster it is travelling, and the further it should go when released. Likewise with the hammer: its head is kept a long way from the body by use of straight arms as acceleration is gained through the turns. The hammer is swung through an angled plane, low at the back of the circle, high at the front.

Throwing the javelin, one of the oldest and most technically demanding events in athletics.

Hurdle Events

The standard hurdles events are the 110m (120yd) and 400m (440yd) for men and 100m (110yd) and 400m for women. They are really sprint races with an added difficulty – or, rather, 10 added difficulties in the shape of barriers which have to be hurdled by every competitor.

The 3000m (2 mile) steeplechase is a gruelling middle distance event with 28 solid timber barriers, plus seven water jumps to be negotiated in all.

The trailing of a leg around the side of a hurdle, rather than over the top, is not allowed, but there is no limit to the number of hurdles which can be knocked down during the race. In the steeplechase, the runners are allowed to put one foot on top of the barriers when clearing them. It is virtually impossible to clear the water jump without putting one foot on the barrier and then driving off hard. There is no penalty for landing in the water – it only slows the athlete down.

The hurdles are arranged on a staggered start around the first bend of the 400m but each one is the same distance from the starting line, so the athlete who rises first at each flight of hurdles is leading. The main aim is not to hurdle as high as possible, but rather to clear the barriers with speed and efficiency and the minimum of interruption to the running action. Time spent in the air is time wasted, and the top hurdlers skim the top of the barriers. The action involves a fast step-over action of the leading leg. A sideways swing of the rear (or take-off) leg then follows through, lifting the thigh as high as necessary (but no higher) to clear the barrier ahead, and to get back into the normal sprinting action between hurdles as quickly as possible.

Cross-country

Cross-country races are held over open country to provide competition on a constantly varying terrain, challenging both in gradient and surface. Most international-class races for men are staged on courses approximately 8–12km (4–7 miles) long, and for women 3–5km (2–3 miles), with the annual world championships taking place each March. In wet conditions, watch for the athlete who appears to glide over the mud rather than get bogged down in it. A relatively fresh runner can be spotted by his ability to produce a high knee lift and vigorous arm drive even on the steep gradient of hills.

Hurdle technique. The same leg leads throughout a sprint race; athletes sometimes change their leading leg in the 400m hurdles.

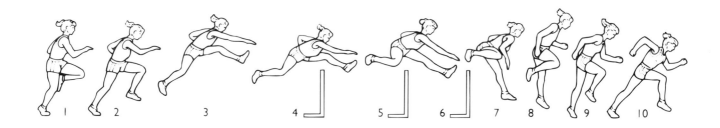

AUSTRALIAN RULES FOOTBALL

ATTRACTING FINALS CROWDS IN EXCESS OF 100,000, THIS IS THE MOST
POPULAR SPECTATOR WINTER SPORT IN THE
SOUTHERN STATES OF AUSTRALIA

The fans expect to see spectacular high marking (catching); bruising body clashes, as no protective clothing is worn; accurate kicks covering in excess of 50m (55yd); high scoring and 100 minutes of non-stop action from the two teams of 18 players plus two substitutes who can go on and off the field. The oval field, which usually doubles as a cricket field, can be up to 180m by 135 (197yd by 148). Four wooden posts stand at each end, with no cross-bars. The inner two posts are the goal posts and the outer two the behind posts. Each post is 6.4m (7yd) apart. A 3m (3¼yd) diameter circle marks the centre of the field and this is enclosed by a 45m (49yd) square. There are further markings in front of the posts for the goal square, 9m (9¾yd) deep.

EQUIPMENT

The ball is oval, like a rugby ball. Sturdy sleeveless guernseys (knitted woollen shirts), shorts, socks and boots are worn, rather like rugby players' uniforms.

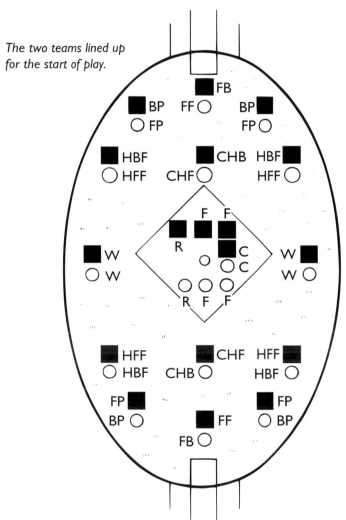

The two teams lined up for the start of play.

FB	full back	CHB	centre half back
FF	full forward	CHF	centre half forward
BP	back pocket	W	wing
FP	forward pocket	C	centre
HBF	half back flanker	F	follower/ruck man
HFF	half forward flanker	R	rover

WINNING

If an attacker kicks the ball between the goal posts a goal (six points) is scored. Any kick at any height counts. A behind (one point) is scored if an attacker kicks the ball between the goal and behind post or if the ball somehow manages to touch a player on its way through the goal posts. If a defender accidentally propels the ball between his own posts, a behind is awarded to the attackers. It is not uncommon for both teams to score in excess of 20 goals in a normal match and as many behinds.

The team with the higher number of points is the winner: e.g.

20 goals (x6) +24 behinds =144 points defeats

22 goals (x6) +11 behinds =143 points

RULES

There are few rules in this flowing game. Players can move the ball by running with it, as long as they bounce or touch it to the ground every 15m (16yd), which can be a pretty skilful move with an oval leather ball! They are allowed to kick the ball and handball (or punch), but throwing the ball is against the rules.

Passing to a team mate is often done by kicking and this produces the characteristic exciting high jump or high mark as players leap to catch the ball. A clean catch gives the player an unimpeded kick. The field umpire gets play under way at the start of each period and after a goal is scored by bouncing the ball in the centre circle where the ruck men try to gain possession.

When a behind is scored, the ball is put into play again by kicking it out of the goal square. Although it looks as if anything goes, free kicks are given for grabbing an opponent above the shoulders or below the knees, and for either not releasing the ball when firmly held or for dropping the ball when tackled.

Lying on the ball, pushing in the back or tripping the man with the ball, or deliberately obstructing the player without the ball – all these are penalized, with a free kick . . . as is time wasting. Punching is forbidden.

A fair tackle of the man with the ball is a shoulder charge, or a hold round the waist.

To complicate matters, some checking or shepherding is allowed. To prevent an opponent from tackling a team mate who has the ball, a player can block him as long as he is within 5m (5½yd) of the ball.

If the ball is kicked out of play on the full, without hitting the ground first, the defender nearest the spot gets a free kick. However, a ball that bounces before going over the boundary line is put back into play by the boundary umpire, who turns his back on the field and hurls it back high over his head after which the players battle for possession.

Time wasting, by arguing with the umpire and similar fouls when free kicks are awarded, is penalized easily – the umpire advances the kick 15m (16yd).

SKILLS & TACTICS

The 18 players each have specific roles. The three forwards are the most creative while the three half forwards have to be elusive.

The three centres need both speed and agility but the three half backs are the spring board needing strength both to clear the ball from the central area and halt attacks. The three full backs must be strong, safe and very reliable as the last line of defence. The stars of the side tend to be a trio that follows the ball all over the field. The ruck or ruck man, usually a very tall player, plus a ruck rover, try to tap and punch the ball to the rover, who then attempts to move the ball around the field.

As the quickest way to score is straight up the middle, the best players tend to be there because this provides the best angle for goal kicking. As goals can be kicked from as far as 50m (about 55yd), play moves quickly. Conversely, in defence the ball is played away from the centre towards the sidelines.

Many of today's teams use the accuracy and fluidity of handball in attack and defence, rather than risk losing possession by kicking. Skilled sides can compensate for their lack of height this way but, despite this, possession changes frequently. There is no offside rule and in good, dry conditions it is a tremendous spectacle to watch; wet conditions, however, can reduce the game to just a muddy kickabout.

Like Gaelic Football and Rugby Football, Australian Rules are direct descendants of the village football matches of the 17th and 18th centuries. A group of cricketers, looking for some winter sport, drew up some rules in the 1850s. The first recorded match between Scotch College and the Melbourne Church of England Grammar School was played over three weekends with 40 players a side. Although Scotch College kicked a goal, the result was a draw. Better rules were written in 1866 and the Victorian Football Association, the governing body of the sport, was set up in 1877.

WORDS

Behind: one point scored when the ball is kicked between the goal posts and behind posts or when the ball touches a player before travelling between the posts **Behind posts:** short posts either side of the goal posts **Checking:** protecting a team mate who has the ball; pushing, shoulder charging or blocking an opponent to prevent tackle **Goal:** six points scored, when the ball is kicked cleanly between goal posts **Goal square:** large rectangle marked out in front of goal posts **Goal umpires:** in their white coats and hats they judge whether a goal or behind has been scored **Handballing:** punching ball out of palm of hand; normal passing, by throwing or passing, is illegal

BADMINTON

THE SPORT BEGAN AS POONA, INVENTED BY BRITISH ARMY OFFICERS IN INDIA,
BUT WAS REALLY ESTABLISHED AT THE DUKE OF BEAUFORT'S COUNTRY
HOUSE AT BADMINTON IN ENGLAND

*B*adminton has some of the overhead powershots of tennis and some of the subtle touches seen in squash. The aim is to volley a shuttlecock back and forth over a 5ft high (1.55m) net with a racket until one player is unable to return it into court.

Like tennis, it can be played by both sexes in singles and doubles. It is unique among racket sports for the ever-changing variety of strokes and the sharp contrast between them. You can smash the shuttle at speeds up to 100mph (160kmph) and in the next stroke caress it over the net with delicate accuracy. The game demands a mastery of deception and tactics, a sprinter's start, a marathon runner's stamina and the sharp reflexes of a panther.

THE COURT

Preferably indoors, the full court is 44ft (13.40m) long by 20ft (6.10m) wide. For singles it is narrower, but the service line goes all the way to the back of the court. There should be a clear space of 30ft (9.14m) above the court.

EQUIPMENT

The lightness and fragility of both racket and shuttle are part of badminton's charm and are the essence of its fast and wristy strokes. Most rackets have metal frames, tightly strung, but weigh no more than 4oz (128g).

The shuttlecock is the most fragile of all the missiles in sport, being basically composed of 16 goose feathers set into a base of domed cork. At the highest level, players sometimes reject a shuttle after a rally or two, and may get through dozens during a match.

WINNING

The first to 15 points wins a game (11 in women's singles) and the first to win two games wins the match. Points can be scored only by the serving side. Service starts from the right-hand half-court. If the rally is won, a point is scored and the server moves to the left-hand court. The same player, alternating sides, continues to serve until a rally is lost. Service then goes to the opponent.

(In doubles, the serve passes to the partner. If a further rally were lost, the serve would pass to the opponents, who continue in the same way.)

The serving side's score is always called first by the umpire: 2–1, 3–1 and then, if the service changes sides, 1–3. The non-server(s) can choose to 'set' in a close game. If the score becomes 13–13, the non-serving side can either play through to 15 points as usual, or decide to play an additional five points, to 18. The non-server also has this choice to make at 14–14, when setting is for three points, to 17. In women's singles, setting is offered at 9–9 or 10–10, for a further three or two points respectively.

RULES

Service must be underarm, with no part of the shuttle above the server's waist and the racket pointing downwards. Both feet must be on the floor within the service area. The receiver must not move before the shuttle is hit, nor take any action that distracts or delays the server.

Players must always hit the shuttle before it hits the floor but must not hit it before it crosses the net, nor touch the net while the shuttle is in play. The shuttle may not be hit twice on the same side of the net, either by the same player or by his partner.

Badminton players need to have greater stamina and agility, strength and flexibility than players of other sports.

The game established by the British aristocracy is now the national sport in Indonesia, the largest country in South East Asia. Thousands play year-round outdoors in local and regional tournaments which produce champion after champion. The greatest of them was Rudy Hartono who won the men's singles title at the All-England Championships eight times between 1968 and 1976. The national team dominates the Thomas Cup, the world team championship.

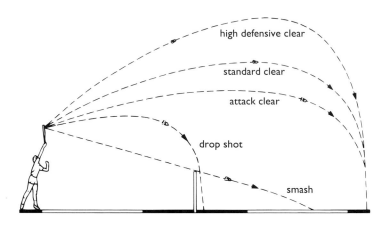

Some of the shots in the armoury of the badminton player.

SKILLS AND TACTICS

Singles

The basic aim in singles is to make an opponent run around the court. Patience and stamina are essential because it can take 10 or 20 strokes to force a weak return or create a vulnerable opening. A smash is then used to try to end the rally. A shuttle decelerates so rapidly that the smash is seldom used from the back of the court except by very powerful players.

Most women lack the power and speed of men, so they cannot finish rallies as decisively. Consequently there are longer, tense battles fluctuating from attack to defence and back to attack. It is a war of attrition in which stamina and concentration matter as much as power.

Women's and Men's Doubles

Positional play here changes rapidly – from side to side when defending, to back and front when attacking. The serves are generally low and to the corners. The receiver tries to meet the shuttle early and hit down or flat to attack. His partner, racket up, waits aggressively at the net, ready to make acrobatic interceptions and dabbing the shuttle down whenever he can.

Mixed Doubles

Delicacy and deception now play a greater part. To prevent the woman being out-gunned by the stronger, faster man, she plays 95 per cent of the game at the net. Though the area she has to cover is small, her task is difficult. Cramped and crouching, she has very little time to decide whether she can intercept effectively or should leave to her partner a shuttle which is travelling twice as fast as it will be when it reaches the man.

With back-and-front play, the sidelines are vulnerable and the man, the sole back-court defender, has to be fast and versatile enough to cover two-thirds of the court.

WORDS

Bird: nickname for the shuttlecock

Clear: overhead stroke hitting shuttle from baseline to baseline, either high (defensive) or flat (attacking)

Dab: shuttle dabbed downwards by net player

Drive: attacking side-arm stroke played flat at the tape height

Drive serve: similar action to low serve, but jab drives shuttle flat and fast

Drop-shot: deceptive overhead stroke hitting shuttle from baseline just

over net

Flick: similar action to low serve, but flicked just above reach of receiver

Lob: underarm clear hit high and deep

Smash: overhead stroke hit downwards powerfully and very steeply

BASEBALL
THIS TRADITIONAL AMERICAN SUMMER GAME IS QUICKER THAN THE EYE,
SO TELEVISION REPLAYS ALLOW VIEWERS TIME TO STUDY
WHAT REALLY TOOK PLACE

A game of strategy and endless permutations between two teams of nine. So difficult to play well and so easy to play for enjoyment, baseball is popular in Latin America and Japan as well as the USA.

Throughout the eight-month season, teams pursue the championship pennant and an ultimate place in the World Series (America's championship playoffs). Individual players also strive for honours in batting, fielding and pitching, the three distinct skills which make up the game. Although baseball stadiums are different sizes, with no uniform distances to the fences, the distances around the bases and from mound to home plate are governed by the same rules.

THE FIELD

This consists of the outfield and square infield, called the diamond. Home plate is a five-sided slab of whitened rubber; canvas bags on the three corners at 90ft (27.4m) intervals mark first, second and third bases. In the middle of the diamond, 60ft 6in (18.4m) from home plate, is the pitcher's mound, approximately 16in (40cm) high.

The playing area is often artificial turf nowadays, but the surface between the bases is dirt, so that players can slide into the base. The vast outfield is surrounded by a fence about 10ft (3m) high. Two lines mark foul territory where any hits do not count, but catches do.

Basic signals of a baseball umpire.

out   safe

time out   strike

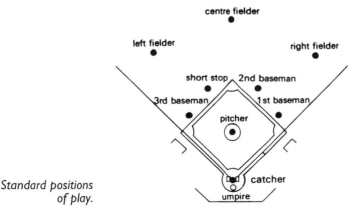

Standard positions of play.

centre fielder

left fielder   right fielder

short stop   2nd baseman

3rd baseman   1st baseman

pitcher

catcher

umpire

EQUIPMENT

A bat about 3ft (1m) long, a ball and a glove made of flexible leather with a webbed pocket between the thumb and first finger are the basic tools of the game.

WINNING

Completing an anti-clockwise circuit of all four bases scores a run. When up at bat, a batter stands at home plate. By hitting the ball safely into fair territory, the batter can run to first base or even further. A single means reaching first base; a double, second base; a triple, third base; and a home run, getting all the way round in one go. Any hit over the fence is automatically a home run, although the batter still jogs round the bases.

Once on base, he is called a runner and must go on to the next base when another runner advances behind him, since two men cannot be on the same base. He may try to steal a base, advancing while the pitcher is delivering the ball. The bases are loaded when a man is on each base.

RULES

A batter can be out in three main ways:
Struck out: Each batter has three strikes before he is out. If a pitch crosses home plate in the strike zone (between the armpits and knees of the batter) and the batter does not swing, that is a strike. Swinging and missing the ball is a strike. The first two foul balls are strikes though subsequent balls hit into foul territory are not counted.
Caught: A ball hit into the air (a fly ball) and caught before hitting the ground.
Off base: Once the ball is hit, a batter must reach base to be safe. He is out when beaten to base by a fielder catching and throwing the ball to the baseman who must be touching the bag. A runner touched with the ball when off base is also out.

A game is made up of nine innings. The visiting team always bats first and once three men are out (irrespective of how many are on bases) the other team bats. When both teams have had three outs, the inning is completed. It is harder to hit than to defend, so the number of runs scored in a game is not very high. Typical scores are 5–3, 7–4 and 3–1. If a team fails to score at all, the winning pitcher has pitched a shutout. An umpire behind home plate judges whether the pitch is good (a strike) or is too high or wide (a ball). Four balls constitute a walk, and the batter goes to first base automatically. He also walks if hit by a pitched ball. Four umpires are stationed around the bases to make decisions, such as whether a runner reaches a base before the ball does.

SKILLS

Batters must judge which pitches to ignore and which will be in the strike zone. Some use sheer strength, often hitting the home runs, others place the ball, using a shorter swing. Fielders are either infielders, who ring the bases, or outfielders. Most outs are at first base, so a first baseman must be sure-handed. The second baseman and shortstop also have to reach balls hit hard and fast into their areas. The third baseman makes long, accurate throws across to first base. All outfield positions need speed and good judgement, to catch fly balls and chase line

drives (on the ground). The catcher, clearly, is a specialist but the pitcher is the most specialized of all. He may use sheer pace (a fast ball) or pitches which swing in the air: the curve moves away from the batter, the drop falls just before reaching the batter, the screwball swings into the batter or the slider, with a late dip away from the batter.

TACTICS

Managers and coaches study where opponents' batters are likely to hit the ball, then place fielders in those spots. The catcher is really the major tactician and he uses coded signs to suggest pitches. The pitcher refuses or agrees with a shake or nod of the head. If the starting pitcher is ineffective or tiring and giving up hits, the coach sends in a relief pitcher.

```
                AMERICAN LEAGUE
Kansas City       000  000  000—0    5   0
Toronto           012  001  31x—8   15   0
   Pichardo, Rasmussen (7) and Mayne; Guz-
man and Borders. W—Guzman, 3-0. L—Pi-
chardo, 0-1. HR—Toronto, T. Ward (2).
Milwaukee         004  000  000—4    7   1
Chicago           100  040  20x—7   13   1
   Boddicker, Maldonado (7), Orosco (8) and
Nilsson, Kmak (8); Stieb, Radinsky (7) and
Fisk, Karkovice (9). W—Stieb, 1-0. L—Bod-
dicker, 0-1. Sv—Radinsky (1). HR—Chicago,
Pasqua (1).
```

Fans follow baseball by reading the box scores (left). These statistical reports show that in the first game, Kansas City were the visitors. Batting first, they failed to score any runs at all. They managed only five hits with no errors. Toronto, the home side, won with one run in the second inning, two in the third, one in the sixth, three in the seventh and one in the eighth. The 'x' in the ninth shows that Toronto did not have to bat in their final inning as they had already won 8–0. Pichardo started pitching for Kansas City, but was replaced by Rasmussen in the seventh; the catcher was Mayne. Juan Guzman pitched a shutout for Toronto, Borders was the catcher. The winning pitcher was Guzman, who had then won all three games in the season; Pichardo lost his only game. Ward scored a home run for Toronto, his second of the season.

WORDS

Bunt: hitting the ball gently to the infield; difficult to do

Error: a mistake, a missed chance of getting a batter out

Grand slam: a home run with bases loaded, making four runs in total

Inning: divided in halves, the top to the visiting team, the bottom to the home team

No-hitter: a pitcher's goal; to give up no safe hits in a game – very rare

Out: the retirement of a batter or runner; three outs end each team's time at bat

Pinch-runner: substitute runner

Strike out: three swings and three misses by the batter; he's out

Basketball appears to be dominated by tall players. However, America's professional league boasts Tyrone Bogues at 5ft 3in (1.6m) as well as 7ft 7in (2.3m) Manute Bol!

BASKETBALL

BASKETBALL ENJOYS A VIGOUR AND CREATIVITY SIMILAR TO THAT OF SOCCER. THE SMALL COURT IS THE SCENE OF NON-STOP ACTION AND CONSTANT SCORING

The fast-action scoring of today's game is quite different to how its inventor, James Naismith, conceived it when he nailed two peach baskets to a balcony at a Massachusetts YMCA in 1892. Each time there was a score, someone had to retrieve the ball with a ladder.

The nations of Eastern Europe present the greatest challenge to the Americans, but none has stood much chance of success against them since the break-up of the Soviet Union.

Basketball is a handling game played by both men and women, with five on each side. They score by tossing the ball through a horizontal hoop 10ft (3.05m) off the floor. This gives a positive edge to tall players and it is not uncommon to find men of 7ft (2.13m) on the court. Much smaller men (and women) with extraordinary skill as play-makers nevertheless prove very effective.

THE COURT

The court is rectangular, with a surface of wood or rubberized composition material. At each end is the target, a metal hoop high above the players. It has a loose string net hanging from it and is fixed to a backboard. The basket protrudes 5ft (1.53m) into the court and the area marked out on the floor under each basket is called the keyhole. No attacking player can stay inside this area for more than three seconds, which helps to keep the game moving.

EQUIPMENT

Other than the court with its baskets and backboards, the individual needs only a pair of athletic shoes with good rubber soles and a simple physical training outfit. The orange ball is slightly larger than a soccer ball and weighs a lot more, nearly 23oz (650g).

Apart from protecting the elbows and knees, with soft material only, a player is not allowed to use any padding.

WINNING

Every time a player shoots the ball into the basket during play, his team gets two points, or three if he is beyond the long-range semi-circle. The ball must go through the hoop from the top and can be bounced off the backboard. A fouled player may be awarded one or more unhindered free throws, taken from the free throw line, each of which is worth one point.

The game is generally in two halves of 20 minutes actual play, though there is now an option of playing four 12-minute quarters, as they do in the US professional game. Extra five-minute periods are played if the score is level at the end of regulation time.

RULES

A squad normally consists of 10 players, but only five are allowed on court at one time. Substitutions can be made at any time and frequently are, to cover injury or exhaustion or for purely tactical reasons. The clock is stopped for these, as it is for 'time-outs', of which each team may take two in each half and one in extra time.

When a team has the ball the players try to move towards the basket by passing or by dribbling the ball, which must be bounced with one hand each time the player takes a step. He must not run with the ball in his hands and as soon as he holds it with two hands he must either shoot or pass the ball.

Attackers who deliberately collide with defenders, or defenders who physically hamper an attacker in the act of shooting, are charged with personal fouls. Once a player has committed five, he can take no further part in the game.

Lesser fouls are known as violations. They are called, for instance, against a player infringing the dribbling rule, or a team that does not leave its own half within 10 seconds of gaining possession, or a player that fails to shoot within 30 seconds (24 under US professional rules).

After a violation, the opposing team is given possession at the point on the sideline nearest the spot where the offence occurred. A team also loses possession if it let the ball go off the court, when the opponents bring the ball back into play at the point where it crossed the line.

SKILLS

Everyone in the team must be able to shoot and to defend. The two forwards and the centre (usually the tallest player) do most of the close shooting, often with spectacular jump shots, where the ball is released high in the air as the attacker leaps above the defence and sometimes above the basket itself. The centre in particular must be extremely good at rebounding – seizing the ball as it bounces off the backboard or the ring after an unsuccessful shot. He is expected to do this at one moment in attack and at the next in defence, at the other end of the court.

The two guards play behind the three forwards. Often smaller and quicker, they are the creative play-makers, who lead the break from defence to attack and whose job it is to pass the ball to the forwards when they are in scoring positions. Speed and deception of dribbling, and accurate passing either in the air or off the ground, are also vital attributes.

TACTICS

A team has three basic attack options. A good passing team, and particularly one with a height disadvantage, may elect to play a slow, patterned game, using a series of different manoeuvres to build up scoring chances. The team takes up as much available time as possible on each offensive movement, since fewer attempted shots mean fewer rebounds that are likely to be grabbed by some of the players from the opposing team.

Tall teams often choose a racehorse style of play, relying almost totally on the fast break. The ball is moved into the attack zone as quickly as possible and the first available shot taken. The team depends on speed to beat the defence, and also height to control rebounds.

Thirdly, a controlled fast break may be used. In this style, a team will advance quickly if the opportunity is there (if the defenders are immediately outnumbered, for example), but may play the slower game if a running opportunity is not present.

There are two fundamental defences: the zone, where a player defends a designated area of the court; and the man-to-man, which involves the close shadowing of an individual opponent. The man-to-man needs five fast defenders and demands greater agility and physical endurance, but is generally thought to be the more effective defence if it can be sustained.

MICHAEL JORDAN Nicknamed 'Air', Jordan dominated the pro game in North America ever since he left North Carolina as the College Player of the Year back in 1984.

His haul of medals and titles is awesome. A member of the US squad that won the Olympic gold medal in Los Angeles, he was immediately named Rookie of the Year after his first season with the Chicago Bulls. Since then this shooting guard averaged over 32pts a game, season after season. In 1990, he piled in 69pts against Cleveland, while his 1986–7 season's total of 3041 pts has only been bettered by Will Chamberlain back in the Sixties.

Annual awards like MVP, Most Valuable Player, were almost taken for granted and his 1992 Olympic re-appearance in the Dream Team of American professionals was another jewel in his dazzling crown.

He shocked the basketball world by retiring in 1993 and taking up baseball. Far less skilled, he played for minor league club, the Birmingham Barons.

Each type of defence can be extended to cover the entire playing surface and is called a press. The zone press can be a very effective action of trapping the opposition in their own half and thus causing a 10-second violation, but it is also vulnerable to the long pass and the fast break.

Individual team members may be given specific tactical roles. A standard offensive play is the pick, where one attacker, without making physical contact, places himself between the defender and the attacker who has the ball, to try to give his team mate an unimpeded shot.

Dr James A. Naismith had a problem. Attendance at the YMCA Training School in Springfield, Massachusetts, USA was falling as the members were bored with doing non-competitive exercises indoors during the freezing winter of 1892. The instructor nailed up a couple of peach baskets at each end of the gymnasium and told the 18 youngsters to toss a soccer ball into them. Basketball was born, but it took a while to realize that it would save time retrieving the ball by removing the bottom of the basket!

WORDS

Assist: a pass that results in a basket being scored

Backboard: vertical board of clear, hard plastic to which basket is fixed

Back court: the defensive zone

Boxing out: keeping the body between the basket and the attacker

Buttonhook: change of direction as player doubles back on himself

Defensive rebound: a rebound caught by defenders

Double team: two defenders marking one attacker, usually the star team player

Drive: to attack at speed

Dunk shot: when a player jumps high and literally stuffs the ball through the hoop

Fake: a feint

Field goal: a successful shot during normal play

Fouled out: player who has incurred five personal fouls (more complex in US) and can take no further part in the game

Free throw: uncontested shot from free throw line; must be taken by player fouled, unless injured

Game clock: runs whenever ball is in play, stops when ball is out of bounds or when foul is committed; so 40-minute game takes about two hours including interval

Goal tending: defender striking ball on its way down to the basket; illegal

Hook shot: when player's back was to the basket and he swivels and hooks ball in with one movement

Jump ball: the method of starting play; ball is tossed up between two players who try to tap it back to their team mates

Lay-up: shot from under the basket after player has dribbled in

Pattern offence: slower attack with players moving to designated spots to execute pre-planned plays

Pick/Screen: offensive manoeuvre in which one player blocks for another, placing himself between the defender and the attacker with the ball

Pressure defence: coverage all over court; usually defenders do not bother to harass attackers beyond the half court line, allowing the 10-second rule to do it for them

Shot clock: the 30-second (24-second in US pro game) clock which limits time a team may possess the ball without shooting; failure to shoot in the allowed time costs possession

Stalling: slowing play down by maintaining possession

10-second line: the half-court line; teams have 10 seconds to cross this line after obtaining possession in the defensive zone

Time out: when play is stopped, often for team to discuss tactics

Travelling: taking more than 1½ steps without dribbling; penalty is loss of possession

Zone defence: when players protect a particular area rather than marking a specific man

BOWLS AND BOWLING

BOWLS AND BOWLING HAVE DEVELOPED FROM THE NATURAL INSTINCT OF
HUMANS TO HAVE FUN BY THROWING STONES AT A TARGET DRAWN
IN THE DUST, OR AT STICKS

Many centuries separate both these games from their origins, but the purpose has never changed: in bowls, to roll large balls as close as possible to a small target ball; in tenpin bowling, to knock down pins by rolling even larger balls at them.

What used to be known as lawn bowls is now even more popular on indoor rinks, where it is played throughout the year. In a variant called crown green bowls, played in the north of England and Wales, the centre of the square green is higher than its edges.

Tenpin bowling takes place in purpose-built halls, with machines to re-position the fallen pins. From its origins in America, it has acquired worldwide popularity and, like bowls, now also sustains many professional players.

Bowls

THE RINK

The game is played up and down 40yd (36.57m) strips called rinks, of which there may be several side by side. Indoor rinks are composed of an artificial green carpet laid on a firm, flat foundation. Outdoors, greens have differing characteristics that are determined by the weather, the soil and the type of grass.

EQUIPMENT

Flat-soled shoes are essential. In formal competition, clubs often insist that both male and female players are dressed all in white and that women wear skirts. Indoor competition dress tends to be more colourful.

The bowls, sometimes known as woods, are now likely to be made of an artificial composition. They are identified by a coloured dot, usually weigh 3–3$\frac{1}{2}$lb (about 1.5kg) and are slightly flattened on one side to produce a bias in travel. This becomes more marked as the bowl loses its momentum, causing the bowl to alter its course by up to 90 degrees just before it stops.

The target ball (the jack) is small and hard, white in colour outdoors and usually yellow indoors.

WINNING

A point is scored for each bowl nearer the jack than the nearest one of an opponent. After all the bowls have been delivered down the rink, the next 'end' is played back the other way.

In singles, each player has four bowls and the first to score 21 points wins. In pairs, each player has four bowls and combines with his partner to score as many points as possible in 21 ends. In triples, each player has three bowls and the team with most points after 18 ends wins. In fours, each player has only two bowls and the points are totalled after 21 ends.

In an indoor variation, singles and pairs (the latter with only two bowls for each player) may compete over the best of five sets, each set determined by the first to reach seven points.

RULES

A tossed coin decides who bowls the first jack; thereafter the privilege passes to the winner of the previous end. The jack must travel at least 25yd (22.86m) from the mat and is centred on the rink wherever it stops. Players must keep one foot on or above this small rubber mat while they deliver their woods. A wood travelling less than 15yd (13.72m) is removed from play, as is one that goes off the end of the rink, unless it has touched the jack on the way.

Opposing players bowl alternately. In pairs, triples and fours, the lead players deliver all their woods before the second players deliver all theirs and so on.

Traditionally, the men's and women's games were kept strictly apart, but there are now some competitions for mixed pairs.

In crown green bowls (usually singles only) play takes place roughly diagonally across the centre of the green. Several games may be in progress at the same time, starting from different points along the edges.

SKILLS

Bowls are delivered with a smooth, underarm action. The player must take account of the speed of the green (which may vary greatly out of doors), and the weight and curve he needs to impart to reach the desired spot. The best players can achieve pinpoint accuracy right down the length of the rink.

The basic shots are the draw, to take the bowl onto the jack; the trail, when the player pushes the jack away from his opponent's bowls and towards his own; and the drive, when a wood is fired hard and straight to break up an end dominated by the opponent.

TACTICS

In pairs, triples and fours, tactics are determined by the 'skip', who always plays last. He is not likely to want all his team to draw to the jack. It may be better to try to remove an opposing wood, or to build a barrier that frustrates opposing attempts to reach the jack.

The side (or the single player) bowling first can choose not only how far to bowl the jack, but also where, within limits, to place the mat. They can thus produce a length to suit their own play, or one that will upset the winning rhythm of the opponents.

Conditions outdoors can vary considerably where wind, rain and sun affect the surface and the trajectory of the bowls. The best players have the skill to play to the conditions; they adjust more quickly and capitalize on their positions.

WORDS

Blocker: deliberately short bowl

Dead bowl: comes to rest too short or outside the rink

Draw: the trajectory of a bowl, including its curve

Fast: a green on which the bowl keeps running

Head: the collection of woods around the jack

Heavy: a bowl delivered too hard

Jack-high: level with the jack

Shot: the bowl closest to the jack

Slow: a green on which the bowl is held back, usually by moisture

Toucher: bowl marked with chalk after it has touched the jack

---

Bowling (Tenpin)

THE LANE

A lightly-oiled wooden surface 3ft 6in (1.06m) wide at the far end of which are 10 pins, each 15in (38cm) high and weighing about 3$\frac{1}{2}$lb (1.59kg). The pins are arranged in a triangle, the apex of which faces the bowler and is 20yd (18.29m) from the line beyond which the bowl is delivered. On each side of the lane is a gutter which catches and removes any bowls leaving the lane.

After every delivery an automatic pin-spotter sweeps the lane of pins knocked down and re-sets those that are still standing. The ball is automatically returned on a raised track.

EQUIPMENT

The bowling ball weighs 16lb (7.26kg) and is 8$\frac{1}{2}$in (21.59cm) in diameter. Three holes, for the thumb and middle two fingers, provide a grip, with the other fingers used for stability. Seriously competitive players use balls made to their own specifications and may have several, of different degrees of hardness, to cope with changing conditions. They also wear special shoes, with a soft leather sole for controlled sliding, and a rubber heel that acts as a brake.

The rest of the necessary equipment is built in at the lane. Apart from the pin-spotting machines, it may include computer-screen scoring and air jets to help dry players' hands.

WINNING

Ten frames comprise a game, and in each frame the bowler is allowed two attempts to knock down all 10 pins. Each pin down is worth one point, but the expert players score far more highly than that through an elaborate bonus system.

If a bowler knocks down all 10 pins with the first ball (a strike), he scores 10 points plus whatever he scores with his next two deliveries. Those scores also count within their own frame. If he knocks down all 10 with two deliveries (a spare), he scores 10 points plus whatever he scores with the next delivery. If there is a strike in the tenth and last frame, an additional two deliveries are also allowed.

A perfect score of 300 points (12 consecutive strikes) is extremely rare, though there are a handful of Americans who have achieved it in three successive games (36 consecutive strikes). A professional bowler expects to average around 220 a game. Compare that to the 90 points that would be scored by a bowler who had just one pin left standing (known as an open frame) on each of his 10 frames.

RULES

Simplicity itself: the ball must be rolled, not thrown; and the player must not step over the foul line when releasing the ball.

SKILLS

Though tenpin bowling can provide enjoyment even for complete beginners, sophisticated techniques are needed at the top level. A good bowler will quickly find each alley's groove, the line that is most likely to lead to a strike, and he must consistently roll the ball on that same line. He is helped in that by small markers set into the lane a quarter of the way down, which the bowler can use as sights.

A strike is not likely to be achieved by rolling at the head pin, but by hooking into the space between the head pin and the pin to the left or right of it. This needs a degree of spin to be imparted to the ball by the gripping fingers. How much spin is necessary depends very much on the condition of the bowling lane.

As the oil that has been applied to the lane dries out, so the friction between the surface and the ball increases and the lane takes more break. All lanes are 39 boards wide and the bowler measures the break by the number of boards across which the ball will turn: on a very oily surface, that might

If a player fails to knock down all 10 pins with the first delivery, the remaining pins (spares) often present an awkward configuration. Pins 7 and 10, for example, are far apart and virtually impossible to knock down with the second and final delivery to achieve a 'spare'. These configurations have colourful nicknames.

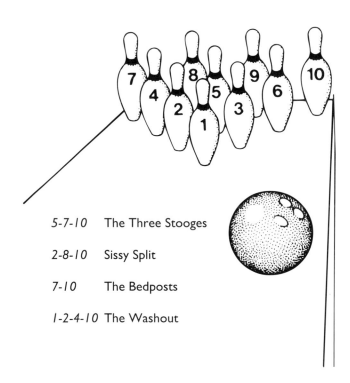

5-7-10	The Three Stooges
2-8-10	Sissy Split
7-10	The Bedposts
1-2-4-10	The Washout

be only three boards; when the oil has dried out, it could produce as much as a 10-board break. The bowler adjusts his style of delivery (and perhaps changes his ball, to a softer or harder one) accordingly.

TACTICS

The object never changes: to knock down every pin with every ball. The only tactical decision the bowler may have to make is if his first ball has left him with an awkward target. Should he attempt the difficult conversion to a spare, or just settle for an open frame?

WORDS

Alley: old-fashioned name for playing area, now called a lane

Foul line: the line the bowler may not step over when delivering the ball; about 16ft (5m) from start of the walk-up area

Frame: the units which make up a game; each consists of two attempts by players to knock down all of the 10 pins

Gutter: channel off the edge of the lane to catch wide balls

Head pin: apex of the triangle of pins, nearest to the bowler

Kegle, kegler: slang names for pin and bowler, derived from old German words

Open frame: when any pins are still standing after two deliveries

Pin-spotter: machine that automatically clears fallen pins after first delivery and re-spots those that are not knocked over; resets all pins after two deliveries or after a strike

Spare: all 10 pins down after two deliveries

Strike: all 10 pins down with first delivery

300 game: the perfect score, achieved with 12 successive strikes

---

The classic, balanced bowling action.

No other sport exposes one competitor against another so cruelly. Ability, bravery, resilience, fitness – all are plain to see in, perhaps, the hardest sport in the world.

BOXING

BOXING IS SIMPLY FIST-FIGHTING WITH PADDED GLOVES. THE GLOVES ARE WORN TO PROTECT THE HANDS RATHER THAN GIVE ADDED WEIGHT TO THE PUNCHES AND, IN FACT, LESSEN THE WEIGHT OF THE BLOWS

It is a simple sport to watch with only two competitors – the boxers – and one official, the referee.

The rules of amateur and professional boxing differ. In amateur boxing the contest or bout lasts only three rounds compared with up to twelve in the professional code. In addition, amateurs are required to wear both headguards and vests. Amateur boxing is most widely followed every four years at the Olympic Games, but there are also amateur World Championships and international matches.

The World Heavyweight Boxing Championship is one of the most prized titles in international sport with a profile to match. When Muhammad Ali was the champion in the Sixties and Seventies it was said he was the most famous person in the world. Outside the ring, boxing thrives on hype and exaggeration, with promoters anxious to sell

tickets to the public and broadcasting rights to television companies. Boxing is a multi-million pound industry with huge financial rewards for those who reach the top in the professional game.

RING

The four-sided fighting area is known as the ring. The area is enclosed by three ropes, stretched between four corner posts, on a raised platform. The ring can vary between 4.27m (4½yd) and 6.1m (6½yd) square in professional contests and between 3.66m (4yd) and 4.88m (5¼yd) square for amateur bouts.

EQUIPMENT

Boxing gloves weigh between 170g (6oz) and 283g (10oz). Hands are further protected by the use of soft bandages and adhesive tape under the gloves. The boxer also wears a gum-shield inside his mouth. It is compulsory for all boxers to wear an abdominal protector cup inside their shorts to protect against low blows. Each boxing federation has its own rules restricting the use of medical substances by seconds or cornermen in order to minimize the risk to the boxer. The seconds' basic equipment includes white petroleum jelly, sterile swabs, a concentration of adrenalin and an ice-bag. All these are used to control the effects of cuts or swelling during the contest.

PROFESSIONAL WEIGHT DIVISIONS (UK, USA)

Flyweight	up to 8st
Bantamweight	up to 8st 6lb
Featherweight	up to 9st
Super-Featherweight	up to 9st 4lb
Lightweight	up to 9st 9lb
Light-Welterweight	up to 10st
Welterweight	up to 10st 7lb
Light-Middleweight	up to 11st
Middleweight	up to 11st 6lb
Super-Middleweight	up to 12st
Light-Heavyweight	up to 12st 7lb
Cruiserweight	up to 13st 8lb
Heavyweight	over 13st 8lb

WINNING

The boxer aims to win a fight either on points by scoring more blows with the knuckle part of the glove on the target area (defined as 'any part of the front or sides of the head and body above the belt line') or to outclass his opponent so that he is no longer able to defend himself.

A knockout occurs when an opponent is unable to get to his feet within 10 seconds of being knocked to the floor. Often the referee decides a boxer is in no fit state to continue even if he is still standing.

As there are four international bodies governing boxing, scoring systems vary. With all bodies, however, the referee and/or ringside judges assess the boxers' performances on a round-by-round basis with the winner of each round being given 10 points, the loser perhaps eight or nine depending on how often he has scored. The round can also be scored even. At the end of the contest the points for each round are added together to decide the winner. A bout can also end in a draw.

World title contests last for 12, three-minute rounds. There is a one-minute rest between each round. Non-title fights last for 10 rounds.

In international amateur boxing the scoring system does not allow for a draw. In the Olympics there are five ringside judges and a referee who does not score the bout.

A boxer may win a fight through a points decision, a knockout, the referee stopping the fight, retirement through injury of his opponent and disqualification. Amateur bouts last for three, three-minute rounds.

RULES

As there are presently four different bodies governing professional boxing – the World Boxing Council, the World Boxing Association, the International Boxing

AMATEUR WEIGHT DIVISIONS (INT'L)

Light-Flyweight	up to 48kg
Flyweight	up to 51kg
Bantamweight	up to 54kg
Featherweight	up to 57kg
Lightweight	up to 60kg
Light-Welterweight	up to 63.5kg
Welterweight	up to 67kg
Light-Middleweight	up to 71kg
Middleweight	up to 75kg
Light-Heavyweight	up to 81kg
Heavyweight	up to 91kg
Super-Heavyweight	over 91kg

Federation and the International Boxing Organisation – interpretations of the rules and judging inevitably differ depending on which organization is staging the contest. Nevertheless, the vast majority of rules remain the same. While watching a bout on television you may see a referee warn one of the boxers. This could be for holding, failing to break from a clinch (close quarter interlocking of the two boxers' arms) punching to the kidneys or striking an opponent who is either down or in the process of getting back to his feet.

In addition, a boxer must not hit below the belt, on the back of the neck, with an open glove or strike with the head, shoulder, wrist, elbow or arm. The opponent must not be hit when the referee has brought the boxing to a temporary halt nor must he be hit after the bell has been rung to signal the end of a round.

Generally the refereeing of amateur international boxing may seem stricter, or fussier, depending on the feelings of the viewer. It must be remembered though that the professional referee is dealing with more experienced fighters competing at a less frantic pace because of the longer duration of their fights.

Boxers only take on opponents of

LENNOX LEWIS
A quick, agile fighter with a devasting right-hand. Born in London, he moved to Canada as a child and first came to prominence fighting for his adopted country in the 1988 Olympic Games in Seoul where he beat Riddick Bowe to win the gold medal in the Super-Heavyweight division. He was awarded the World Championship in February 1993 when the IBF, WBA, and WBC champion Riddick Bowe relinquished the WBC crown rather than agree to fight against him. Now based in the UK, he defended his crown successfully for the third time in May 1994, taking his unbeaten record to 25 wins.

Muhammad Ali was The Greatest, the most famous person in the world, his face instantly recognizable in the remotest villages on earth. As Cassius Marcellus Clay, he won the Olympic gold at Light-Heavyweight level in 1960 and immediately turned professional. Early in 1964 he upset Sonny Liston to win the world heavyweight crown, the first of 25 controversial world title fights spread over 16 years. His only major loss was to Joe Frazier, later reversed. His last two defeats were as an over-the-hill veteran. In between, the American converted to Islam, refused to serve in the US Army and was stripped of his title for three and a half years. Remembered as much for his publicity stunts, predictions and poetry, Ali was a superb athlete with remarkable speed and reflexes for a heavyweight.

comparable weight so there are many weight division limits. Boxers are required to be inside the necessary limit on the morning of the fight.

SKILLS

Orthodox boxers score most of their points using a left lead or jab, with the right hand following up with heavier blows after the left has made the initial opening.

A southpaw or left-hander is a boxer who stands right foot forward and leads with his right hand. He is often considered to be a tricky opponent for orthodox boxers to counteract effectively.

There are three basic punches: the straight blow or jab, the hook and the uppercut, which is delivered with bent knees and the hand brought up to hit the chin or the body of the opponent.

'Any fool can fight but very few can box' is an old adage worth bearing in mind when watching the sport. The boxer's principal aim is to hit his opponent without being hit himself. Apart from blocking punches with his arm and shoulder he will also try to duck and slip punches with small movements of the head. Body punches, used to draw an opponent's stamina, can be blocked with the elbow as well as by pushing the blow aside with a half-open glove.

A boxer will often feint or pretend to throw a punch in order to land a blow with the other hand. Boxers will practise for hours to perfect combination punching, a rhythmic sequence of swift consecutive blows to the head and body.

Counterpunching is vital. One of the best known and most difficult to perfect is the right cross over the opponent's left jab, where the boxer hopes to slip the left lead and then pivots round to hit hard with a right counter.

The best counter against the southpaw is the left hook coming from outside the southpaw's line of vision.

WORDS

Canvas: the floor of the boxing ring

Combination: a rapid series of punches

Distance: the full number of rounds scheduled for the contest

Gumshield: guard for the teeth worn by boxers inside the mouth

KO/Knockout: when a boxer is hit so hard he cannot get back to his feet and defend himself within

10 seconds

Purse: prize money put up for a fight by the promoter

Ring: where the contest takes place

Seconds: boxer's assistants

Spar: to practise boxing, usually wearing protective headgear

Standing count: where a boxer, despite not going on the floor, receives a count from the referee who must then establish whether the

fighter can defend himself

TKO/Technical Knockout: when referee stops the fight because the boxer cannot defend himself

Towel, throw-in: when a boxer's seconds indicate they no longer want the fight to continue

Weigh-in: usually held on the morning of a fight. Needed to check that a boxer is within the correct weight category

CANOEING AND KAYAKING

THE SPORT DEVELOPED THROUGH THE BIRCH-BARK CANOES (SINGLE PADDLE) OF AMERICAN INDIANS AND THE SEAL-SKIN KAYAKS (DOUBLE-BLADED PADDLE) OF THE ESKIMOS. THESE REMAIN THE BASIC CRAFT OF THE SPORT, WHICH HAS SEVERAL WIDELY DIFFERENT DISCIPLINES

Those most often seen are the Olympic events of sprint racing and slalom. Sprint racing is held, like rowing, on a flat water course, while slalom takes place on short natural or artificial downhill courses full of swirling water, rocks, rapids and 'gates' through which the competitor must pass.

Both sexes compete (though not against each other) in kayaks, but only men race in canoes. The classes are identified by the letters 'C' or 'K', followed by a figure for the number of competitors in the craft – for example K1, C2 or K4.

THE COURSE

Flat water racing is held over distances from a straight 500m (550yd) to a 10,000m (6-mile) circuit, as well as over marathon distances. Wild water races are usually contested over about 8km (5 miles), while a slalom course may be anything between 300m and 800m (about 350–900yd). In the two latter disciplines, events are graded according to the severity of the course. Competitors start at intervals, racing against the clock.

EQUIPMENT

There are specialized craft for each form of racing. Slalom canoes and kayaks are as short as possible – no more than 4m (13ft) for a K1 – but must withstand impact with rocks. Fibreglass is the usual construction material. Competitors wear buoyancy aids, crash helmets and a kind of waterproof skirt (a spray deck) to prevent rough water rushing in. Sprint craft are longer and sleeker; the K4 can be up to 11m (36ft).

The single-bladed paddles for canoe racing have a rounded grip at the top of the shaft to help the 'digging' motion. Kayak racers use a long, double-bladed paddle. For paddles and for the craft, minimum weight with maximum strength are the aims.

WINNING

Straight sprint racing requires the competitors to stay in their lanes and get to the other end first. It is usually run in heats but (unlike athletics) stages a repechage, or rerun, for the losers, giving them a second chance to reach the final.

In wild water races, a kind of cross-country event for canoeists, the competitors start at one-minute intervals and the one recording the shortest time wins. It is in slalom racing, the most exciting of all disciplines, that complexities arise.

Competitors start at 45-second intervals. Up to 30 numbered 'gates' may be hanging over the course, just above the water. These are pairs of poles through which the racer must pass without touching either pole with his body, his paddle or his boat. Some are deliberately hung immediately after a hazard – a drop over a rock ledge, for example – and some have to be negotiated upstream rather than down; they are painted in red-and-white stripes and the downstream gates are coloured in green and white.

A judge sits on the bank close to each gate. Each one touched brings a five-point penalty, and 50 points are deducted for missing a gate, taking one in the wrong order or passing through it in the wrong direction. The competitor's finishing time is expressed in seconds, to which the penalty points are added. The competitor with the lowest number wins, but everyone gets a second run, the better score to count.

WORDS

Back-paddling: pushing paddle forward to reverse direction

Brace: recovery stroke to prevent canoe capsizing

Draw stroke: paddle dug in wide of the boat to pull it sideways

Eskimo roll: used to right an overturned kayak

Free gate: with black and white stripes, can be entered from either direction

Gate: two poles hanging freely over a slalom course, through which the competitor must pass

Grade: river rapids are graded from one (easy) to six (impossible)

Portage: carrying the craft round awkward obstacles

Telemark turn: a fast turn using the paddle as a pivot

RULES

There is no restriction on the design and construction of any type of racing canoe, but it has to conform to minimum length and weight restrictions. In flat and wild water racing, but not slalom, there is a maximum length restriction.

In all rough water racing, the craft must be 'unsinkable'. A capsize in which the competitor parts company with his boat disqualifies him from that run in slalom, but in wild water racing he is allowed to get back in without help and carry on. All he loses is the time.

SKILLS

All forms of canoeing are physically very demanding and, in terms of all-round muscular strength and heart-lung endurance, canoeists rank highly. The upper body has to be especially powerful, but leg muscles are used to anchor the body and enable the canoeist to rotate his trunk, and stomach muscles to resist the rotating caused by the pushing and pulling of the arms.

Nothing demonstrates the strength of a canoeist better than to watch him turn against a torrent and steer through an upstream gate in slalom, using only two strokes for the manoeuvre.

Strength above all is needed for any racing paddler, but rough water racing also demands an acute ability to read the swirling water, possessing lightning-fast reactions to counter any problems and mishaps on the course.

TACTICS

Like a distance runner, the so-called 'sprint' canoeist must judge when to make his greatest effort in order to produce the maximum psychological effect on his rivals. The downstream canoeist is engaged in a permanent tactical battle with the water, trying to find the best line through the

hazards, always having to wrestle hard against the opposing elements.

In addition, the tactics of the slalom canoeist alter according to the temperament of the competitor and the state of the competition. Some use the first run to achieve the fastest possible time and hope they won't incur any penalties; some prefer to try to achieve a clear run first, and then try to improve on their overall speed the second time around.

Flat water canoeing demands all-round physical strength with particular emphasis on the upper body, torso and legs.

When a cricket match is over, the next one is played on a different strip of newly rolled and mown turf.

CRICKET

CRICKET IS AN IMMENSELY COMPLEX GAME WHICH HAS EVOLVED SINCE ITS ORIGINS MORE THAN 250 YEARS AGO

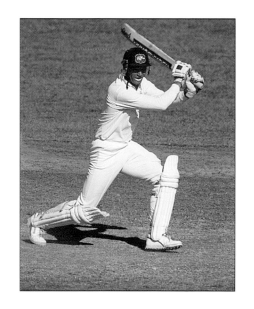

It must be the only game in the world where play stops for lunch and tea. Not only that, but a top-class match played over as many as five days often does not produce a result.

In recent years, one-day cricket, which nearly always produces a winner, has grown in popularity and has become vital to the commercial success of the game at professional level. Every four years international teams compete for the World Cup which consists of a series of one-day matches.

Traditionally the game has been played over three, four or, at international level, five days but there is no international cup competition for the longer form of the game. Five-day matches between international teams are known as 'test matches' but there are currently only nine countries which are allowed to play them. Zimbabwe is the latest country to be given test match status.

Cricket demands great concentration and patience from those who play and watch – a day's play often lasts for more than six hours.

It is hard to think of another sport where the weather conditions play such an important part in the progress of a match. Cricket is rarely played in the rain, or in dim light, although many one-day games, especially in Australia and South Africa, are now played under floodlights to encourage more spectators to attend matches in the evening after work. Sunny weather or overcast conditions during the course of a match can affect the way a game is played, but despite the importance of the weather, cricket is played in countries with differing climates such as England, the West Indies and India.

THE FIELD

Cricket is played on a large grass field with most of the action taking place on a strip of specially rolled and mown grass. The strip is known as 'the pitch'. The pitch, which is 22yd (about 20m) long and about 3yd (3m) wide, plays a vital part in the game because the ball is bounced off it. How it reacts to varying weather conditions often determines the course of a game.

Three stumps are placed in the ground at each end of the pitch. These are known as the wickets. The stumps are 28in (about 81cm) high and make a target 9in (about 23cm) wide. Two small pieces of wood called bails rest on top of the stumps.

EQUIPMENT

The basic requirements for cricket are a bat and ball, two sets of stumps and protective equipment for the batsman. The bat is made of willow and can vary in weight according to the preference of the batsman. The ball has a cork centre wrapped with twine and is covered with leather which is dyed red. The ball weighs between 5½ and 5¾oz (around 156–160g).

Although the players on the team usually dress in white clothing, in one-day games many cricket teams are increasingly wearing coloured clothing.

To protect themselves against the hard ball, batsmen wear pads on their legs, a thigh pad, protective gloves, an abdominal protector and normally a helmet. The wicket-keeper, who stands right behind the stumps when the ball is being delivered by the bowler, also wears pads on his legs and specially reinforced gloves.

WINNING

The basic aim of cricket is to score more runs than the opposing side. The game is played between two teams of 11 players. One team bats and attempts to score as many runs as possible while members of the other team bowl at the batsmen in an attempt to get them out. Cricket is made up of overs with a bowler delivering six balls from one end of the pitch followed by another bowler delivering six from the opposite end.

There are always two batsmen out on the field, one at either end. To score a run after one batsman has hit the ball, they must both run to the opposite end. If a batsman hits the ball over the edge of the field, the boundary, he scores four. If the ball goes over the boundary without bouncing the batsman scores six. However, a batsman does not have to run if he hits the ball.

LAWS

The laws are administered by two umpires. They are the sole arbiters of any decision that has to be made. They decide when a batsman is out, after one of the bowling side has appealed by shouting 'How's that'; they decide when play should stop, either for rain or bad light, and when it should resume.

The main aim of the bowling side is to dismiss, or get out, the batsmen from the opposing team. In cricket, there are 10 ways of getting a player out. The most frequent are as follows:

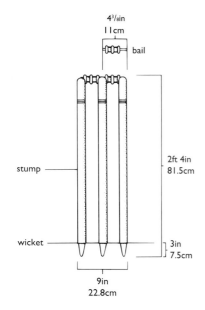

4³⁄₈in 11cm · bail · 2ft 4in 81.5cm · stump · wicket · 3in 7.5cm · 9in 22.8cm

The bowler's target is the wicket; as long as just one bail falls, the batsman is out.

Bowled: the bowler beats the batsman, the ball hits the stumps.

Caught: the batsman hits the ball which is caught before it touches the ground. This can be a high ball caught near the boundary or a fast-travelling chance a few feet from the bat.

L.b.w.: leg before wicket is, simply put, when the batsman's leg prevents the ball from hitting the wicket.

Run out: if the batsman fails to get to his end in time, he is run out if the ball breaks the wicket. He is in (not out) if the bat he is holding is actually grounded beyond the popping crease (the painted white line in front of the stumps).

Stumped: if the batsman steps out of his ground, usually deceived by the angle of the ball, the wicket-keeper stumps him by breaking the wicket with the ball (or a hand holding the ball).

With the exception of one-day matches, both teams have two innings. The bowling side needs to dismiss 10 of the opposition's batsmen before they have the opportunity to go in and bat themselves.

In exceptional cases, usually when a team builds a high score, it can declare its innings closed before all its batsmen are out.

SKILLS

The batsman: His job is to score as many runs as possible before being out. The main attacking shots are the drive, a stroke played with the full face of a vertically straight bat, the pull, a cross-batted shot which goes to the leg-side of the field, and a cut, which goes between third man and cover point.

The bowler: His job is to take wickets and prevent the batsman scoring runs. There are many different types of bowlers. A fast bowler can attempt to defeat the batsman by the sheer speed of his delivery. A medium-pace bowler will try to dismiss the batsmen by getting the ball to swing in the air or to change direction off the pitch when it lands. A spin bowler will hope to deceive the batsman by getting the ball to turn sharply off the pitch.

RICHIE RICHARDSON
One of the world's outstanding batsmen, Richardson is instantly recognizable, with his wide-brimmed maroon sun-hat. Despite making his Test match debut for the West Indies on their 1983–4 tour to India, he remained in the shadow of the well-known Viv Richards for several years until he replaced his fellow Antiguan as the West Indies captain in 1992. He immediately led the side to victory in Test matches against South Africa, Australia and Pakistan. A naturally aggressive batsman, he's also played more than 150 one-day internationals. In 1993 he became only the second overseas cricketer to play the sport for the Yorkshire county side.

AUSTRALIA v ENGLAND (Third Test)
Played at Sydney on January 4, 5, 6, 7, 8, 1991
Match Drawn. Toss: Australia.

AUSTRALIA

Batsman	Dismissal	Runs	Dismissal (2nd)	Runs
G.R. Marsh	c Larkins b Malcolm	13	(2) c Stewart b Malcolm	4
M.A. Taylor	c Russell b Malcolm	11	(1) lbw b Hemmings	19
D.C. Boon	c Atherton b Gooch	97	(4) c Gooch b Tufnell	29
A.R. Border*	b Hemmings	78	(5) c Gooch b Tufnell	20
D.M. Jones	st Russell b Small	60	(6) c & b Tufnell	0
S.R. Waugh	c Stewart b Malcolm	48	(7) c Russell b Hemmings	14
G.R.J. Matthews	c Hemmings b Tufnell	128	(8) b Hemmings	19
I.A. Healy†	c Small b Hemmings	35	(3) c Smith b Tufnell	69
C.G. Rackemann	b Hemmings	1	b Malcolm	9
T.M. Alderman	not out	26	c Gower b Tufnell	1
B.A. Reid	c Smith b Malcolm	0	not out	5
Extras	(b5, lb8, nb8)	21	(lb16)	16
TOTAL		518		205

ENGLAND

Batsman	Dismissal	Runs	Dismissal (2nd)	Runs
G.A. Gooch*	c Healy b Reid	59	c Border b Matthews	54
M.A. Atherton	c Boon b Matthews	105	(6) not out	3
W. Larkins	run out	11	lbw b Border	0
R.A. Smith	c Healy b Reid	18	(5) not out	10
D.I. Gower	c Marsh b Reid	123	(2) c Taylor b Matthews	36
A.J. Stewart	lbw b Alderman	91	(4) run out	7
R.C. Russell†	not out	30		
G.C. Small	lbw b Alderman	10		
E.E. Hemmings	b Alderman	0		
P.C.R. Tufnell	not out	5		
D.E. Malcolm	did not bat			
Extras	(b1, lb8, nb8)	17	(lb1, nb2)	3
TOTAL	(8 wkts dec)	469	(4 wkts)	113

ENGLAND	O	M	R	W	O	M	R	W
Malcolm	45	12	128	4	6	1	19	2
Small	31	5	103	1	2	1	6	0
Hemmings	32	7	105	3	41	9	94	3
Tufnell	30	6	95	1	37	18	61	5
Gooch	14	3	46	1				
Atherton	5	0	28	0	3	1	9	0
AUSTRALIA								
Alderman	20.1	4	62	3	4	0	29	0
Reid	35.1	9	79	3				
Rackemann	25.5	5	89	0	3	0	20	0
Matthews	58	16	145	1	9	2	26	2
Border	19	5	45	0	9	1	37	1
Waugh	14	3	40	0				

FALL OF WICKETS

	A	E	A	E
1st	21	95	21	84
2nd	38	116	29	84
3rd	185	156	81	100
4th	226	295	129	100
5th	292	394	129	–
6th	347	426	166	–
7th	442	444	166	–
8th	457	444	189	–
9th	512	–	192	–
10th	518	–	205	–

Umpires: A.R. Crafter and P.J. McConnell

A cricket scorecard. Australia won the coin toss and batted first, scoring 518 runs, including 21 extras (5 byes, 8 leg-byes and 8 no balls). In their second innings, Australia changed their batting order, Healy batting third (3). Needing 255 to win, England ran out of time. The bowlers' statistics record O (overs bowled), M (maiden over), R (runs conceded) and W (wickets taken).

The fielder: His job is to prevent runs by stopping the ball and to take catches when the batsman hits the ball in the air.

TACTICS

Batsman: A batsman will usually score slowly at the start of his innings and increase his scoring the more he gets used to the conditions and the quality of the bowling. No two batsmen are the same. Some are naturally aggressive and attempt to score quicker than others. All, though, have the same aim in mind – to score as many runs as possible.

Bowler: Any bowler has techniques he uses to dismiss a batsman. A fast-bowler, for example, can intimidate the batsman by bowling at his head and body. He can also try to deceive the batsman with changes of pace. Spin-bowlers have variations; sometimes, in the case of the leg-spinner, being able to turn the ball different ways. One of the bowler's weapons is to bowl accurately and frustrate the batsman into making a mistake.

WORDS

BATTING

Collapse: when several batsmen are all out in quick succession

Duck: out for no runs

Innings: refers both to the individual effort of a batsman and the collective effort of the team

Opener: one of the two men who bat first

Tail ender: one of the last to bat, usually a bowler

BOWLING

Bouncer: a fast ball that is pitched short and lifts towards the batsman's upper body and head

Full toss: a bad ball that does not bounce before reaching the batsman

Maiden over: an over in which the batsman fails to score a run

Wide: an off-course ball that the batsman can't reach

FIELDING

Bye: when the ball evades the wicket-keeper and the batsmen complete a run without the ball actually having been hit

Howzat/How's that: an appeal made to the umpire by the fielding side, meaning 'is he out?'

Leg-bye: when the batsman runs, after the ball has hit any part of his body

CURLING

A FORM OF BOWLS ON ICE PLAYED WITH 40LB (18KG) STONES AND
NOTORIOUS FOR THE FRENZIED SWEEPING THAT ACCOMPANIES THEM

Curling has been played in Scotland for centuries and has spread to North America, across Europe and as far as Australia. The oldest relic of the game, the Stirling Stone, bears the date of 1511.

No longer played on frozen lakes (unless covered by at least six inches of ice), it is now a highly-competitive rink game for teams of four. There are annual world championships for men and women where extraordinary skills are evident, but at heart it remains one of the most sociable of all sports. Though less accessible than bowls, it has the advantage of lacking the formalities of that game. Curling can also boast a repertoire of some four hundred songs written about, and dedicated to, the sport!

The tee or button at the centre of each target is only 12 inches in diameter.

THE RINK

The area of ice used for a game is known as a rink and is about 138ft (42m). Several may be laid side-by-side. The ice must be kept in perfect condition so that the polished base of the stone slides on it with as little resistance as possible.

At each end of the rink is a target (the house), a circle on the ice 12ft (3.66m) in diameter within which are some concentric coloured circles. The centre circle, known as the tee, is 12in (30.48cm) across. The two tees should be 114ft (34.75m) apart.

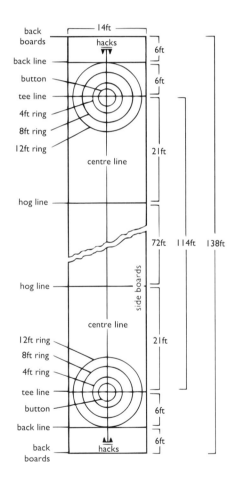

EQUIPMENT

Traditionally, the stone is a round and polished block of granite, though stones of iron are used in Canada. A metal striking band encircles it, to save wear and tear from the frequent collisions with other stones. A detachable handle is bolted into its centre, by which the player projects it. Matching stones are provided at the competition venue, as is the foothold on the ice (the hack) from which play starts.

Players wear odd shoes: one has a sole that can grip the ice, the other a sole that slides on it. In serious competition, these different shoes can prove vital. So is the broom that every player holds at all times, though the once-obligatory bottle of Scotch is seldom seen.

WINNING

As in bowls, the object is to get the stones down the rink and as near as possible to the target (called the button in North America). Each stone from one team nearer to the tee than the nearest of the opponents' stones scores a point. Stones that are not inside the house do not score any points. Matches are usually played over 10 ends (heads), the winner being the team that score the highest points in total, not necessarily the one winning the most heads.

Each player delivers two stones, playing them alternately with his opposite number on the other team, so that by the time the two captains (skips) have played, there may in theory be 16 stones around the head. In practice, several of these will by then have been knocked behind the house, and taken out of play.

RULES

In his delivery, a player may retain contact with the stone as far as the hog line, 33ft (10.06m) down the rink. From that line, other members of his team may sweep the ice ahead of the stone as far as the tee. From there, the opposition may sweep to encourage the stone to travel out of the house. Stones not reaching the far hog line are then removed from play.

SKILLS

The skip, from the far end, indicates with his broom the point to which he wants the stone aimed. From a crouching position with one foot on the hack, the player draws the stone back and with a smooth underarm swing sends it on its way. Sliding on one foot and with the other trailing behind him, the player will travel with it to the hog line, the handle still under his control. The moment of release and the turning of the handle determines the amount of draw to one side or the other.

Then the sweepers take over. Many scientific theories have been advanced as to why vigorous scrubbing of the ice immediately ahead of the stone should so affect its travel, but it clearly does. The sweepers, guided by roars from the skip, can add yards to the distance a stone travels or precisely influence its direction.

TACTICS

Though 15 stones have been delivered when the last player projects the final stone, it is often that one which decides the head and is the only one to score. Tactics will have

Players seem to will the stone to be on target.

determined that. If the first stone has drawn to the tee, the next player tries to remove that stone.

If he fails, the skip may call for a guard – a shorter stone to protect the first one – or perhaps for another stone within the house but far enough apart from the first so that the opposition could not clear them both with one stone. The tactical battle between the opposing skips is never-ending: where and how should they deploy their weapons, the massive stone and the mighty broom?

WORDS

Bonspiel: match between two clubs featuring several teams

Broom: for sweeping the ice ahead of a stone; usually made of horsehair or synthetic fibre, sometimes of besom or corn-stalk

Button: see Tee

Crampit: see Hack

Draw: curve in trajectory of stone achieved by turning handle on delivery

Grand Match: gathering of many hundreds of curlers on a deeply-frozen lake somewhere in Scotland

Hack: metal foothold from which curler delivers

Head: series of 16 stones delivered to the house

Hog: stone that fails to reach hog line and is removed from the ice

House: the circular target on the ice

Lead: first player on a team

Pot-lid: stone exactly on the tee

Rink: both the area where the curling game is played and also a team that is playing it

Skip: captain of a team, and last man to play

Strike: fast stone thrown to knock another out of position

Tee: centre of the house

Cycling's popularity boomed in the 1890s after the invention of the pneumatic tyre by one John Dunlop, a Scottish vet living in Belfast. Legend has it that he first made an inflatable tyre for his son's tricycle.

CYCLING

BEST-KNOWN FOR ITS MASS START ROAD RACES, OF WHICH THE MOST
FAMOUS IN THE WORLD IS THE ANNUAL TOUR DE FRANCE, CYCLING IS ALSO
SERIOUSLY CONTESTED BY AMATEURS AND PROFESSIONALS ON PURPOSE-BUILT
TRACKS KNOWN AS VELODROMES

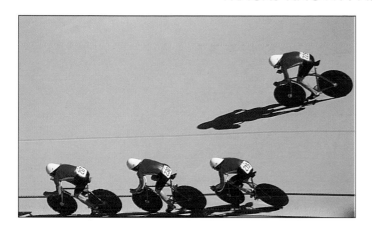

In Western Europe in particular, many professional cyclists are highly-paid and celebrated athletes.

The road race at a major competition such as the Olympic Games usually consists of several circuits of a public-road course that has been completely closed to traffic. A road race lasting a number of days, such as the Tour de France – which lasts 26 days and covers about 3500km (2200 miles) – is known as a stage race. A set distance is covered each day over public roads on which (the cyclists hope) a rolling closure has been applied, the authorities clearing the road well ahead of the travelling circus and re-opening it after the last vehicle has passed. Some regions may be more cooperative than others.

Track racing, in its various forms such as sprint, pursuit and time trial, is a more specialized business in which modern technology plays a much greater part than it does on the road. The machines used are precision-engineered from highly-sophisticated materials, as was startlingly demonstrated at the Olympic Games in Barcelona with Chris Boardman's Lotus bike with its revolutionary design.

Chris Boardman's revolutionary Lotus bike was the talking point of the 1992 Olympics.

Track Racing

THE TRACK

The standard length of a championship track is 333m (about 365yd), but many are shorter than this and some longer. Indoors or out, most are made of narrow hardwood planks and consist of two straights parallel to each other, inclined to at least 12 degrees from the horizontal, and two very steeply banked bends – perhaps rising to an almost unbelievable 55 degrees.

Three lines are painted round the track. The blue band on the inside of the circuit marks the end of the competitive area. The continuous red line just above it is known as the sprinter's line and the blue line a third of the way up the bank as the stayer's line, below which a sprinter may not be passed.

EQUIPMENT

The advanced racing cycle is a wondrous machine of carbon fibre, disc wheels and aerodynamic design, unlike anything seen on the road. Lightness with strength is the aim, and these bikes have neither gears nor brakes. The fine tyres are stuck firmly to the rims, so the whole wheel has to be changed after a puncture.

WINNING

Sprint: a knock-out competition between pairs of riders, with each round the best of three heats. Though the distance is usually three laps, it is not until the last that the racing begins. Until then, the riders play cat-and-mouse, often standing still on their wheels to dare the opponent to go in front.

Pursuit: two riders start on opposite sides of the track and the winner is the fastest over the designated distance, or the one that catches up with his opponent. In team events, the winners are the first to get three of their four men home.

Time trial: amateurs race one at a time against the clock for 1km (1100yd) and the fastest wins.

Points: after a mass start, the first three over the line on each lap score points, which are doubled on the final lap. The winner is the highest points scorer.

RULES

Sprint: the lead rider must travel at least at walking pace. During a standstill, he is penalized if he moves backwards more than 20cm (approx 8in), by being forced to lead for a lap. The heat is re-started in the event of a fall, puncture or mechanical trouble.

Pursuit: in individual heats the race is re-started if there is a fall, puncture or mechanical breakdown in the first 30m (32yd); after that, the rider must drop out.

Time trial: in the event of a fall, puncture or mechanical trouble, the rider may re-start. However, two re-starts are the maximum that is ever allowed.

SKILLS & TACTICS

In the two-man sprints, the race is usually won by the man who swoops right down from behind off the top of the track. In the mass-entry points race, it is the fast, final sprint at the end of each of perhaps 175 laps that determines the ultimate winner.

Road Racing

THE COURSE

Road race circuits or courses are chosen, where possible, to include a mixture of flat roads, hill climbs and descents. In world championship races the road must never be less than 5m wide (16½ft), and it must be at least 8m (26ft) in the last kilometre before the finish line. Maximum distances in world championships vary considerably between the sexes and are: women 70km (45 miles); amateur men 190km (119 miles); professional men 280km (175 miles).

EQUIPMENT

Road machines are stronger and heavier than track bikes, and their two chain wheels and collection of sprockets give the rider up to 20 gears to choose from. They have quick-release hubs for wheel changes at the roadside, and special accessories to take drinking bottles.

The road racer carries some food in the back pockets of his jersey for the race's duration, has chamois leather inserts in his shorts to prevent any saddle-chafing and steel plates on his shoes to slot on to the pedals. He wears light gloves for extra grip and, essentially, a crash helmet.

WINNING

Stage races (those that last more than one day) have winners in several classes. The overall winner of the whole race is the rider whose daily stage times, added together, are lower than those of any other competitor. The overall team winners are decided by adding together the times of the best three men of each team on each stage.

There is a points winner, the rider who has accumulated the lowest total of actual placings in each day's riding, regardless of time. There is a King of the Mountains, who has collected most points on the designated hill climbs; and a Hot Spot Sprint winner, who will have collected most points at the designated sprint spots on each daily run. Apart from the overall points winner, all those classifications also occur in one-day road races.

RULES

Dangerous riding is not allowed, such as boring into a pack or switching in front of others. Taking pace from, or hanging on to, vehicles is banned, and so is pushing another competitor. But riders are allowed to help one another by exchanging food and drink, or waiting to pace back into the bunch a rider who has had a puncture or an accident.

WORDS

Bit-and-bit: groups of riders taking turns to share the pace at the front

Break: group of riders who are moving clear of the main field

Bunch: the largest group on the road

Commissaire: race referee

Domestique: rider whose duty is to look after the team's stars

Echelon: formation used to combat wind

Honking: standing on the pedals, usually on stiff climb

Musette: rider's feeding bag, collected during racing

Off the back: riders who have fallen behind the main field of cyclists

Prime: pronounced 'preem' – a point on the course at which there are special prizes to be won

Yellow jersey: worn by the race leader

SKILLS

Stamina is the greatest asset a road racer can wish for, and to acquire that he must spend thousands of miles on the road in training – probably as much as 150km (90 miles) almost every day of the year. Without that hard-won cycling strength, all his guile and experience will count for little.

TACTICS

The road racer must use his wits all the time. He needs to decide which break is worth joining and which is likely to prove a waste of energy; when he should leave a pack and go out on his own; where he needs to position himself if he is looking for sprint or climb points, or if there is going to be a sudden rush for the finish. The stage racer has even more to think about, for his racing will be influenced by the relative and cumulative times of his closest challengers.

In the end, it is team work that makes the difference in what appears to be an individual sport. Stage races are contested by teams, each with a star rider. The star's team mates are called domestiques, expected to cycle ahead and shelter the star from the wind, for example.

Cyclo-cross, Mountain Bikes

Just as runners, horses and motorbikes race across country, so too do bicycles. Traditionally, cyclo-cross has been the international sport where competitors combine pedalling with frantic sprinting carrying their lightweight bikes over obstacles and up muddy hills.

Artificial obstacles are put in the way, such as a gate or a felled tree, forcing riders to dismount and carry their bikes. According to international rules, these must not force riders to 'perform feats of acrobatics'.

Since the mid-Eighties, the sturdy mountain bike has inspired new and separate international competitions, complete with a World Cup and World Championships.

Cyclo-cross riders tend to race over several circuits of a short course, while mountain bikers have longer circuits of 8km (about 5 miles) where there is less running but more severe hills. As well as cross-country events, mountain bikers also compete in downhill events, with savage twists and bends, and in the USA, hill climbs.

CHRIS BOARDMAN It is difficult to tell who got most publicity at the Olympics in Barcelona – Boardman or his bike! The young 23-year-old Manchester Wheeler rocketed to victory in the 4000m individual pursuit setting world record after world record. He was even the first man to catch his opponent in an Olympic final. Yet successes had been rare for the 1.75m (5ft 8in), 72kg (11st 4lb) amateur – he won a bronze medal in the 1986 Commonwealth Games and came fifth in the 1991 World Championships. The bike changed all that. Lotus Engineering of motor racing fame built the carbon-fibre monocoque with only half a front fork and Boardman got the best out of it. 'All I thought of in the final was one word: Fight!'

DARTS

DARTS HAS GROWN FROM BEING A GAME PLAYED LARGELY FOR FUN IN CLUBS
AND PUBS TO BEING A HIGH-PROFILE, HIGHLY-REWARDED,
PROFESSIONAL ENTERTAINMENT

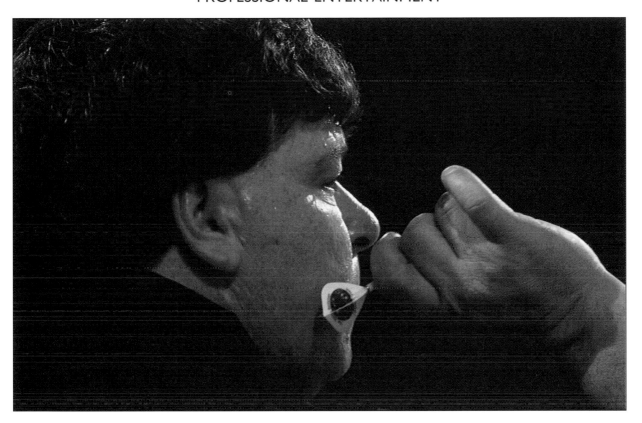

Once television recognized the dramatic potential of the game, and how easy it was to screen, the skills of the best players – most of them British – became familiar to a wide audience. The exposure drew sponsors, and at the 1992 World Championships there was £130,000 in prize money. With exhibition games, another source of income for the top players, the simple activity of throwing arrows at a board can now bring a very comfortable living.

The lack of athleticism among some of its leading participants led to doubt about the game's claim to be a serious sport; however, the governing body has worked extremely hard to improve the image of professional darts. Nowadays it is very much a family sport.

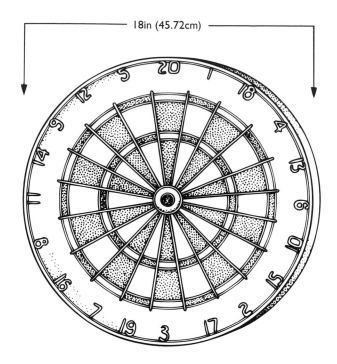

18in (45.72cm)

THE BOARD

The normal 'clock board' is 18in (45.72cm) in diameter. It used to be made of cork, or even of an elm log, but is now usually made of compressed fibres, with the various scoring segments delineated by a wire framework (spider). Each one has a value from one to 20 clearly marked on the edge of the board, but this is doubled if the dart lands within a narrow strip round the perimeter of the circle and trebled if it lands in a narrow strip nearer the centre of the board. In the centre is the tiny bull's eye (50 points) with a small outer ring worth 25.

The board is hung on a well-lit flat wall or stand with the centre of the bull 5ft 8in (1.73m) above the floor. Players throw with their toes touching or behind the back edge of a raised strip on the floor called an 'oche' (pronounced 'ockey' and now frequently called 'hockey'), placed 7ft 9¼in (2.37m) from the face of the board.

EQUIPMENT

Most professionals use darts made of tungsten alloy and weighing less than 1oz (28g). The material enables the darts to be very slim, making it easier for the player to group three darts together in one small target – the treble-20, for instance. They are then balanced by plastic flights attached at the tail of the shaft.

WINNING & RULES

Each player in turn throws three darts. The object is to reach an agreed total (usually 501 or 301) in the fewest possible darts, but the method of recording the score is unusual. The total appears at the top of each player's board, and at the end of each turn his score is subtracted from it. Thus the player can always see what his target is. The importance of this is that his final throw must reduce the target to exactly zero, and must be achieved by throwing a dart into a 'double' segment.

'Double top' (double-20) is a favourite finish, because most players find this one the easiest double to hit. Double-16 is also popular, because should the double be missed and single-16 scored, there remains double-eight, and so on to double-four, two and then one. Hitting the bull's eye counts as a score of double-25.

Tournament matches are usually decided over a number of sets, each set being the best of five games (legs). World championship matches are always played over five sets in the early rounds, seven in the quarter-finals, nine in the semi-finals and 11 in the final. So competitors who are playing in the closest possible final would have had to play 55 legs of 501 up, a severe, nerve-racking challenge to anyone's stamina and concentration.

SKILLS

The throwing skills are obvious, particularly if you have ever watched a player total 501 in nine darts – the equivalent of the 147 maximum break in snooker. What can sometimes seem even more amazing is the ability of the player, in the course of a three-dart turn, to perform mental arithmetic so swiftly that he knows what to aim for in order to leave him with a double for the next dart.

TACTICS

Professionals always concentrate on treble-20. Three darts in that little bed bring the maximum score of 180, and though that may not happen very often, consistently accurate throwing should produce an average of 100 per turn (two single-20s and one treble), which is the least score that all top players would expect.

The throwing action must be almost mechanically repetitive, even under pressure.

Sometimes a player will find himself in a bad patch in which he never finds the treble-20. A switch to treble-19 does not lose him much and may help cure the problem. The hardest part of the whole battle often proves to be the double needed to finish, and this is when a clear head and absolute concentration prove to be a player's greatest assets.

WORDS

Bull: the half-inch (1.27cm) spot at the centre of the board, worth 50

Bust: to score more points than needed to go out; player then loses the rest of his turn

Check-out: to finish; a 15-dart check-out is to win in only 15 darts

Double: a dart landing in the outer ring of the board

Double start: a game where players are required to hit a double to start

Double top: double-20, which is situated at the very top of the board

Flights: the three feathers, now usually plastic, that balance the dart in flight

Flying start: a game where players start without having to score a double

Leg: one game, of 501 in tournament darts

Oche: raised strip on the floor behind which the player must stand to throw

Set: decided by the best of three or five legs

Spider: wire mesh that marks out all the segments on a board

Three in a bed: three darts in the same double or treble segment

Toe the oche: to begin play, e.g. 'Toe the oche at 11am'

Ton: 100 scored

Too hot: a throw that busts

Treble: a dart which lands right in the inner ring of the board

Wire dart: a dart that bounces out of the board, usually because it has hit the wire; may not be thrown again

Man and horse have worked in harmony for centuries. Advice on how to ride and train was written by Xenophon, a Greek, as long ago as 365BC.

EQUESTRIAN EVENTS

SHOW JUMPING IS THE BEST KNOWN OF THE MANY COMPETITIVE FORMS OF THIS SPORT

Show jumping pits horse and rider against a series of fences and the clock, testing jumping ability and speed round an intricate indoor or outdoor course. Points are deducted for knocking down fences or exceeding the time limit.

Three-day eventing is a tremendous and complex test of the all-round skills, courage and stamina of both horse and rider. The best known part is the 8km (5 mile) cross-country gallop, which is in fact the last part of a gruelling four-phase speed and endurance test. It takes place on the second day, and it is usually then that the whole event is either won or lost.

On the third day is a fairly easy show jumping course, designed to test the suppleness of the horse, and on the first day is the dressage test. Perfection is the aim here, achieved by coordination and control on the part of the horse and absolute understanding between horse and rider.

Show Jumping

THE COURSE

Though indoor arenas are more familiar to television viewers, many of the major events of the world take place outdoors, in arenas three times as big. Some horses prefer the tightly-disciplined manoeuvres necessary indoors while others – often the larger horses – do better in the wide-open spaces.

The course designer uses a variety of fences, some big, some small, and places them to test the ingenuity and ability of the competitors without eliminating too many.

EQUIPMENT

At international level, the rider wears a reinforced cap, white shirt and tie, jacket, breeches and boots. The horse needs to have a bridle, saddle and protective coverings for his forelegs.

WINNING & RULES

The aim is to clear all the obstacles in the right order and inside the time limit. Four faults are imposed for knocking down any part of a fence or landing in the water (or on the landing tape); three faults for the first time a horse refuses a fence, six for the second and elimination on the third; and eight faults for a fall, of horse or rider.

If two or more competitors finish equal, a jump-off is held on a shortened course when speed as well as faults may decide the winner. Riders therefore concentrate on trying to get a clear round (no faults) the first time out and a fast clear round if they reach the jump-off.

There are special events in which speed and agility play a part from the beginning, and there are also puissance contests which test high jumping ability only. These end with only two fences which are progressively raised,

HENDERSON MILTON On Friday 18th September 1992 at Donaueschingen in Germany, the outstanding grey horse, Henderson Milton, confirmed his position as the best show jumping horse ever by becoming the first show jumper in history to win over £1 million in prize money.

The late Caroline Bradley bought Milton as a six-month-old foal, and her diligent schooling nurtured Milton's outstanding ability. When John Whitaker took on the horse in 1985, he started him off with small indoor shows. On his first trip abroad, however, Milton showed that he was a horse for the big occasion with big crowds – he came third in the Berlin Grand Prix, his first-ever international event. A star was born.

The dazzling grey, with a mischievous sense of humour that includes removing rugs and bandages when bored, is a star of Grand Prix classes and now competes as Everest Milton.

WORDS

Box: enclosure where event riders prepare for the speed and endurance phases and where horses are examined before the cross-country

Broken down: describes a horse that has badly strained or ruptured its back tendons

Circling: refusing an obstacle by circling before it

Combination: an obstacle comprising two or three fences within 12m (13yd) of each other

Jump-off (or barrage): a second (or later) round in which those lying equal first compete against each other

Over-reach boots: rubber rings worn by horses to prevent the toe of a hind foot injuring the heel of a fore foot

Oxer: fence comprising poles and hedge; double oxer has poles on both sides of the hedge

Passage: a slow, very elevated trot used in dressage

Piaffer: similar to passage, but performed on the spot

Pirouette: dressage movement in which horse turns a full circle, pivoting on the inside hind leg

Puissance: contest to judge jumping ability only

Running out: refusing to jump an obstacle by riding past it

Spread: any fence combining width and height

Tendon boots: worn by horses to prevent the toe of a hind foot injuring the back of a foreleg

Treble: three obstacles close together

---

like the human high jump bar, until only one competitor clears them.

SKILLS & TACTICS

Before each competition, the rider walks the course carefully, pacing the distances between fences that are particularly close together to decide whether the horse will need a shortened, normal or lengthened stride. Such decisions have to be communicated to the horse at the right time, which the most stylish riders manage to do with the minimum of movement.

There is no perfect build for a show jumping horse, but it must be brave and have plenty of spring in its hindquarters. An experienced horse will not need much prompting about the point of take-off, which is usually one-third of the height of the fence away from its base.

When speed is known to be a decisive factor, the top riders try to save time by cutting corners to shorten the designated route. Those who are drawn to ride early in an event try to jump with such speed and precision that they demoralize all their remaining opponents.

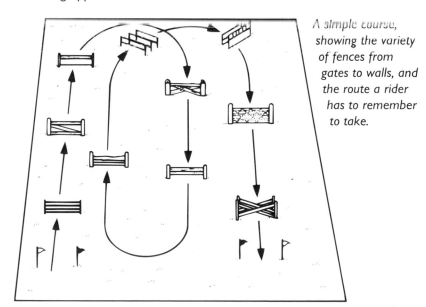

A simple course, showing the variety of fences from gates to walls, and the route a rider has to remember to take.

Dressage

The horse and rider are required to perform a set pattern of complex moves which the rider has memorized. The horse's actions must be rhythmic and precise, moving sometimes in a straight line, sometimes at an angle and sometimes in a circle. It will have to change step, to pirouette and to trot on the spot. Each of some 20 moves are marked by the judges, who even study the hoof prints in the sand to assess the perfection of movement. For this event, both horse and rider are beautifully groomed and the rider remains as still as possible.

Three-day Event

These competitions open with a 10-minute dressage test. The second day is divided into four parts, all timed independently, that are designed to test the speed, endurance and jumping ability of the horse. On the third day

Eventing demands a considerable amount of courage from both the horse and the rider.

there is a traditional show jumping competition over a comparatively simple course. On each day of the event there is a different form of dress that riders are expected to wear.

Day two opens with Phase A, in which 16–20km (10–12½ miles) of roads and tracks must be covered at a rate of 240m (262yd) per minute, a brisk trot or canter. Phase B is a steeplechase course of about 4km (2½ miles) in which four fences are each jumped three times at a gallop. This is followed by a repeat of Phase A.

There is then a break of only 10 minutes, during which time the horse is checked for fitness to continue by a veterinary surgeon before the gruelling final phase, an 8km (5 mile) gallop across country with solid, unyielding fences and walls, water jumps, steep banks and drops. For each second over the time limit, the rider receives 0.4 of a penalty point. Refusal to jump at a fence costs 20 points, a fall within the penalty zone around each fence costs 60 points, and taking the wrong course at any time results in immediate elimination.

Riders try not to gallop the horse all out, in order to conserve its energy throughout this demanding day. They look for short cuts in which to save time on the cross-country section, but this often means tackling the set obstacles at their most difficult point. Both horse and rider need not only exceptional stamina, but supreme courage.

Under international rules, all riders in senior three-day events must have reached their 18th birthday and must carry a minimum weight of 75kg (165lb, or nearly 12st) for all sections of the competition except the dressage. For the lighter female riders, this often means the addition of saddle weights.

FENCING
TO TRAIN FOR WAR AND FOR DUELLING, COMBATANTS PRACTISED WITH BLUNTED OR COVERED WEAPONS, AND SO MODERN FENCING AS A SPORT EVOLVED

Fencing today is a worldwide sport that retains much of the flourish and exhilaration of the duel, but the danger of injury is slight.

Apart from its considerable physical demands, it offers a mental challenge of the highest order. Acute concentration is necessary throughout the bout – even one second's relaxation may prove too much – and the fencer is constantly analyzing defence and attack to devise tactics to outwit the opponent.

Over the years, the romantic traditions of the sport have been well preserved in France and Italy. Their fencers, of both sexes, tend to be among the best in the world as well as the most colourful.

THE PISTE

Fencing is confined to a mat (piste) 2m wide (6ft 7in) and 14m long (46ft), which for the purposes of electrical scoring is covered by solid metal plates.

EQUIPMENT

Over a protective undergarment (plastron) the fencer must wear a white jacket and knee breeches made of man-made fibres, usually Kevlar, a leather glove on the fencing hand and a large rigid mask with a wire mesh visor.

Three weapons are used, each with different characteristics, and each needing a different style of fencing: the foil evolved from the light, practice weapon of the 17th century, the épée from the heavier duelling sword and the sabre from the cavalry sabre. All the types consist basically of a blade, a guard and a handle.

This is the defensive box, the imaginary area defining the sabre target. Every attack is matched by a parry, the defensive action taken to deflect or block the attacker's blade. The position of the hand and the angle of the blade vary according to the zone attacked. Antique French words are still used for specific zones: prime is the first position protecting the left-hand side of the body; seconde is the lower right-hand side; tierce is upper right; low tierce guards against a lateral cut; quarte, the fourth position, protects the upper left-hand side, while quinte, the fifth position, protects the head.

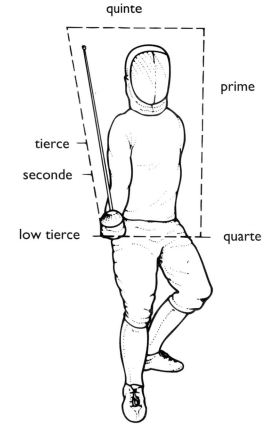

quinte

prime

tierce

seconde

low tierce

quarte

When electronic scoring apparatus is used, the fencer is plugged into a cable which runs up his back and down his fencing arm to connect with his blade. The cable is connected to a spring-loaded spool at the back of the piste, which takes up the slack as a fencer starts to retreat. Hits that are made on target are then automatically registered on a scoreboard. They are recorded for the successful hit against the opponent, so the competitor with the higher score would be winning.

WINNING

Matches at top level are decided over nine minutes, with one-minute rest periods after three and six minutes. The winner is deemed to be the first to score fifteen hits or the one who is leading at the end of nine minutes. Competitions are often played in a series of pools in which the participants all have to fight each other to determine the overall winner.

In foil and épée, hits are scored with the point only; in sabre, with the point, the whole of the front edge or the leading third of the back edge. The targets differ too: in foil, the whole of the trunk, front and back; in épée, every part of the fencer; in sabre, every part above the line of the hips, front and back.

RULES

Every bout is controlled by a president, but judges have been superseded by impartial electronic apparatus nowadays. In foil, if both fencers are hit simultaneously, the attacker alone scores points. The president must decide which fencer first straightened his arm with the point continuously threatening the target. Though fencers may side-step or turn slightly, they can never reverse their actual positions during a bout. If a fencer is forced back over his rear limit line twice, a penalty hit is then conceded.

SKILLS & TACTICS

What surprises most people when they see fencing for the first time is how violent and aggressive it is. Although foil and sabre are difficult disciplines to understand, because of rules governing right of way, epee is straightforward sword-fighting which explains its popularity in international competitions.

The sport demands poise, balance, muscular control and a mind and body so completely in harmony that many of the complex fencing movements are carried out automatically, leaving the brain free for analysis. A fencer's mind is never still. By reasoned observation or by intuition, he knows when to attack. At the same time, he is reading his opponent's mind and body and deciding when to step in, and how far, in order to disconcert his opponent's preparations to attack.

He must deceive without being deceived. While developing his own tactics, he must prepare counter-tactics to meet the lightning-fast reactions of his opponent – which may themselves be nothing more than clever deceptions to draw him into making a mistake. This may be a particularly difficult sport to master, but it is seldom ever a dull one, and you need only look at a fencer at the end of a long bout to see how intensely demanding it is.

Left-handers have done remarkably well in international competition over the years. So much so that ambitious and demanding parents have often insisted that their right-handed children learn how to fence left-handed in order to gain an advantage on their opponent. On rare occasions this extreme application of tactics has been known to pay off!

WORDS

Assault: a bout

Attack on the blade: preparation to attack by beating or pressing against the opponent's blade

Balestra: a short jump forward

Barrage: a tie or fight-off

Broken time: a deliberate pause between two movements of an attack

Compound attack: one which includes one or more feints

Corps à corps: when two fencers come into bodily contact

Engagement: the crossing of the blades in contact with each other

Feint: a movement of the blade to resemble an attack, the purpose of which is to draw a reaction

Flèche: an attack made by running rather than lunging

Judges: now superseded by the electronic scoring apparatus

Lunge: classical leg action to enable the fencer to reach his opponent

On guard: the prepared position at the start of a bout, to which the fencer will always return between his attacks

Parry: defensive, deflecting action with the sword

Phrase: sequence of fencing

movements exchanged between both fencers

Piste: the area on which fencers fight

Preparation to attack: a blade, body or foot movement which opens the way for an attack

President: the controlling official at a bout

Riposte: the offensive action which follows a successful parry

Second intention: today, this phrase often describes a successful response when an attack is interrupted can counter-attack

Touché: the word used to acknowledge a hit

FACT FILE

The invention of gunpowder triggered the start of swordfighting, with defence as important as attack. The handguard was invented by a Spaniard in about 1500, but France and Italy are recognized as the cradle of this science, which was taught in fencing schools in the 16th century. The following century, swordfights were staged in London, as is today's televised wrestling, with choreographed encounters. The sport plays down its roots in the duels fought by gentlemen to avenge their honour, preferring to extol its virtues of keeping fit, both mentally and physically.

It may look like all-out warfare, but American football is the most organized and analyzed sport in the world. Every move is planned by coaches who decide the tactics which are delegated to the quarterback.

AMERICAN FOOTBALL

DEVELOPED FROM RUGBY UNION OVER A CENTURY AGO AS A GAME FOR AMERICAN COLLEGE STUDENTS, THIS IS NOW A FEROCIOUS PROFESSIONAL SPORT DEMANDING EXCEPTIONAL STRENGTH AND SPEED

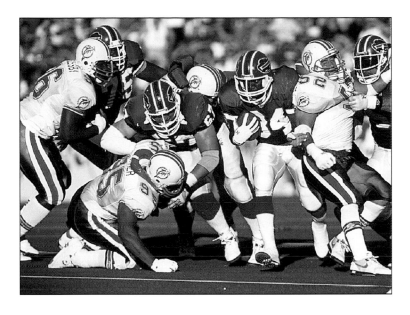

Every strategy on the field is planned by coaches on the sidelines, so that it is almost like a violent game of chess. Quite simply, 11 men attempt to carry an oval ball over their opponents' goal line by passing or running with it. The opposition is allowed to tackle them, and so effective are they that teams are given four attempts at moving the ball a mere 10yd (about 9m) which is why the 100yd (92m) long field is marked with stripes at 10yd intervals.

Play starts and stops every few seconds with players regrouping before starting another play. The violent collision of the players as they try to batter their way upfield has produced helmets and padding that make the already oversized athletes look positively superhuman. Although the two teams can each have only 11 men on the field at any one time, every player's role is highly specialized and the coach has a pool of 45 players that he can call on to carry out his tactical plans. Many players are on the field for just seconds before trotting off as colleagues come on to deal with a new situation. The team with the ball is known as the offense, the opposition as the defense.

THE FIELD

Traditionally played on grass, more and more teams use artificial surfaces. Only the space above the cross-bar and between the posts of the H-shaped goals counts when kicks are taken. Lines mark off the field into 5yd (4.6m) sections for the added benefit both of the spectators and the players who use the gridiron lines as a guide to whether a team has made all or part of the necessary 10yd (9.1m) to be able to retain possession.

The quarterback is the key player, initiating all the moves in American football.

EQUIPMENT

A helmet, equipped with a face mask, protects the head from direct blows. Also mandatory is a mouthpiece, usually dentally fitted. Players then strap on shoulder pads, kidney pads, thigh pads, knee pads; heavy tape protects any joint which can be bent in the wrong direction. Cleated (studded) shoes, a light, numbered jersey and tight-fitting pants complete the outfit.

WINNING

Play starts with a kick-off from the 35 or 40yd line, giving possession to the opposition straight away because they usually catch the ball. Then they try to advance the ball upfield at least 10yd in four attempts called downs. If they succeed they have four more attempts at another 10yd. If they fail, they give the ball to their opponents where it lies. If there seems little chance of making the 10yd in four downs, a team will give up possession by kicking the ball as far as possible away from their own goal line, forcing the opposition to begin their attack deep in their own half of the field.

There are two ways of gaining the 10yd. Holding the ball tightly, a player can run upfield as far as he can before being stopped by a tackle. The second and more spectacular way is by passing the ball, throwing it forward through the air to a receiver. This move often covers an area of more than 30yd (27.4m) in one fell swoop. However, if the ball is caught by the defense (an interception) they take over possession. If no-one catches the ball, the pass is incomplete and no yardage has been made, but a down has been used up.

In any four downs, running and passing plays are mixed, to try to confuse the defense. Taking the ball across the opposition's goal line scores a touchdown, worth six points. Each touchdown may be converted by a place kick taken in front of the posts, worth an additional point.

If attackers get near their opponents' goal line but cannot make the requisite 10yd, they can attempt a field goal. This is worth three points and is kicked from any spot on the field. The ball is snapped back by the center to a player who holds it for a specialist kicker to strike from distances as far as 50yd (about 45m) away from the goal line.

One other way of scoring involves the defense. If a player carrying the ball is forced backwards behind his own goal line and tackled, he gives away a safety, two points, to the other team.

A game has four quarters of 15 minutes each, a nominal time of an hour; but the clock only runs when the ball is actually in play, so most games in fact last for nearly three hours. If at the end of this time the score is tied (level), an additional 15 minutes of football will be played, the first score producing a winner of the match and ending the very long game.

RULES

Although there seems to be more violent physical contact in football than most other similar sports, deliberate roughness, such as punching, kicking and tripping are always strictly forbidden. The umpires, dressed in black and white striped shirts, throw a yellow flag or handkerchief on the ground when they spot an infringement of the game's rules. Because the game is based on the ideal of advancing just a few yards at a time, penalties are easy to award.

If the offending team is on the attack, they would be moved back 5, 10 or 15yd (4.6, 9.1 or 13.7m) depending on the seriousness of the offence committed. So a team might find itself trying to make a distance of 20yd (18.2m) on the next play with only three downs left. If the defending team then breaks the rules, the attackers could then be moved upfield 5, 10 or 15yd, so making their first down automatically.

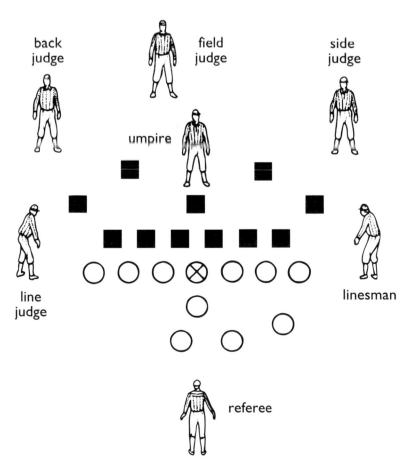

A simple line-up; the center, marked with an x, has the ball.

SKILLS & TACTICS

Once a player has caught the ball on a kick-off he tries to run up the field towards the opponents' goal line, while his team mates block opponents trying to tackle him. Sometimes a player catching the ball from the kick-off runs all the way to score a touchdown, but usually he is tackled soon after catching the ball. A player can keep going even if only half-tackled, the referee stopping play when his forward progress is halted. The players then go into a huddle for the quarterback to give the next play.

The defenders often do the same though this only takes a moment as the defensive formation is fairly standardized. Then both sides line up facing each other about one foot (about 30cm) apart at the line of scrimmage. This imaginary line runs through the tip of the ball straight across the field. It is from this line that the ball must be advanced 10yd (9.1m). On the sidelines two men carry a 10yd-long chain which has a tall pole with a flag on it at one end (which is

WORDS

Backs: two types – big and strong for straight ahead running and blocking; smaller and quicker for wide running

Down linemen: defenders who adopt a crouching stance opposite the offensive line. They try to detect where a play is going and stop the advance of the forwards and running backs

Field goal: worth three points, is a place kick from anywhere on the field that goes between the posts

Fumble: when a runner loses possession of the ball before he is stopped by tacklers. A free ball; everyone goes for it

Incomplete pass: a forward pass that is caught by neither an attacker nor a defender, a down is used up, the yardage is the same

Line backers: men in the 6ft 4in (2m) 225lb (100kg) range, fast enough to catch running backs and defend against passes, strong enough to fight off the blocks of 275lb (125kg) opponents and then make some tackles

Linemen: the biggest men in football; often ranging in height to 6ft 8in (about 2m) and weighing close to 275lb (125kg). Their strength and size keeps equally big men away from their backs and pass receivers

Pass receivers: although the ends and wide receivers specialize in catching forward passes, nowadays running backs are also key pass receivers

Punt: a kick from the hand that usually takes place on a fourth down; good punters average about 40yd (36.5m)

per kick, while good punt returners are happy to average 10yd (9.1m) per return

Quarter: the unit of play – 15 minutes

Quarterback: The key man on the side, needing tactical awareness for deciding the attacks. He must be able to pass accurately, often throwing overhand 60yd (54.8m) and quickly, having only three seconds at most to release the ball. He must be able to run with the ball and withstand hard tackles

Safeties: defenders who stay with speedy receivers, trying to prevent their catching a pass

Safety: attack is trapped behind its own goal line, costing two points

Time out: clock is stopped for coaching staff to consult players

placed level with the line of the scrimmage) and a similar pole to show how far the team in possession has to go.

The scrimmage is quite formal. Everyone on both teams must be behind the line of scrimmage. The center has his hands on the ball. The quarterback stands behind him and shouts a series of coded instructions for specific moves or plays, say '59-red-blue-hut!' On the word 'hut' the center snaps the ball back between his legs straight into the quarterback's hands and play is under way. Many of the moves are executed so quickly that only the television slow motion action replay can really show the quarterback's sleight of hand. He can fake a hand-off (disguise handling the ball) to a running back or drop back to position himself for a forward pass.

As players are allowed to block opponents, the man with the ball will often follow a colleague whose job is to clear a path for him through the opposition.

Sometimes players attempt to cover only 2 or 3yd by squeezing through a small gap in the defensive wall. For the long forward pass, receivers sprint upfield, away from the line of scrimmage, and run a pattern designed to throw off any pass defenders. Defenders can use their arms to tackle but the offensive team must not hold; blocking from behind (clipping) is illegal, as is pass interference, interfering with a man trying to catch a forward pass. The only ways a defender can stop a pass getting to a receiver are to block him straight after the snap, or to get in between him and the ball. Best of all, he might try to intercept his opponent's pass!

The best teams are the best-drilled teams, able to carry out the military-like manoeuvres dictated by the coaches. When both sides are equally adept then a single mistake, a flash of individual brilliance or the skill of a kicker can make the difference between victory and defeat.

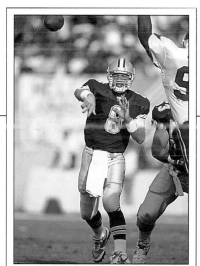

TROY AIKMAN

The statistics say it all: in the 1993 Super Bowl, the Dallas Cowboy's quarter-back attempted 30 passes, completed 22 for 273yd (249.5m) and four touch-downs. In only his fifth season as a pro, the 6ft 4in (1.93m) 222lb (101kg) Oklahoman has already broken club records set by the legendary Cowboy Roger Staubach and was the key player in sending the young Dallas squad back to the top. His collegiate career (at Oklahoma and UCLA) was so successful that he was rated the third best passer in college history.

Turning pro, he soon won a reputation both for accuracy and tenacity – he is rarely intercepted and has often initiated 'come-from-behind' wins in the final quarter.

Football's stars are among the most recognizable and marketable in the world. No wonder Gary Lineker, the former England captain, moved to Japan to develop the game there.

FOOTBALL

FOOTBALL IS KNOWN AS 'THE PEOPLE'S GAME' BECAUSE OF ITS ALMOST UNIVERSAL POPULARITY THROUGHOUT THE WORLD. ANYONE CAN PLAY IT. ANYONE CAN UNDERSTAND IT

Football is played everywhere and enjoyed everywhere. Its basic appeal is its simplicity. Its laws are straightforward and it can be played anywhere from the street to the local park, to hundreds of magnificent stadiums around the world. To succeed at the highest level, footballers require many qualities: skill in controlling the ball, balance, speed, athleticism, anticipation and physical courage. Given a certain level of fitness, there is scope for the short or the tall, the wiry as well as the muscular. Diego Maradona, who helped Argentina to win the World Cup in 1986, was a short, powerful player; Franz Beckenbauer, who captained West Germany to success in 1974, was tall and elegant.

The spectators at big professional matches contribute to the entertainment. The roar of the crowd along with the colourful banners and scarves all add to the excitement and tension. The explosion of noise when that tension is released by the scoring of a goal is one of the game's big attractions for many supporters. The World Cup, which takes place every four years, rivals the Olympic Games as the world's biggest and most popular sporting event.

NICKNAMES

British clubs are often referred to by their nicknames. Among the most colourful are:

ENGLAND
Manchester United: The Red Devils
Norwich: The Canaries
Newcastle United: The Magpies
Arsenal: The Gunners
Everton: The Toffeemen
Sheffield United: The Blades
Southampton: The Saints
West Ham United: The Hammers
Portsmouth: Pompey
Millwall: The Lions
Brentford: The Bees
Stoke City: The Potters
Bolton Wanderers: The Trotters
Bury: The Shakers
Luton Town: The Hatters

THE FIELD

Football has traditionally been played on grass although several clubs have experimented with 'plastic' or 'all-weather' pitches. No manufacturer, though, has so far been able to produce a synthetic surface that reproduces the bounce or feel of a grass surface. Sides that play all their home matches on an artificial pitch have a definite advantage, so in England, clubs in the top leagues have been forced to replace their plastic pitches with grass.

The 1994 World Cup finals saw the use of an indoor stadium for the first time in the competition's history.

EQUIPMENT

Football kit, like the game itself, is not complicated. The 10 outfield players of each team all play in the same coloured shirt, shorts and socks. The goalkeeper must wear a shirt that does not clash with the shirt colour of either side. Boots are light and cut away at the ankle. All players must wear shin-guards under their socks.

Shirts normally bear the name of a club's commercial sponsor. This income has become vital for many smaller professional teams who, despite small crowds, often have to pay players large wages.

The ball is spherical and traditionally has been made of leather. Nowadays balls are coated with a synthetic film to stop them soaking up moisture so that they remain relatively light and lively.

WINNING

A football team consists of 11 players, only one of whom, the goalkeeper, can touch the ball with his hands while the ball is 'in play'. Games last for 90 minutes with matches split up into two halves of 45 minutes. The team which scores the greater number of goals wins the match.

Goals are achieved by propelling the ball into the opposing team's net, usually by kicking or heading it. Only the deliberate use of hands is prohibited. Under pressure, a defender may concede an own goal, turning the ball into his own net. For a goal to be awarded, the whole of the ball must cross the whole of the goal line.

The most common form of competition for a number of teams wishing to compete against each other is a league. Usually teams play each other twice during a season, once on their home ground and then on their opponents' ground. In most leagues in the world, two points are awarded for a win and one for a draw, but in countries such as England attacking play is encouraged by awarding teams three points for a win.

When all matches have been played, the team with the most points wins the league. Teams that finish level on points are separated by 'goal difference'. That is determined by subtracting the number of goals a team has conceded from the number it has scored. The team with the greater goal difference finishes higher in the league.

Another popular competition is the knockout tournament. Teams are paired together by means of a draw. The winners, either after a single match or after the scores in home and away matches are added, go through to the next round and another draw is made. Normally the eventual winners of the tournament receive a silver cup, so this type of competition has come to be called cup football.

From time to time, the sudden death element of cup football allows a lesser, unfancied team to beat more distinguished opposition. Knockout competitions provide the drama of the unexpected. League contests, in which everyone plays each other, reduce the element of chance and generally reward the best team over a long period. Cup matches that finish level after 90 minutes are often decided by another 30 minutes of play called 'extra time'. If the scores are still level at the end of this period matches are settled by a penalty competition. Both teams take five penalties each with the team scoring the most winning the match. Recently, many matches in the finals of the World Cup have been decided on penalties and, as a result, football's governing body, the FIFA, has considered many rule changes in an effort to encourage teams to attack more during the normal playing time.

LAWS

Football is governed by 17 laws. The first six merely define the field of play, the ball, equipment, the players and officials who arbitrate during a game. Other laws relate to such technicalities as the duration of the game and the start of play. Before a match, the two team captains spin a coin to decide who has the choice of either kicking off or picking which end to defend. A strong wind or sun in one direction could influence this decision. Teams play 45 minutes each way with a break for half-time of between 10 and 15 minutes. The duration of a half-time break is often influenced by preferences of television companies when matches are being televised live. In general, only two laws give rise to argument but they are enough to make refereeing no job for the sensitive One is Law 12, 'Fouls and Misconduct'. This forbids kicking, tripping and punching for example, as well as handling the ball and other less physical offences such as swearing and time-wasting.

If the transgression is serious, or persistent, the offender will be officially cautioned (shown the yellow card) or sent off the field (shown the red card). Players are now shown the red card if they deliberately foul an opponent when a goal would almost certainly be scored. This attempt to stop what is known as the 'professional foul' is designed to increase the number of goals

scored and prevent the employment of cynical tactics. Law 12 has also been amended to prevent a goalkeeper touching the ball with his hands when the ball has been deliberately kicked back to him. The 'back-pass' rule has become popular with spectators, if not the players, because the ball is in play for longer. The second source of contention is Law 11 which carefully details when a player is offside. Basically, a player is offside when the ball is played forward to him in his opponents' half and there are not two opponents between him and the goal. A player, though, cannot be offside from a throw-in, corner kick, or a goal kick. A linesman, who adjudicates on offside decisions, must be sharp-eyed to spot when a player is offside. His ability to make the right decision can be crucial. With fewer goals being scored, especially in international matches, it has been suggested that the offside law be abolished or modified.

Certain offences within the penalty area are punished by a penalty kick – in effect a free shot from a spot marked 12yd (about 11m) from the goal which can only be defended by the goalkeeper. Otherwise play starts after a foul with a free kick; the team offended against resumes play with a stationary ball at the place where the infringement took place. The opponents must be 10yd (about 9m) away from the ball at freekicks. When fouls occur near the penalty area this gives the attacking team an excellent opportunity to score. Several players, such as the former French international Michel Platini, are known as 'free kick specialists' because of their ability to strike a stationary ball into the net from just outside the penalty area. Experts often bend the ball round defensive players. If the ball goes over the side line (touch line) a throw-in is awarded there against the side that last touched the ball. Any player can take it, and throw the ball two-handed over

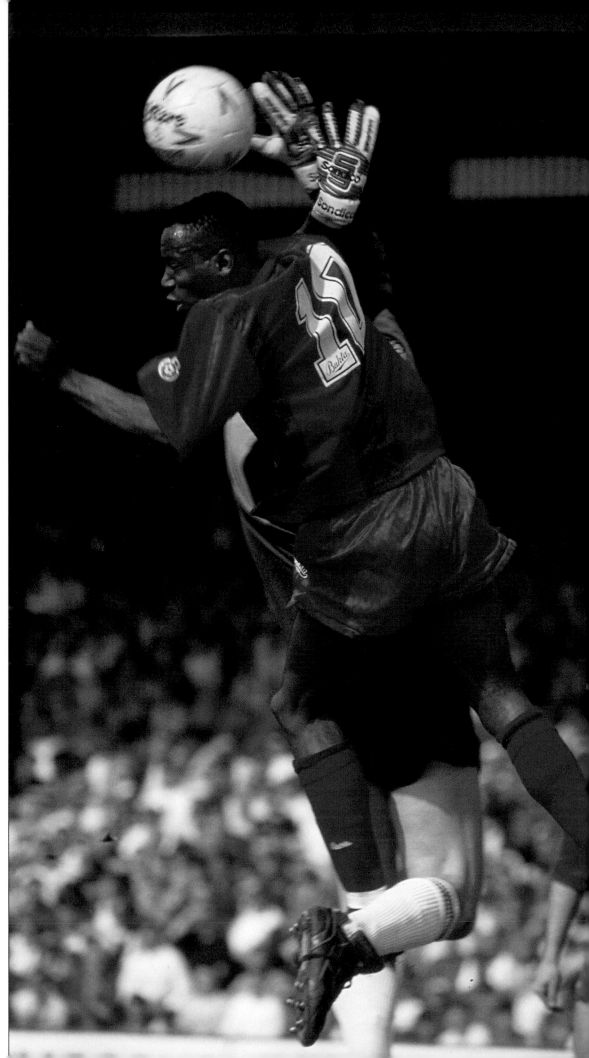

Football demands high skill coupled with physical fitness and bravery. At the highest level, players perform twice a week, month after month. One day they might be representing their club in a league match; a few days later it could be a European Cup tie, and soon after they could be on international duty: each time, a different set of circumstances and conditions, even different team mates. And, all the time, the fans demand victory. The stakes (and wages) are high, so strikers are expected to risk all to score. Goalkeepers in particular have to ignore all the advancing opponents, and keep both eyes on the ball.

his head and back into play. If a defender is the last person to touch the ball as it goes over the goal line, then a corner kick is given to the attacking side, taken on the side of the field where the ball went out of play. If, however, an attacker is the last one to touch the ball before it goes over the goal line, then a goal kick is awarded to the defending team. The goalkeeper usually takes this, placing the ball in his goal area and either booting it upfield, or often just tapping it to a colleague (who must stand outside the penalty area) who plays it back to the goalkeeper. He then has the easier job of kicking the ball downfield.

SKILLS

Goalkeeper: must be brave and agile. Needs good judgement in jumping, diving, catching or punching the ball. His ability to position himself correctly is also vital. The change in the law which prevents goalkeepers handling back-passes means that goalkeepers now have to be able to kick the ball clear under extreme pressure.

Defenders: must have the strength to tackle firmly and the pace to match the speed of an opposing attacker. An ability to head the ball well is essential among central defenders.

Midfield players: must be complete all-rounders, reinforcing defence or attack as required. Stamina, imagination and accuracy with long and short passes are important.

Strikers: Ideally they should be fast, skilful and strong and have the ability to make half-chances into goals. Bravery is essential.

Common to all players are the many ways in which to control and kick a ball. All the great players tell tales of practising with a tennis ball on the way from home to school, in the playground and in the back yard. The learning process goes on and on, so that a ball can be trapped instantly and passed to a colleague all in one movement. The chest, thigh and foot are all used to bring a ball under control. Kicking the ball with the inside or outside of the foot makes it curve left or right; there has to be the ability to flick a ball delicately or hammer it goalwards from 40yd (about 36m) out. Heading skills have to be equally refined: sometimes for a defensive clearance; at other times heading firmly downwards to beat the goalkeeper's dive. A subtle nudge of the head can be sufficient to deflect a crossed ball into the path of a colleague – or straight into the net. As in all sports, the best professional players can make it look too easy!

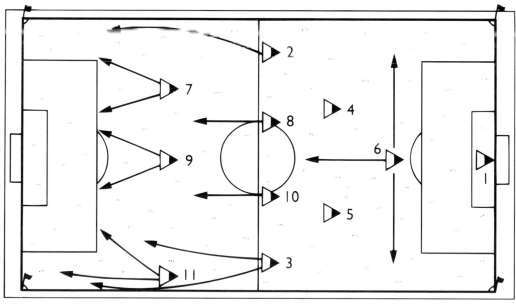

Commentators often refer to an 'extra' or 'spare' defender called the sweeper whose role is to plug gaps in defence or initiate attacks. Number 6 is the sweeper who is able to cover back to left and right, or to attack up the middle. Numbers 2 and 3, the full backs, can push up to support the midfield or attack knowing that the sweeper is covering.

The offside law is the hardest to understand. Many teams deliberately trap opponents offside by moving defenders upfield simultaneously. When attacker 7 passes the ball back to team mate 9, defender 6 tells his team mates to push up together, putting attackers 10, 11, and 7 offside. Free kick to the defenders.

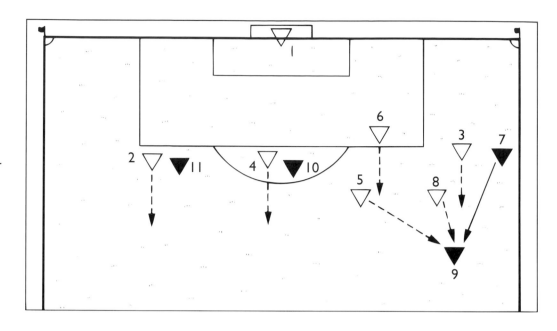

THE WORLD CUP FINALS

◆ First played in 1930, the winners were Uruguay

◆ Brazil is the only country to play in all 14 tournaments

◆ Three nations have won three times: Brazil, Italy and West Germany

◆ Gerd Muller scored a record 14 goals in 1970 and 1974

◆ In 1958 and 1962, Brazil went undefeated through the finals, playing 13, winning 11 and drawing twice.

WORDS

Corner: a means of re-starting play after the defending team has played the ball over its own goal line

Cross: a ball kicked into the penalty area by the attacking team from a position wide and deep into their opponents' half

Direct free kick: a free kick from which a goal may be scored without another player touching the ball

Indirect free kick: a free kick from which a goal may not be scored until another player, from either side, has touched the ball

Mark: a defensive technique where a player will stay as close as possible to his opponent in order to stop or disrupt the progress of an attack

One-two: a quick exchange of passes between two players in which the second returns the ball to the first

Professional foul: a serious, deliberate foul which prevents the probable scoring of a goal and results in the player committing the foul being sent off

Red card: shown to a player by the referee to indicate the player is being sent off

Sweeper: a spare defender without specific marking responsibilities. Usually the last man in defence in front of the goalkeeper

Throw-in: a means of re-starting the game after a ball has crossed the touchline. The ball must be thrown from behind the head with both hands

Winger: an attacking player who operates mainly near the touchline

Yellow card: shown to a player by the referee if the player has committed a bad foul. If the player is shown another yellow card he will be sent off. If a player collects several yellow cards during a season he will be suspended from playing for a specified number of games

TACTICS

Modern football is intensely competitive. Professional players often say their game is 'all about winning'. But, because it is easier to defend with organization than attack with imagination, much football strategy is negative. Nevertheless, teams and players that have captured the imagination of the football public have been notable not only for winning, but winning with flair and style. Few teams have reached the pinnacle of excellence achieved by Brazil in winning three World Cups between 1958 and 1970 and few players have matched the brilliance of the team's main inspiration, Pelé. At various times, Hungary and Holland, at international level, and Real Madrid, Ajax of Amsterdam and Bayern Munich at club level have also shown a spirit of adventure in which skill and resolution have been thrillingly blended. And from time to time exceptionally gifted players come to the fore. Dutchman Johann Cruyff was the star of the Seventies, Diego Maradona of Argentina the star of the Eighties. The Nineties is still waiting for such a player to emerge. As the game gets quicker and players get fitter it has become increasingly difficult for teams to be successful by playing a carefree, open attacking game. A mixture of determined defending and judicious attacking is now the order of the day. At international level, West Germany – now Germany – has been the most successful at adapting to this method of play, reaching five of the last seven World Cup finals and winning the competition twice. Managers spend much time on the training ground working out methods to defend successfully. In the modern game much emphasis is also placed on turning free kicks and corners (set pieces) into goals.

Different countries have developed different styles of play. In England, teams tend to play the ball forward quickly and over longer distances. In Italy or France, sides employ a much more measured build-up with the players performing a series of patient, short-passing moves.

DAVID PLATT

After an unsettled start to his career, Platt has now emerged as one of England's most accomplished players. His talent was spotted early on when he was on Manchester United's books as a youngster, but he was transferred to lowly Crewe Alexandra for £40,000 without playing a first-team match. After scoring 55 goals in 134 games for Crewe he was signed for Aston Villa by Graham Taylor.

He first came to prominence at international level in the 1990 World Cup finals, when he scored vital goals to help England into the semi-finals. An all-action player, he moved to Italy in 1991 for the sum of £5$\frac{1}{2}$ million.

The idea of a professional golf circuit developed in the USA. Although every continent has its own tournaments, only Europe can rival the USA when it comes to big tournaments.

GOLF

From such crude beginnings, the game has now become a much more sophisticated sport.

Physical it may be, with a golfer walking, on average, 5 miles (about 8km) during a round, but it is also a thinking game. Ninety-five per cent of golf is mental. It takes intelligence to work out the best place to hit a drive, the best way to play a hole. Scoring well needs more than just good driving. The game demands complete concentration for as long as maybe four hours – concentration on the apparently simple task of getting a small ball into 18 separate holes in as few strokes as possible.

The top male professionals can earn millions in prize money, setting their sights on the four most important tournaments or majors: the Open Championship in Britain, the US Open, the US Masters and the US PGA (Professional Golfers' Association)

Championship. The best women compete for their own majors. A golfer is always on his own – if he plays badly, he can only blame himself. Golf is a simple game, confusing only because of the special language.

THE COURSE

The standard number of holes on a full course is 18. Each is made up of three distinct sections: the tee, the fairway and the green. The tee is a flat area about 6yd (5m) square where the golfer strikes the first shot at each hole. The golfer hopes the ball lands on the fairway, the stretch of ground that runs from the tee to the green. The grass here is cut short, but is bordered on both sides by rough or longer grass which starts about 3in (8cm) in height and can become knee deep. There is a premium, therefore, on driving accurately off the tee to make the next shot easier.

In addition to the rough, there are other hazards to be avoided – hollows filled with sand called bunkers, water hazards such as lakes, streams and ditches, as well as trees and bushes. All these are strategically placed by golf course designers to catch the badly-aimed or poorly-struck ball.

The third part of a hole is the green which has the actual hole, 4¼in (10.8cm) wide, sunk in it, marked with a tall stick and flag. Greens are deliberately smooth to allow the ball to run along the ground to the hole. On average about 50ft (15m) across, they often undulate or slope gently.

EQUIPMENT

A golf ball is 1.68in (43mm) in diameter and is dimpled to make it fly through the air with aerodynamic efficiency. On the course, golfers are allowed a maximum of 14 clubs, each designed to strike the ball in different ways in different conditions. They may use as many as four woods with big, solid heads that maximize distance. There are 10 irons, numbered one to 10, with varying degrees of loft (elevation) which are normally used from the fairway. The higher the number, the greater the degree of loft and the shorter the distance the ball will travel.

WINNING

Most important golf championships are decided by stroke-play, with players adding up their scores for each of the 18 holes, and the lowest total winning. In big tournaments, four rounds of 18 holes, played over four days, decide the winner.

To tell how well a golfer is doing at any stage of a round, each of the holes has a par rating. This is the score a good golfer should make. There are three ratings – par 3, par 4 and par 5. A par 3 is up to 250yd (228m) long from tee to green. The green should be reached with one shot, leaving two putts to make par. A par 4 hole is from 251yd (229m) up to 475yd (434m), while the par 5 hole is anything over 475yd.

A typical par-4 hole of 444yd with a dogleg to the right.

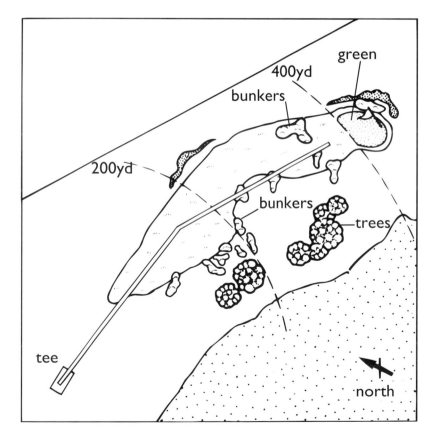

RULES

Rule one emphasizes the simplicity of the game which consists of playing a ball from the teeing ground into the hole by successive strokes in accordance with the rules. The next 40 rules deal with the awkward situations that golfers get themselves into, as well as, for instance, the limitations on equipment. Only one replacement is allowed if a club is broken accidentally when hitting a shot. Other rules cover good manners, requiring that players do not try to upset opponents in any way or waste time.

The ball must always be played from where it lies, from where it landed. If it is impeded by branches or long grass, that is just hard luck on the golfer. Loose stones, leaves or twigs can be removed but at no time must the ball be moved or else the golfer suffers a penalty of one stroke, which is added to the score. At times, of course, the ball lands where it is impossible to play – behind a tree, in a pond, even out of bounds or off the course, for instance. Then stroke and distance come into play. If a drive is hit out of bounds, a player can use another ball and drive off

---

WORDS

Ace: a hole in one

Address: a golfer's stance before hitting ball

Albatross: a hole completed in three shots less than par

Birdie: a hole completed in one shot less than par

Bogey: a hole completed in one shot more than par

Borrow: the slope on a green

Caddie: person employed to carry clubs and give advice on shots

Chip: a shot hit with a lofted iron close to the green

Cup: another name for the hole

Divot: a sliver of earth taken up when an iron shot is played correctly

Dogleg: hole with sharp bend to left or right between tee and green

Eagle: a hole completed in two shots less than par

Etiquette: the rules by which golf should be played

Fore: a warning shout before a drive or shot is played

Handicap: not used in professional play, where all players are of equal ability; in amateur games, a system of bonus strokes is used so that players of differing standards can meet on equal terms

Marshal: official who keeps spectators in order at all the tournaments

Nineteenth hole: popular name for the bar in the golf clubhouse

Open: a tournament open to amateurs and professionals

Pin: another name for the flag in the hole

Playoff: when two or more players finish with the same score at the end of tournament, they play extra holes. It is sudden death: the first to win a hole wins the tournament

Tee: the area where a golfer strikes the first shot at each hole; or, the small wooden or plastic peg on which the ball is placed for this first shot

Wedge: 10 iron

JACK NICKLAUS

◆ Nicknamed the 'Golden Bear', the American is rated the greatest player in the history of golf. No one can match his record of 20 major titles:

◆ US Masters: 1963, 1965, 1966, 1972, 1975, 1986

◆ US PGA Championship: 1963, 1971, 1973, 1975, 1980

◆ US Open: 1962, 1967, 1972, 1980

◆ British Open: 1966, 1970, 1978

◆ US Amateur: 1959, 1961

again. This would be counted as the third stroke – the first drive plus a penalty stroke. If the ball is in an awkward lie, a player can move two club lengths away and drop the ball. Although this also incurs a penalty of one stroke, it could be a safer course of action than trying to hack the ball out of trouble. If there is any snow, ice or a pool of water on the green due to extreme weather or poor drainage, a player can move the ball to another spot and drop it without incurring a penalty, as long as the new position does not have the advantage of being nearer the hole.

SKILLS & TACTICS

While average amateurs strive to hit the ball reasonably straight, professionals may not always want to. If a hole curves to the right or left a shot may be shaped to go in that particular direction.

If a golfer fades a ball, the shot he has made goes intentionally from left to right; if overdone, this becomes a slice or cut shot in which the ball moves much more dramatically from left to right and generally into trouble.

Many golfers, on the other hand, play a natural draw, a shot that intentionally moves from the right to left. If not carefully controlled, this shot then becomes what is known as a pull or hook.

On average, a golf professional will drive a ball 280yd (255m), but downwind this could approach as much as 400yd (360m) if the fairways are sunbaked.

At the highest level, all the best golfers in the world can drive, chip and putt in all weathers, on all surfaces and in any country. The winner will be the player who, on the day, is most confident and able to withstand the mental pressure of sinking a putt that could be worth a million dollars!

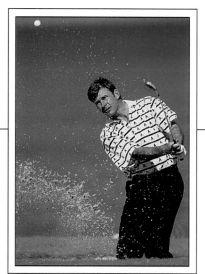

NICK FALDO

Faldo is Britain's most successful golfer since the war. He turned professional at only 19, winning his first tournament the following year along with the title 'Rookie of the Year'. Always a diligent and reliable player, he had the courage to re-model his swing action in mid-career under the tuition of golf guru David Leadbetter. The change of style has resulted in him winning five major championships and the extra title of 'World's Number One'. He was a key figure in all the European's Ryder Cup triumphs in the Eighties. In 1992 he became the first professional player to win more than £1 million in prize money on the European tour in a single season.

GREYHOUND RACING

THE GREYHOUND AS AN ANIMAL CAN BE TRACED BACK 7000 YEARS, AND FOR MANY CENTURIES WAS USED FOR HUNTING AND COURSING

In London in 1876 an attempt was made to introduce 'simulated coursing', the forerunner of greyhound racing, over a straight 400yd (365m) track with an artificial hare mounted on a rail. 'The new sport is undoubtedly an exciting and interesting one,' wrote The Times. *The idea was not pursued, and in America the modern sport was born at a circular track in Emeryville, California, in 1919. The mechanical hare moved to Britain in 1926 and it soon raced around the world.*

Much greyhound racing survives only through the betting industry, to the extent that some meetings are held in such locations and at such a time that hardly any of the public are present at all. The tracks are licensed and the dogs registered, but the races are held solely to provide results for the bookmakers and the punters.

THE TRACK

Racing takes place on an oval track with a circumference between about 400 and 550yd (366–493m), around which the artificial hare is made to move on an electrified rail. The surface is usually of turf, sand or cinders. The dogs start in traps from behind which the hare commences its run, on the inside of the track. When the hare is about 12yd (11m) in front of the traps, their doors automatically open to let the dogs out.

EQUIPMENT

Racing greyhounds, which may be in several shades of colour but seldom grey, are thoroughbreds built entirely for speed. They usually begin to race at 12 or 15 months, according to national rules; their age being reckoned from the first day of the month in which they were born. All dogs must be registered with the racing authority, and for every dog there is an identity book. This is its passport to the racing world, within which is recorded details of its birth, parents, measurements, colouring and racing record. The book is never left in the hands of the dog's owner, but is produced every time it races. An official checks the identity of every dog in the paddock immediately before a race starts.

Dogs wear coloured jackets bearing numbers corresponding to the position of the trap in which they are drawn, and are always muzzled. Kennel hands (often kennel maids) parade the dogs before the race, giving punters a chance to pick their fancy. They put them in the traps and are at the trackside to collect them again when the hare disappears and the dogs do not know where to go next.

WINNING

Race timing is automatic, with a device that is set in motion as the trap doors open. There is a judge at the winning post and a photo-finish camera to help him. Races are held over distances varying from 230yd (210m) to 1200yd (1097m), and usually with a maximum of six or eight runners.

There are several categories of race. Some countries use a grading system, in which dogs of the same grade compete against each other. The winners advance a grade, repeated losers go down a grade. Often there are races just for dogs trained by trainers licensed at the racecourse concerned, as well as open races for greyhounds in the charge of any licensed trainer. There are also handicap races, in which one or more dogs have to run the full distance (from the inside traps) and the others are given starts of varying distances according to form; and there are also races over hurdles.

'No race' may be declared if there is a defect in the starting mechanism or in the running of the hare, which has to be kept reasonably near the leading greyhound. A 'no race' can be rerun at the same meeting.

RULES

Every effort is made by the authorities in countries where greyhound racing is well organized to ensure there is no return to the dubious practices of years past. Apart from the identity book check before every race, all dogs are officially identified and weighed before the first race of any meeting. A dog whose weight varies more than a specified amount from its last running weight is withdrawn. A veterinary surgeon examines them then, and again immediately before a race; between those examinations, each dog is kept in an individual kennel, which may be locked at the request of the owner.

Racecourses should be approved by the governing body, which demands a high standard of operating procedures and a minimum number of officials. As in the horse racing world, owners and trainers are liable

to disqualification if they run a dog at an unauthorized course, or if they engage in any improper or fraudulent practices.

It a dog runs outside the defined track, whether or not it finishes the race properly, it is regarded as not having completed the course. A dog that fights during a race is disqualified. Repeated fighting will result in permanent exclusion.

SKILLS

The speed with which a dog is blessed is more of a talent than a skill, but it can be breathtaking. Dogs have been timed at up to 45mph (72kmph) on the straight, and at nearly 39mph (63kmph) around a four-bend track. The skill of a good trainer is unquestioned. It is his job to keep the dog in perfect racing condition and to persuade the animal to release that natural speed whenever the door of the trap opens.

When greyhound racing first began in America, live hares were used, which was presumably a strong incentive to a dog to get there first. By breeding and training, the dogs now seem prepared to chase the mechanical hare around the track not just for a sprint of half the circuit, but (in a marathon) for three circuits of the track. They have the skill, but without the benefit of a jockey it cannot be easy to give them the will.

TACTICS

Inevitably, this is a matter that can only be discussed between dogs, but you can watch one exercising its native intelligence and cunning for tactical purposes. Like an athlete, a greyhound will go for that position in the field most favourable to its particular style of running. That may be on the rails, giving it the shortest distance to cover; or on the outside away from the other runners.

The first bend is often the one that sorts out the wise heads from the rash ones. Coming so soon after the start line, the dogs are still bunched when the hare goes round the bend. This is the moment when the dogs are liable to get in each other's way, and when you will often see the class dog either anticipating the bend or keeping clear of trouble and streaking away from the mob as soon as the track straightens out again.

All racing greyhounds are trained to react instantly to the opening of their traps.

Gymnastics features different skills on different equipment. Top left: the pommel horse; top right: the asymmetric bars; bottom left: the beam; bottom right: the rings.

GYMNASTICS

It is one of those rare sports in which there is no confrontation between competitors – who are, indeed, not competing so much as performing to the highest degree of perfection they can muster. No stop watch or tape measure can prove who the winner is. That is a matter of opinion, and we rely on the expert judges to get it right, just as we do in the performance sport of ice skating.

There are several branches of the sport, of which outstandingly the most popular is artistic gymnastics. Even that is different for men and women, for there is little common ground between the sexes other than extraordinary agility and their use of both the floor and the vaulting horse. On the men's six pieces of apparatus, they demonstrate controlled strength; a much more artistic element is included in the women's standard four exercises.

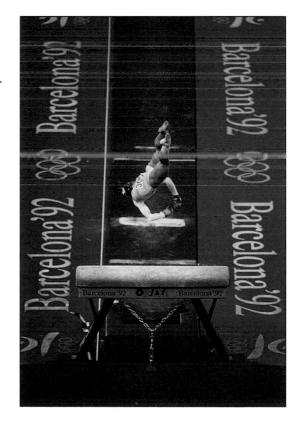

Women also compete on the Olympic programme in rhythmic gymnastics, the most lyrical of all forms.

Artistic Gymnastics

THE APPARATUS

For men: a floor mat 12m square (about 13yd); a well-padded vaulting horse 1.35m high (4ft 5½in) and 1.6m long (5ft 4in); parallel bars, adjustable in width but 1.75m (about 5ft 9in) above the mat and 3.50m long (11ft 5½in); a pommel horse, lower than the vaulting horse but with two parallel handles in the centre, 40–45cm apart (approx. 16–18in); the rings, a pair swinging freely 2.75m (9ft) above the floor; and the high bar, at the same height as the rings.

For women: the same floor mat; the same vaulting horse, but at only 1.2m high (3ft 11in) and set across the run instead of along it; the beam, 5m long (16ft 4½in), 1.2m (3ft 11in) above the floor and only 10cm (less than 4in) wide; and the asymmetric bars, which are a parallel pair with one 2.4m high (7ft 10½in) and the other 1.6m (5ft 4in).

EQUIPMENT

Both men and women wear leotards, one-piece costumes made from stretchy material which normally have shoulder straps for men and (usually) sleeves for women. To this men must add white trousers, though shorts are allowed for floor and vault. Bare feet are often seen, but socks or flexible shoes are recommended. For rings and bars, competitors will wear leather hand guards and rub magnesium carbonate onto their hands (and often on the equipment as well) to absorb sweat and therefore improve their grip on the apparatus.

WINNING

The judging and marking of gymnastic exercises is an extremely complicated matter, the details of which vary between sexes and according to the apparatus. While it is not possible to generalize with absolute accuracy, the following notes give a reasonable picture of the operation.

Six judges, drawn randomly from different countries, judge each exercise. From their scores the highest and lowest are disregarded and the final score is the average of the other four. It is intended that this system should eliminate any outstanding bias, one way or the other, conscious or subconscious; and even beyond that, the referee (head judge) will query any remarkable discrepancy in the scores.

The judges are helped by a technical assistant whose job it is to check that the requirements of each exercise have been met and to assess the content value of each exercise against a predetermined difficulty factor. The judges thus start with an idea of the maximum possible score for the exercise, and deduct from it a number of points for any faults they see.

With the World Championships of 1993 a new code of points was introduced. This included the awarding of a 1.0-point difficulty bonus, which made it much harder for the gymnast to reach the 'perfect' score of 10.00. Indeed, it was never achieved at all in those championships.

In major tournaments such as world and Olympic championships, all competitors perform all the apparatus exercises. After the qualifying rounds, those with the highest combined scores (perhaps 24 or 36 of them) move on to the all-round final. Earlier scores count for nothing here, and each gymnast has to perform again on each apparatus. The competitor with the highest aggregate score is the all-round champion, the most prestigious position in the sport.

The top few scorers in the qualifying round on each individual piece of apparatus (perhaps six or eight of them) advance through to the apparatus finals. Each one eventually produces a champion, and the all-round champion may not necessarily be among these particular competitors.

RULES

Each element in a performance is awarded a degree of difficulty, decided by the international governing body. Each routine has to contain a set number of elements from each category.

Floor: The routine must last between 50 and 70 seconds and must include tumbles, balances (held for at least two seconds), height in somersaults, movements requiring suppleness and those requiring strength. Men must include three acrobatic sequences. A major element of dance and consecutive leaps is included for women, which should be performed in harmony with the music.

Vault: a springboard is used for take-off and every part of the vault will be marked, from take-off through the flight to the landing. Women are allowed two vaults, of which the average mark counts.

Parallel bars: precise, continuous swinging movements are necessary, as well as lateral movement and flight, when contact is lost with either one or both hands.

Pommel horse: all parts of the horse must be used, with the legs continuously swinging without touching the horse. Most important are double leg circles, with the legs horizontal and together. The pommel is the downfall of many a good gymnast.

Rings: swinging movements, handstands and demonstrations of strength (such as the crucifix position) must be included. All stationary positions must be held for at least two seconds.

High bar: the routine consists of continuous swings, forwards and backwards, changes of grip and twists. The gymnast must release and then regrasp the bar at least once during the routine.

Beam: flexibility, concentration, rhythm and expression are necessary. There must be a leap, a handstand and also elements of dance and good balance.

Asymmetric bars: the gymnast must perform 10–12 continuous movements without stopping for any pauses, with a maximum of four movements on the same bar. The best performances include at least three releases and regrasps.

SKILLS & TACTICS

The young women appear to defy gravity and never lose their balance; the men exhibit a strength and control that seems magical. Even top-class competitors can commit major errors, occasionally coming to a complete halt or falling off their apparatus (notably off the women's beam and the men's pommel horse), and to succeed they must carry on, immediately putting such disasters behind them.

To win a major tournament, a gymnast must display elements of great difficulty and complexity as well as virtuosity. Tactically, these are vital when a rival is leading and only an exercise of greater difficulty will give the competitor a chance to score more highly.

The flexibility of young gymnasts on the beam defies belief.

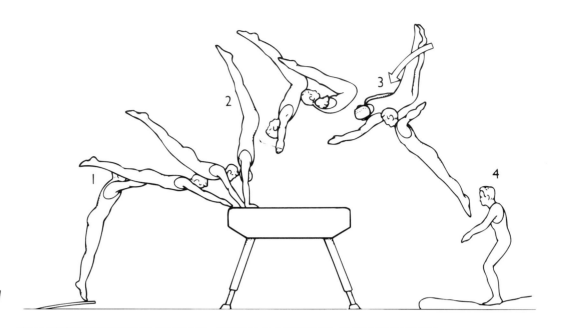

Every element of a vault contributes to its success: take-off, flight, contact and landing.

WORDS

Amplitude: desirable quality indicating that movements are fully and freely expressed

Bridge: arching the body up on hands and feet, with the chest upwards

Croup: part of the long vaulting horse nearest to the performer

Crucifix: forming the shape of a cross while on the rings, the body remaining vertical with the arms extended horizontally

Dislocation: hanging by the arms in front of the bar, with the hands gripping backwards

Dismount: way of getting off any apparatus

Flic-flac: a backwards handspring

Hang: when the body is entirely below the bars or rings (the opposite of 'support')

Layout: the body fully extended

Neck: part of the long vaulting horse furthest from the performer

Pike: a 'V' made by bending the body forward at the hips with both legs straight

Planche: supreme test of strength and balance by lifting the body on the arms alone and keeping it horizontal

Reuther board: springboard used for mounting apparatus

Roundoff: tumbling move in which the body twists 180 degrees as it rotates forward 360 degrees

Scale: balancing on one leg

Sole circle: revolution on the bars in which the feet as well as the hands remain on the bar

Straddle: spreading the legs wide apart

Support: basic position on bars and rings, in which the shoulders are above the hands and the arms are completely straight

Travel: the gymnast's movement along the pommel horse

Tuck: often seen in somersaults, in which the knees are brought as close as possible to the chest

Walkover: a cartwheel on the spot, backwards or forwards, but head-on rather than sideways; free or aerial walkover, one without using the hands

Rhythmic Gymnastics

Rhythmic gymnastics has its roots in the 'free expression' gymnastics developed in the mid-19th century by the Swedish master, Per Henrik Ling, who wanted nothing to do with the strength elements being introduced at the same time in Germany. Originally known in the English-speaking world as recreative gymnastics, the idea of free movement to music found great favour in France as 'gymnastique moderne'.

As modern rhythmic gymnastics it has had its own world championships since 1963 and made its Olympic debut at Los Angeles in 1984, by which time it was known simply as rhythmic gymnastics.

It is performed only by women, and always to music, on a mat 12m (13yd) square. The composition and choreography of the exercise (which lasts between 60 and 90 seconds) has to correspond in rhythm and character to the chosen musical accompaniment. Its most striking aspect is the use of accessories: individual competitions are held with ball, clubs, hoop and rope. The most beautiful of all, the ribbon, is generally now reserved for group exercises, and the effect of six women weaving complex and integrated patterns with ribbons 6m long (19ft 6in) is just dazzling to watch.

The essential element of all the exercises is easy, rhythmic grace. The performer and the apparatus are as one, flowing and swooping, soaring and diving. Neither the equipment nor the gymnast must ever be still for a moment and yet the exercise should never give the impression of involving either haste or energy.

The ball is rolled along the floor and over the body, bounced, thrown and caught – but never with a grip. Clubs are thrown, twisted and twirled. While the hoop is up in the air the gymnast herself may be rolling head over heels on the ground; while the hoop rolls along the ground, the gymnast may leap over it or dive through it. Even the rope which is used must never be still, and one movement with the rope is expected to merge seamlessly with another.

Rhythmic gymnastics has a balance and grace that attracts older women to continue performing in the sport.

As players have become fitter and more powerful, so the ball is hit harder.
Evasive action is sensible rather than cowardly!

HOCKEY

HOCKEY IS PRIMARILY A TEST OF SKILL RATHER THAN STRENGTH, WITH THE MOST SUCCESSFUL PLAYERS ABLE TO HAVE A SEEMINGLY MAGNETIC CONTROL OF THE BALL WITH THEIR STICK

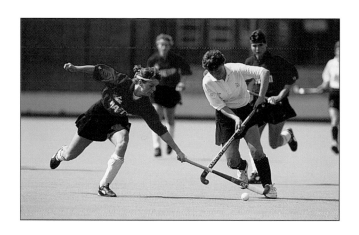

Played between two teams of 11, the object of the game is to propel a small, hard ball with a stick curved at one end into the opponents' goal. Curiously, only one side of the stick can be used to hit the ball. The game lasts for two periods of 35 minutes. The use of artificial pitches has increased the pace of the game with the ball moving across the surface at speeds far greater than can be achieved on grass. The near perfect surface means fewer errors are made in stopping or controlling the ball which, as a result, is in play for a greater percentage of the game. While making the game more attractive to spectators this does make greater demands on the fitness of the players. In poorer countries of the world, such as India and Pakistan, artificial pitches are sometimes too expensive to lay down. These countries are now struggling to maintain their former dominance of the sport.

At the highest level of the sport, the majority of goals come from the penalty corner, also known as the short corner. Consequently, increasing emphasis is placed on developing accurate short corner routines in all the current hockey training.

THE FIELD

The goals in hockey are much smaller than in football. The posts are 4yd (3.6m) apart with a horizontal cross-bar 7ft (2.1m) from the ground. A backboard, 19in (48cm) high and 4yd (3.6m) wide, lines the back of the net.

THE EQUIPMENT

The stick can weigh no more than 28oz (793g) and no less than 12oz (340g). The curved head is made of wood and the striking face is flat. The average length of the stick is 3ft (90cm). The ball is usually white and should weigh no more than 5¾oz (163g) and not less than 5½oz (156g), the same as a cricket ball.

WINNING

In hockey, the team which scores the greater number of goals is the winner, with all goals being of equal value. Unlike most games, a goal in hockey can only be scored from within a restricted area, the shooting circle.

The only exception to this rule is that no goal can be scored directly by a player taking a penalty corner. If you see the goalkeeper stand aside and let the ball enter the goal you can be sure he believes the ball has not been touched by an attacker inside the circle.

RULES

The most common infringement is 'feet'; when the ball touches a player's foot, a free hit is awarded unless any advantage is incurred by the opposition. The penalty for most fouls is a free hit which is taken from where the infringement occurred. Dangerous play can result in a player being 'sin binned', or prevented from playing for a short period.

In certain circumstances the umpire may award a penalty corner. A penalty corner has become the most common way of creating a goal. A player of the attacking team pushes or hits the ball from a spot on the back-line. The ball must be stopped just outside the D before it is dribbled or passed into the shooting circle. If the ball goes 5yd (4m) beyond the D, it does not have to be stopped. The players of the attacking team must remain outside the circle until the ball has been played. The defending side can only have five players, including the goalkeeper, on the goal line. The rest must be in their opponents' half of the field. If a defender commits an intentional foul inside his own circle the umpire can award a penalty stroke to the attacking side. The penalty stroke is a push, flick or scoop stroke taken from a marked spot 7yd (6.4m) in front of the goal.

WORDS

Indoor hockey: Six-a-side game that is popular in Europe as a winter training exercise, it now has tournament status. It helps develop skills as the ball must be pushed, not hit, and can only be lifted when shooting within the circle

Mixed hockey: popular recreational game, now with international status. Played with a set number of men and women on each side

Overlap: when defender moves to join in attack, providing extra attacker

Push: propelling the ball along the surface and not in the air

Scoop: propelling the ball into the air with a fast shovelling movement of the stick

Trapping: stopping the ball motionless with the stick

SKILLS

While possession of the ball is important, against well-trained teams it is not enough. It is also necessary to beat an opponent while keeping full control of the ball.

An attacker needs the shooting skill and flair to take his chances. Some players also specialize in converting a penalty or penalty corner, often under great pressure.

Tackling, or dispossessing an opponent, is another important skill. When making a tackle a player must always ensure he is well-balanced before he starts.

Because hockey can only be played with the left-hand face of the stick, the ball is mainly played on the right side of the body. However, the ball often has to be played from the left side and this requires the ability to turn the stick quickly. Players on the left side of the field, in particular, must develop the skill of using the reverse stick.

The dazzling dribbles that were part of the South-Asian game are now rarer as they are more easily stopped on artificial grass.

TACTICS

In recent years the defensive systems used by the top teams have become more sophisticated. Most teams now employ a rigid marking system. The defender's aim is to mark an opponent man-for-man to prevent him gaining clean possession. The only defender who positions himself according to the location of the ball is the sweeper who covers his team from behind to gather any loose ball or tackle an opponent who has broken free of his marker.

In attacking against a marking system, players try to evade their marker by deft changes of speed and direction of running. As this is difficult, the ball is often passed into open space for a team mate to run into it. With more and more time being spent on fitness and tactics it has become more difficult to score goals from open play. However, recent law changes have reduced the influence of obstruction, making play more fluid, with more rapid passing and longer possession of the ball.

As penalty corners provide the majority of goals, defenders have to be on their mettle.

The Romans are credited with the idea of horse racing in Britain after shipping Arab horses across from Gaul. The first race meeting was in Yorkshire back in AD210.

HORSE RACING

ACROSS THE WORLD, THERE CAN BE FEW SPORTS THAT INVOLVE THE PUBLIC
MORE THAN HORSE RACING

To satisfy the millions who bet on races, many of the daily newspapers devote more space to racing than to almost any other sport.

Flat racing generally draws the biggest crowds, perhaps because it takes place in the warmest weather. In Europe the flat season runs from March to November, with many important events between May and July. The National Hunt racing season, incorporating hurdling and steeplechasing, stretches from the end of August to early June, with most of its big prizes coming between October and April.

On-course betting is an integral part of the racing scene. Rows of bookmakers stand on boxes beside blackboards on which they chalk the names of the horses and shout the odds offered against them. In recent years there has been a great increase in off-course betting, with licensed 'betting shops' to be seen in most towns.

Because the British royal family has had a close interest in flat racing for nearly 500 years, it has remained a magnet for nobility, aristocrats and those who wish to be thought of as such. This is particularly true of fashionable courses such as Ascot and Goodwood in England, and Longchamp in France. Many thousands of the British public flock to the two most famous races in the world, the Derby at Epsom and the Grand National steeplechase at Aintree, Liverpool.

Flat Racing

THE COURSE

There is no standard length to a course, nor a standard shape. In any meeting, individual races may vary in length from half a mile (800m) to 2 miles (3200km). The surface is usually dirt in America and grass in Europe, though all-weather tracks are also proving very popular. Starting stalls are now commonly used everywhere, producing the fairest start conditions.

EQUIPMENT

Jockeys wear 'silks', the jersey in the identifying colours of the owner of the horse, as well as thin white breeches, thin black leather boots, goggles and a crash helmet; they carry a short whip.

The saddle may weigh up to 7lb (about 3kg), but lead weights may have to be carried under it if the jockey's weight does not match up to the race requirement.

WINNING

First past the post is the winner, though the racecourse stewards may disqualify a horse that has not run by the rules, whether or not there has been an objection from another rider. If the winning margin is as little as 'a short head', the photo-finish camera is always consulted.

No horse may race until it is a two-year-old (the birthday is presumed to be 1st January of the year of foaling in the northern hemisphere, and 1st August in the southern hemisphere). Few races are for all-comers. The Derby, for example, is for three-year-olds, and the Oaks and the 1000 Guineas are for fillies only. There are special weight-for-age races for maidens (horses that have never won), when every horse of the same age carries the same weight; handi-cap races, in which the heaviest weight is allocated to the horse with the best record; and selling races, the winners of which are offered for sale.

Jockeys balance like gymnasts urging their mounts to go faster.

THE CLASSICS

England has five flat-racing Classic races, all for three-year-olds. Most are 200 years old.

Spring
The 2000 Guineas (1809)
1 mile, Newmarket
The 1000 Guineas (fillies) (1814)
1 mile, Newmarket

Early June
The Derby (1780)
1½ miles, Epsom
The Oaks (fillies) (1779)
1½ miles, Epsom

Autumn
The St Leger (1776)
1¾ miles, Doncaster

The Derby has given its name to Classic races in about every racing nation in the world. Yet the name of the first Derby was decided on the toss of a coin between Lord Derby and Sir Charles Bunbury . . . so Americans would be celebrating the Kentucky Bunbury every year, had the coin fallen in a different way!

RULES

Flat racing is governed by the Jockey Club, the members of which are not likely to be jockeys. Its stewards are present at every meeting to enforce the rules of racing. 'Bumping and boring' in the final stages is the most common transgression, and if the stewards think there has been deliberate interference, they may disqualify the horse or (for reckless riding) decide to suspend the jockey. All jockeys, complete with their saddles, have to weigh-in before the start of a race and weigh-out immediately after it, to make sure that all the conditions of the race are met in full.

SKILLS & TACTICS

The most skilful jockeys are those who consistently persuade horses to run at their best. This is usually through a combination of riding style, tactical awareness and a close appreciation of the nature of the individual animal – in which the advice of the trainer proves to be vital.

Hurdling

Hurdle races range from 2 to 3½ miles (3200–5200m) and are suitable for horses of three years and over. In a two-mile race there are eight hurdles about 3ft 6in high (1.07m), light enough to be knocked down without causing any damage to the horse. The jockeys are much bigger in size than their colleagues on the flat and the horses are stronger, carrying higher weights of 10–12½ stone (64–80kg).

In the colder and wetter weather of the National Hunt season, jockeys are allowed to wear jerseys for extra warmth rather than the usual thin silks. The greater demand for sustained stamina in these longer races, often over very heavy ground, means that it is quite a common event to see a horse coming through right from the back of the group to win the race.

Steeplechasing

THE COURSE

The strange name of this sport originated in informal cross-country races using a distant steeple as the target, and the courses have not got any easier. Steeplechasers have to be bred for the job and at least four years old before they start. Distances range from 2 miles (3200m) to the 4½ miles (7250m) of the Grand National and if the fences are not jumped cleanly, the horse may fall or the jockey be unseated.

Steeplechase courses are a severe test of stamina, strength and courage. The 12 fences in a two-mile race are 4ft 6in high (1.37m) and include one water jump 15ft wide (4.57m) and two open ditches. These are the toughest obstacles on the course: the fence itself is preceded by a ditch 4ft wide (1.22m) with a guard rail 18in high (46cm) situated in front of it.

SKILLS & TACTICS

Falls are frequent, and one of the jockey's greatest assets is to be able to keep his seat on a stumbling horse. A fallen jockey is allowed to remount and finish the race, in the unlikely event that he can catch his horse. It is just part of the hard luck of the game if any other riders are brought down by a faller.

Tactics play a greater part in steeplechasing than in any other form of horse racing. Starts are frequently untidy and there is no draw for starting position, but there is little call for a horse to be away like an arrow, as there is in flat racing. Keeping out of trouble is the best way for a jockey to help his horse, and trying to give it a clear view of the fence ahead – very difficult with a big field. It is more important for a horse to be a good jumper than to be a fast runner. A fence cleanly taken not only avoids a fall, but can mean two lengths gained.

Steeplechasing requires great strength and courage from both horse and rider. Although the sport of racing from village church to village church (or steeple to steeple) originated in Ireland, it was in 1830 that Thomas Coleman of the Turf Hotel in St Albans, north of London, opened a circular steeplechase course. In this way, paying spectators could see the action more clearly. The idea was an instant success and over 60 courses were then built in the next decade. Cheltenham and Aintree were amongst those inspired by the landlord's brainwave and remain as the twin pinnacles of all National Hunt racing.

WORDS

Allowance: weight allowance to inexperienced apprentice jockey

Ante-post betting: betting before the day of the race

Apprentice: jockey who has not ridden 75 winners

At the distance: with a furlong (201m) to go

Chaser: stoutly-bred horse that runs over fences

Colt: male horse less than four years old

Come through late: come from behind

Draw: starting position of each runner

Filly: female horse less than four years old

Flight: line of hurdles

Going: state of the ground (e.g. firm, good, soft)

Guard rail: take-off rail in front of a fence

Handicap: race where horses of different ability are differently weighted

Handy: in touch with the leaders

Jockey Club: governing body of racing

Members' Club: the most expensive viewing enclosure available

Objection: when a jockey complains to the stewards and winning bets are suspended

Pace: speed of the race (e.g. 'off the pace', not keeping up)

Paddock: parade ring where horses are viewed

Photo-finish: used in 'short head' finishes to determine the winner

Plates: the horse's lightweight shoes

Put to stud: to retire a horse from racing and use it for breeding

Scratch: withdraw horse from race

Selling races: lowest class of race; the winner is offered for sale

Silver Ring: the cheapest viewing enclosure

Spread a plate: lose a shoe

Starting price: the odds as the horses leave the post

Stewards' enquiry: determines the result of an objection

Sweating up: when a horse gets nervous before a race

Under pressure: horse being ridden hard

Under starter's orders: when the white flag is raised, just before the off

BETTING

Bookmakers (bookies) have to balance their books, by working out how they can afford to pay out on winners and still make a profit on the money they receive from punters. Therefore they offer long odds (say, 100–1) on an outsider, a horse with little or no chance of winning. By contrast, the horse expected to win has the shortest odds (say, 2–1) and is the favourite. Punters can bet on a horse to win, or by paying extra, bet each way. In this case, if the horse fails to win but still finishes in the first three or four, the punter receives about 25 per cent of the odds.

Before a race, the odds are constantly changing as betters decide to back their fancy and the bookies juggle the mathematical chances of making a good profit.

LESTER PIGGOTT Piggott won the first race of his phenomenal riding career in 1948 at Haydock as a 12-year-old. Champion jockey 11 times, he's ridden a record 30 Classic winners in England, including nine Derby victories. His most famous triumph was on the great Nijinsky in 1970. After a short spell in prison for tax evasion problems, he astounded the racing world by returning to the saddle in 1990 at the age of 54. He then went on to win a string of top races including the Breeders' Cup Mile in 1991 and the 2000 Guineas on the horse 'Rodrigo de Triano' in the following year.

Ice hockey's goalminders are dressed like gladiators. As well as special face masks and padding, they use different gloves – one as a stopper on the stick hand, the other to catch the puck.

ICE HOCKEY

SAID TO BE THE WORLD'S FASTEST TEAM GAME, ICE HOCKEY MAKES
SPECTACULAR VIEWING

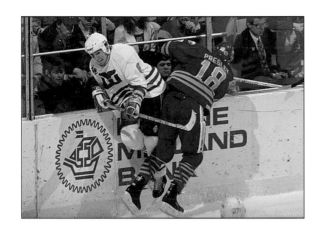

The players skate so quickly and hit the puck so hard it is sometimes difficult for the eye to keep up with the action. The result of such frenzy within a tightly confined area (less than a quarter of the size of a soccer pitch) is a multitude of collisions, many of them not always accidental. Retaliation is swift and sometimes violent.

Ice hockey dates, as you might expect, from the time two field hockey teams decided that, if they used a flat puck instead of a ball, they could play on a frozen surface. That seems to have been in Ontario, Canada, in 1860, though it was 20 years before an ice hockey club was formed. Canada and then the United States became, and remain, the home of the game, but by the end of the century it had spread to Britain and beyond.

The popularity of ice hockey in North America soon led to professionalism. The National Hockey League is now a multi-million dollar business across most of that continent and ice hockey, with baseball, American football and basketball, is one of the four most outstandingly important games of the region.

THE RINK

Ideally, the playing area should be 200ft long and 85ft wide (61m by 26). It should be surrounded by a continuous barrier board, rounded at the corners and up to 4ft (1.22m) high. The puck rebounds from the board, remaining in play. The goals are about 10ft (3m) in from the back barriers, so that play can take place behind them. The goals are very small, 6ft wide (1.83m) and 4ft high (1.22m), but the puck is still shot into them quite frequently.

The rink is divided into two halves by a red line, and into three equal zones by two blue lines. These are used to control the offside rule. The centre circle is for re-starting play after a goal, and the two face-off circles in each defensive zone for re-starting play after a foul.

EQUIPMENT

The puck is a flat-surfaced disc of vulcanized rubber only an inch thick (2.5cm) and 3in in diameter (7.6cm), weighing about 5½oz (156g). Sticks are usually of laminated wood, the goalminder's being wider and heavier than the others. Skates are notable for their short and very thin blades, only one sixteenth of an inch (1.5mm) wide. Again, the goalminder's are different, wider and lower and with extra stanchions joining the skate to the boot to prevent the puck passing under his feet.

All players are heavily protected against injury, with padded guards for shoulders, elbows, knees and shins, and thick gauntlet gloves. Goalminders go even further. They live behind a padded suit of armour, and most wear their helmets over substantial face masks.

WINNING

As in field hockey, you win by scoring goals. They can only be scored when the puck has been struck by a stick, not a foot, and do not count if an attacking player is within the goal crease, a semi-circle of 4ft radius (1.22m) in front of the net. It is not only the name of the scorer who receives official credit. As in basketball, the player who passed the puck to him (if any) is credited with an 'assist'.

If an attacking player is fouled when in a scoring position in front of goal, with no player but the goalminder between him and the goal, the referee will award a penalty shot. From the centre face-off circle, a player takes the puck up the ice with only the goalminder to beat; and the goalminder must not move out of his goal crease until the puck crosses the blue line.

RULES

There are only six players of each team on the ice at a time (usually a goalminder, two defencemen, two wings and a centre), but there may be 20 in the squad. The pace of the game demands frequent substitutions, at the discretion of the coach. Whole forward lines may be changed together, or even the entire five outfielders; or just one man, because of injury or exhaustion.

There are three periods of 20 minutes' actual playing time each, and the teams change ends after each period. Each period begins with the referee dropping the puck on the ice between the sticks of the opposing centres. When play stops for a foul, it is then re-started with a face-off from whichever of the special circles is nearest to the point where the foul occurred. Other than that, the puck only becomes dead when it is hit over the barrier.

The penalty box at the side of the rink is well used. There are four infringement grades for which players can be banished. **Minor penalties:** two minutes in the 'sin bin' are incurred for fouls such as elbowing, charging, tripping, raising the stick too high, deliberately hitting the puck out of the rink, hooking an opponent with the blade of the

---

WAYNE GRETZKY

Until this Canadian came on to the scene, only kings and warriors had been dubbed 'The Great One'; but Gretzky is the most dominant player in history. In 10 years with the Edmonton Oilers (1978–88) and subsequently with the Los Angeles Kings, the brilliant centre posted records as the all-time scoring leader in points and assists. In 1986 he scored a season's record of 215; in 1982 he notched 92 goals and in 1986 provided 163 assists. No wonder he was voted MVP, most valuable player in the National Hockey League, a record nine times (1980–87, 1989). He helped Edmonton win the Stanley Cup five times.

stick, 'boarding' (pushing an opponent intentionally against the barrier) and falling on top of the puck to stop play – only the goalminder is allowed to do that. Boarding is such a frequent offence that referees tend to overlook it unless it is notably vicious.

No substitute is allowed for the player sent off, but if the opposition scores during his absence, he can return immediately. A goalminder incurring a minor penalty is allowed to stay on the ice; his coach withdraws an outfield player instead.

Major penalties: five minutes is imposed for 'rough play', which loosely covers any of the above offences if they are particularly violent. If two opposing players are serving a major penalty simultaneously (for fighting each other, for instance), substitutes are allowed for both of them. If the goalminder incurs a major penalty, a penalty shot is awarded against his team.

Misconduct penalties: ten minutes in the 'sin bin' are given for abusive language or insubordination towards a referee. Again, the goalminder escapes banishment, a team mate being sent off instead.

Match penalties: in extreme cases of violence, with deliberate injury or intention to injure, the referee may banish a player from the arena for the rest of the game, and the player cannot appear in any subsequent match until his case has been dealt with by a disciplinary committee. A substitute is allowed five minutes after the offender has been sent off.

The offside rule is framed to encourage the attacking side to keep skating forwards. Remember the three zones into which the rink is divided? Beyond the halfway line, a player with the puck can only pass to a team mate who is in the same zone; he must not hit the puck ahead to a player in the attacking zone, but must himself be the first player into that zone. In defence, however, a player can pass to a man in his own half of the rink. He may not, in a tight situation, whack the puck down to the other end of the rink ('icing').

SKILLS

Brilliant skating ability is essential for the top-class player – skating at high speed forwards, backwards or sideways, with the puck under control and the head up, looking for the colleague to whom he will pass. Even defenders, usually bulkier than the forwards, are expected to be able to take the opposition by surprise with a fast break up the ice to score.

The most obvious tactic used by ice hockey players is the body check, a method of blocking that is legal as long as it is made by the shoulder or the hip, and is not made from behind.

WORDS

Boarding: forcing an opponent onto the barrier boards

Body check: blocking an opponent with hip or shoulder

Box system: defensive ploy by short-handed team

Butt-ending: hitting opponent with the end of the stick; a major penalty

Flashing: chopping the opponent's wrists with the stick

Icing: when defender hits the puck right down the rink; illegal

Powerplay: all-out attack

Screening: blocking the goalminder's view

Slapshot: full-blooded drive, not a flick

Spearing: driving stick into opponent's stomach; illegal

1. goalminder
2. right defence
3. left defence
4. centre
5. right wing
6. left wing

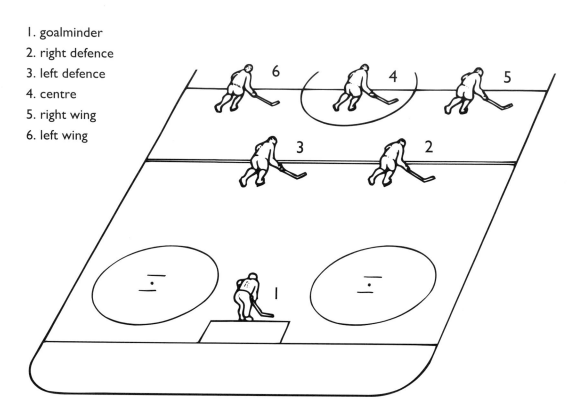

How an ice hockey team lines up. The circles near the goalminder are for re-starting play after a foul.

TACTICS

Tactics are largely in the hands of the coach, with his weapon of ceaseless substitutions. For instance: an opponent is sent to the sin bin; the coach calls for a powerplay, sending on five attacking men; the defending coach puts on his 'penalty killers', four men who play the box system, forming a square to keep attackers away from the danger zone.

Suppose the referee spots a defender fouling a player who is not in possession of the puck. The ref puts up his hand, but allows play to continue as long as the attacking team has possession. Suddenly, their goalminder leaves the ice and a sixth attacker comes on, a big advantage for the

team. There is no actual fear of the opposition scoring, because as soon as the attackers lose possession of the puck the whistle blows for the earlier offence.

Ice hockey is played at great pace, using both physical strength and subtle finesse with the tiny puck. Few individuals have both attributes. Those that do, like Wayne Gretzky and Mario Lemieux in North America, make the difference between a good team and a great team. Opposing coaches can try all sorts of tactics to stop them but few succeed.

If one or even two men are asked to mark a star, then the defensive balance is upset, allowing the star's team mates more freedom. It is impossible to stop a genius!

ICE SKATING

ICE SKATING TAKES MANY FORMS, FROM EXCITING RACING TO STYLISH,
ARTISTIC INTERPRETATION THAT IS VIRTUALLY BALLET ON ICE

Few sports have proved so universally popular among television viewers as figure skating, from which the 'figures' element has been removed for most competitions. It does not need intricate knowledge of the sport for the spectator to revel in its beauty and excitement.

Separate competitions are held in men's and women's solo skating, in pairs and in ice dance. Each one is sub-divided: the individuals and pairs skate one short programme, during which they must perform certain pre-set movements, and one longer programme in which they are free to skate as they wish. Ice dancers have three sections: the compulsory dances, the set pattern dance (in which all competitors perform the same tempo dance, but choose their own music), and the free dance.

Artistic Skating

THE RINK

The usual area for international competitions is a rink 60m (200ft) long and 30m (100ft) wide, with rounded corners. The ice must be perfectly flat and competitors are expected to use the whole of it.

EQUIPMENT

The blade used for figure skating is slightly longer than the boot to which it is fixed, and has small teeth at the front end which help in spins and jumps. The blade is about 3mm wide ($^1/_8$in), with a hollow groove along its underside which gives the blade an inside and an outside edge. There are guards that clip on to the blade when not in use, some of which are made to enable the skater to walk on them when necessary.

The boots are extremely important. They must fit tightly around the instep and over the ankle, but should not squeeze the toes. Other clothing for the ordinary skater is a matter of personal choice and practicality, but top-class performers seem to compete in appearance as much as in skating. Some women's costumes have become eye-catchingly theatrical.

WINNING

All results in international figure skating depend on the opinions of a panel of nine judges, each one from a different nation. Each element of the competition is marked separately, and each is awarded one score for technical merit and another for artistic presentation, each from a possible total of 6.0. Each judge clearly displays the chosen score, either on an electronic board or by holding up cards.

After each section of the competition, each judge adds his or her two marks together to produce an order of competitors. To determine the overall winner of any category, the marks are mathematically adjusted so that each section receives its agreed weight of importance. In solo and pairs skating, the short programme marks are worth 33.3 per cent of the whole,

*A typical ice skating jump:
the Axel Paulsen.*

left
forward
outside

left
forward
outside

right
backward
outside

and the long programme 66.7 per cent.

There is a slight variation to this in the marking of ice dancing. The three dances which together form the compulsory section are each given a single score out of 6.0, and that section carries 20 per cent of the whole marks. The original set pattern (30 per cent of the whole) has two marks, for composition and presentation, and the free dance programme (50 per cent) is marked for technical merit and artistic impression.

In all categories, the winner is the one placed first by the greatest number of judges.

RULES

Solo skating: Each competitor is allowed two minutes in which to include seven obligatory movements (specified jumps, spins, spirals and so on) to music of his or her choice. Faults in any part of the performance are penalized by the judges deducting decimal fractions of a point from the 6.0 technical and 6.0 artistic maximum scores.

The long free programme offers women four minutes and men five in which to devise performances that show off their talents. They may use whatever moves they think they are capable of demonstrating effectively, in whatever order and to whatever music they like. Inevitably, this is the part of the programme where even the unskilled viewer at home fancies that he can spot the winner.

Pairs skating: In the short programme, each pair of competitors (mixed sex) must link six specific moves within a two-minute time limit. In the long programme, they have five minutes to display their best lifts, spins and spirals together, as well as to impress the judges with synchronized solo skating movements while skating apart (shadow skating). Good pairs skating demands close teamwork, harmony and understanding as well as split-second timing and anticipation.

Ice dancing: The basic difference between dance and pairs skating lies in the strength

and athleticism of the latter in the free programme, which should include spectacular lifts. In ice dancing, the lifts should be 'small', with the man's hands no higher than his shoulders; and because it is supposed to be a dance on ice, the couple will be penalized if they spend too much time apart, or are apart by too great a distance.

Women are expected to show both artistic skill in interpreting the music and explosive, athletic jumping if they are to win medals.

Torvill and Dean revolutionized ice dancing, yet other couples now present even more ambitious programmes.

In the first section, compulsory dance, the judges particularly look for close proximity between the skaters, and for correct timing and placement of steps, just as for competitors on a dance floor.

More originality is expected in the next section, where the dancers must stick to the pre-determined rhythm but are free to create their own steps and choose their own music. The absolute freedom of choreography and choice of music (but no vocals) for the four-minute free dance led to the memorably beautiful performances of the British pair, Torvill and Dean, who took ice dancing to levels of all-round perfection never before achieved.

SKILLS

The technique of top-grade ice skating alone demands an application that is hard to understand. It is not just that good skaters seem as secure on blades half as thick as a pencil as most of us are in boots on the pavement. The speed and facility with which they skate forwards, backwards and sideways is a skill that many can acquire; but perfection in spins and jumps seems just miraculous.

A spin should generally consist of six full rotations, and should be carried out literally on the spot and apparently without effort. That goes too for the sit-spin, where the skater starts upright and then sinks slowly, spinning on one leg – an amazing test of strength and control. Jumps must achieve real height and a clean, faultless landing to score well, and many top skaters manage this with mid-air acrobatics as well.

The skater who is going to succeed must then add grace, balance and artistic interpretation. The position of the head, the carriage and movement of the body, the way the hands are held all contribute greatly to the overall effect, and indeed are used to conceal the immense physical accomplishment of the exercise. Everything must be made to look so easy in this gymnastic ballet on ice.

WORDS

Arabesque: long sustained gliding edge with body stretched forward and the free leg raised high behind the skater

Axel: jump from outside forward edge, with one-and-a-half midair rotations, landing on back outside edge of opposite blade

Bracket: half-turn from one edge to the opposite edge of the same blade

Broken leg spin: sit spin with free leg extended to side or behind

Camel: spin in an arabesque position

Chasse: three-step dance sequence with disengaged skate passing the other

Cherry flip: (see toe jump on page 117)

Choctaw: dance turn wherein blades and direction are changed simultaneously to opposite edge

Cross-foot: spin executed on flat of both blades, with legs crossed and toes together

Crossover: a stroke where the free foot crosses in front of the skating foot

Death spiral: pairs skating move, with man acting as pivot while woman rotates around him

Double jump: any jump which has an extra midair rotation

Flying camel: jump variation of a camel spin

Flying sit spin: a long loop jump landing into a sit spin

Lasso lift: pairs move involving side-by-side, hand-to-hand position from which woman is lifted up overhead to rotate one-and-a-half times, while partner's arm is outstretched in a lassoing pose

Layback: one-foot spin with torso bent backwards

Layover: one-foot spin with torso bent sideways

Loop jump: take-off from outside back edge, rotating once before landing on the outside back edge of the same blade

Lutz jump: counterwise jump from a fast back outside edge of one blade, using the other toe as lever to achieve a reverse midair rotation, landing on back outside edge of the opposite blade

Mohawk: dance half-turn when skates and direction change simultaneously to opposite edges

Overhead axel: pairs lift begun from woman's forward outside edge, from which woman is rotated one-and-a-half times above partner's head, his arm supporting her armpit, landing on back outside edge of woman's opposite blade to the one from which she began

Parallel spin: executed on flat of the blade, with upper body and non-skating leg parallel to the ice (also called camel spin)

Rocker: one-foot turn, reversing direction with no change of edge

Salchow: jump executed from inside back edge of one blade, rotating once before landing on outside back edge of opposite blade

Sit spin: executed with the free leg extended forward and the skating leg well bent, with body crouched over skating knee

Spiral: any gliding movement with the body in sustained pose

Split jump: jump in which the skater achieves a splits position

Split lutz lift: pairs move achieved from backward side-by-side position, beginning and ending on woman's back outside edge

Spreadeagle: skating heel to heel and in line

Throw axel: spectacular pairs move achieved by the man throwing the woman through the air from the force of his axel jump, his partner landing on a true edge

PERFECTION

Jayne Torvill and Christopher Dean revolutionized the sport of ice dancing. Statistics show that they won four world championships (1981–84), the Olympic gold in 1984 and the World Professional title in 1985. However, it was their lyrical *Bolero* and entertaining *Mack and Mabel* that gave ice dancing a worldwide audience. In Sarajevo, they scored the first-ever maximum score for artistic impression — all nine judges giving them six out of six. Some newspapers sent their ballet critics to review

Short-track speed skating has rocketed in popularity, encouraged by its acceptance as an Olympic sport in 1992 at Albertville. Long-track skating has taken place outdoors for decades, but is limited to cold-climate countries. As more and more indoor rinks have been built around the world, so more and more youngsters have enjoyed racing one another over the tight, covered ovals. The style of racing, with its massed starts and elbow-to-elbow finishes, is not only easier to understand but generates excitement and risk, giving it instant appeal.

Speed Skating

Speed skaters on a 400m (438yd) circuit are said to be the fastest self-propelled humans in the world. They have reached speeds above 48kmph (30mph) and can cover 1500m or a mile about one minute faster than a track athlete. These long-track skaters, with their skin-tight, streamlined costumes, lean into the job and consume the ice with what seem to be huge, easy strides.

Short-track speed skating is an altogether more frenzied affair, with a bunch start and often a bunch finish. The skaters hurtle round a tight indoor circuit, fighting for position on the bends. It is not uncommon to see a skater on the outside of the bunch flying off into the barrier. Races generally take place over 500 and 1000m (550 and 1100yd), with relay races covering 5000m (3 miles) for men's teams and 3000m (nearly 2 miles) for the women.

Long-track racing is almost bound to take place outdoors, on artificially frozen oval circuits. There are not many of these – most being in Scandinavia and other parts of northern Europe – which makes training difficult for some and restricts the spread of top-class competitors. In Norway and Holland in particular, the speed skating rinksides attract as many supporters as ice hockey matches do.

This form of ice racing used always to be with a massed start, first past the post the winner, and that tradition was maintained in the United States longer than anywhere else. But now the time of each competitor decides the winner, and two of them are drawn to skate together, in separate lanes and against the clock. Each time they complete a circuit the two change lanes, with responsibility for a clean changeover being the main responsibility of the man from the inside track.

They skate on long, straight blades that are no more than about 8mm thick ($^1/_{32}$in), using an easy, economical style. On the straights both hands are usually clasped behind the back, but as they approach a bend (they always race anti-clockwise) they lean in to the left and rhythmically swing the right arm. Races for men are over distances from 500 to 10,000m (550yd to 6 miles), and for women from 500 to 5,000m (about 550yd to 3 miles).

World and European championships comprise events over four distances for which points are awarded, the champion being the competitor with the best points rating overall. In the Olympic Games, no overall champion is recognized and there are gold medals for each separate event.

There is a surprising correlation with cycling, which uses the same muscles. Men and women have won titles in both sports.

MORE WORDS

Toe jump, flip jump: any jump attained by assistance from the saw-toothed point of the blade
Triple jump: any jump with two extra midair rotations
Twist lift: pairs move involving one or more midair rotations by the woman while descending to land on a true edge
Twizzle: one-foot dance turn involving a full 180-degree rotation of the blade, almost on one spot
Walley jump: the only major counter-clockwise jump apart from the lutz, begun from a backward inside edge and landed on the backward outside edge of the same blade

This sport has been nicknamed the 'Champagne of Thrills' because bobbers touch 100mph (160kmph) as they hurtle down icy tracks. The steel and fibreglass bobsleighs are built on two axles; the rear is fixed and the front is used for steering. Smooth rounded runners are placed along the bobs . . . but brakes are used only in emergencies! A far cry from the day when an Englishman called Wilson Smith strapped two sleds together to go down the Cresta Run . . . back in 1888!

Luge

The course averages 1000m (about 1100yd) in length, with at least a dozen bends.

The single seater luge is restricted to 22kg (about 48lb) and the double to 25kg (about 55lb). If the rider (stripped) weighs less than the maximum weight allowed he/she may add half of the difference by wearing a weight-belt of some sort – usually around the waist.

There are standard single-seater championships for men and women and also two-seater events for men. Results are decided by lowest aggregate times achieved during four descents (singles), or two descents (doubles). To start, the rider sits on his luge then pulls away using two metal hoops set in the ground and uses the wire brushes on his knuckles to give himself an extra push on the ice for the first few yards.

The luge is flexible, so the rider steers by pulling up the runner on the side to which he intends turning, at the same time pushing the front end of the opposite runner inwards. If the driver puts his weight over the outer runner, it will slide faster than the inner runner. As the luge is travelling so fast (about 120kmph/75mph) only the slightest correction is needed to alter its course – just tilting the head one way is often enough!

Bobsleigh

International championships comprise four runs for each sled, the lowest aggregate time deciding the winner, and even after four descents the outcome may be determined by mere hundreths of a second.

Any advantage which heavier crews may have is eliminated by rules stipulating the maximum combined weight of bobs with their crews as 630kg (1389lb) for fours and 390kg (858lb) for twos. Within these limits, additional weights may be bolted to the sled to assist a lightweight crew.

Crucial seconds can be saved in steering – going into turns at the correct angle without rising higher up the banking than necessary. Synchronizing weight transference to control movement and assist the steering is more pronounced in four-man crews, when the two middle men play a vital role. The faster the sled goes, the more the crew has to lean inwards as one man. Most important of all is the start. The electric timing begins 15m (about 16yd) after the start and all riders including the driver have to push the sled forward without rocking the sled or getting in each other's way.

The Cresta Run is a steep, twisting icy run down the side of a mountain in Switzerland which is home to one of the most exclusive clubs in the world, the St Moritz Tobogganing Club. A mere 600 members including film stars and aristocrats continue the hair-raising racing that began in 1884 when a Major Bulpetts from England built the course. Now it is about 1200m (three-quarters of a mile) long with a drop of some 153m (500ft) and a dozen hairpin bends, with legendary names like Church Leap and Shuttlecock.

Luge riders lie on their backs and peer between their toes.

MARTIAL ARTS

DEVELOPED IN THE FAR EAST AS METHODS OF ARMED AND UNARMED COMBAT, THE MARTIAL ARTS HAVE BECOME POPULAR SPORTS AROUND THE WORLD

Although for some practitioners there is a religious dimension, martial arts like judo, karate and taekwondo were developed by peasants who were banned from owning weapons. Other martial arts like kendo use simple wooden staffs both for self-defence and attack.

Once Western sportsmen and, to Japanese surprise, Western sportswomen, had learned the techniques, the pupils began to beat the old masters. Their physical conditioning and aggression overcame subtler, traditional skills. Now the Japanese and Koreans have learnt from the Europeans, and the pendulum is swinging back their way.

Even the Japanese sport, sumo, has a challenge from foreigners. Despite its intricate rituals and oversized heroes, sumo's giant wrestlers have been joined by a Hawaiian American weighing over 39st (248kg).

Judo

Often described as 'two men in pyjamas fighting without pillows'; instead of throwing pillows, their intention is to throw each other to the floor. As in boxing and karate, the two players fight for a fixed period of time (five minutes for men, four for women at the Olympics) unless a decisive throw, hold, strangle or armlock ends the bout, as a knockout does in boxing.

THE MAT

The sport, which originated in Japan about 100 years ago, takes place on an area of matting 16m (17½yd) square. The contest area in the centre is marked by a metre-wide (about 3⅓ft) red band. The contest referee awards scores and penalties and ensures the safety of the competitors. However, any decision he makes may be overruled by the agreement of both line judges. They note when a player goes outside the area and spot any infringements or scores that go unnoticed by the contest referee. Competitors never argue with officials . . . ever!

EQUIPMENT

The judogi consists of white baggy trousers and a loose-fitting, strong cotton jacket tied at the waist by a red or white belt which distinguishes one competitor from the other. A buzzer, bell or hooter is used to indicate a contest is over.

WINNING

The Japanese tradition of the sport is maintained through customs and language. First, the players bow to the referee and each other; then the referee shouts 'Hajime!' (begin). Judo means 'the gentle way' but the players attempt to get a good grip on the other's jacket (usually the lapel and the end of the sleeve), then try to upset the balance using a variety of throws and holds to throw the opponent onto the floor.

A player scores an ippon (outright win) by correctly executing a throw that hurls an opponent flat on his or her back; by holding an opponent down with his back to the ground for 30 seconds; or gaining a submission when the opponent gives in, indicated by tapping either his opponent's body, his own body or the mat with a hand or a foot. A bout can also end when a player scores two waza-aris.

Judo requires both strength and balance.

A waza-ari is one grade lower than an ippon, and requires a high degree of skill. Perhaps an opponent is not thrown fully on his back or lands on his side; if an opponent is pinned to the ground for 25–29 seconds, this is waza-ari. Yet a further grade down is a yuko. Again, a throw may not be executed well enough for a waza-ari or an ippon, but an opponent held down from between 20 and 24 seconds would concede a yuko. A koka, the lowest score, is awarded whenever a player is knocked to the ground and lands on his bottom, not flat on his back, or is held down for 10–19 seconds.

Once a player scores two waza-aris, the fight is over. Although any number of yukos and kokas can be amassed, these are beaten by just one waza-ari. Similarly, just one yuko betters any number of kokas. If the scores are level at the end, the referee calls 'Hantei!' The two line judges then pick as a winner the player who has been more aggressive and initiated more attacks. The referees raise their white or red flags, which correspond to the players' belt colour. Most contests tend to finish decisively, with ippon or waza-ari. When the referee calls 'Sore-made!', the bout is definitely over.

RULES

The referee can award penalties to any player who breaks the rules or is not seen to initiate any attacks. The lowest penalty score is a shido (the equivalent of a koka), followed by a chui (equivalent to a yuko). A keikoku warning is equivalent to a waza-ari and a hansoku-make is a disqualification. So a combination of a waza-ari score with a keikoku penalty against the opponent would automatically win the contest. Penalties are awarded for moving outside the contest area or any other breach of the rules (e.g. hitting or kicking), or the use of techniques illegal to contest judo, such as bending the fingers, or attacking the face.

SKILLS

Look for the player who seems to be dominant and more aggressive, the one who takes a firm grip on his opponent's jacket first. Usually a superior judo player will stand more upright, while his opponent bends forward to prevent himself from being thrown; his attacks will look more decisive and stronger. As the contest proceeds, fitness begins to tell. The weaker player appears to be in pain, breathes heavily and

WORDS

Dan: a top degree of proficiency
Dojo: practice hall
Judoka: contestant, player
Kansetsuwaza: armlocks
Matte!: Wait! Called when the holds look inconclusive, when players go over the edge of the allowed contest area, costumes become undone, etc; the players start again in the centre of the mat
Ne-waza: groundwork
Osaekomi!: a hold has been applied; the timekeeper then starts the clock to time its duration

Shai: a contest
Shimewaza: strangleholds
Sono-mama!: Do not move! Freeze!
Sore-made!: That is all! The contest is over
Tachiwaza: standing or throwing techniques
Yoshi!: Unfreeze

does not attack. As well as several attacking moves, there are also a series of defensive ones designed to counter opponents' aggressive advances.

Judo players talk about throws and holds. These are innumerable and few, if any, can execute them all perfectly. Players attack from the front, the side, and even use sacrifice throws, dropping to the floor before throwing an opponent, using various parts of the body (legs, hips, hands, etc) as specific levers.

If the throw is perfect and merits ippon, the bout is over. With holding techniques, the idea is to pin an opponent down on his or her back for 30 seconds. Strangles are only allowed on the neck (never the head) and even the loose judogi can be used to apply a strangle. Armlocks can only be applied to the elbow joint, so wrist locks and shoulder locks are actually illegal. There are straight and bent armlocks, both of which are painful and can force a submission, or even cause a broken arm.

TACTICS

If a player is better at groundwork than throws, he may concede a small score in order to get a chance of fixing a hold, strangle or armlock. All the tactics are geared towards moving the opponent into a position where the strongest technique can be used against him or her. This is why there often appears to be little definite activity, apart from pushing and pulling, especially in cases where both the opponents are very familiar with the other's particular strengths and weaknesses in the sport.

Top-class players tend to use combination throws where the first move is aimed at confusing an opponent before a quick change in the technique style puts him off balance and he is then thrown before he knows what is happening.

At the highest level, international players know each other's styles and preferred tactics thanks to television – coaches study videos, analyzing the best way to beat opponents.

NICOLA FAIRBROTHER A journalist who was 'more interested in headlines than by-lines' when she went to Barcelona for the first official Olympic competition for women's judo. At 22, she won the silver medal at lightweight – under 56kg (8½st) – as part of a British women's team that hit the headlines through bad luck and bad decisions. A promising gymnast, Fairbrother switched to judo but she only began winning tournaments aged 15. In 1987, despite winning the European junior title at under 52kg (8st) she was tempted to give up judo when she faced tougher opponents. In 1993, however, she confirmed her potential by winning the World Championship under 56kg.

Karate

Karate ('empty hand') derives from a mixture of the ancient Chinese martial art kempo and the disciplines of yoga.

A karate expert is in complete control both mentally and physically as he tries to manipulate the mind and body of his opponent. In competition, his techniques are completely controlled to stop a fraction of an inch from the target – no actual contact is allowed.

The three attack techniques are thrust, blow and kick. These attacks can be delivered to the upper part of the body (including head, face and neck) or the middle of the body (including chest, abdomen and back). An opponent will try to read these attacks, and defend accordingly. Each player is therefore constantly trying to outwit as well as to outfight his opponent.

The object of each three-minute karate match is to score points by penetrating the defence and accurately executing these attacking techniques to any of the prescribed target areas listed above. When such an attack is effectively carried through, a point is awarded. Three points are needed to win a match. If neither contestant scores three points within the three-minute time period, the two judges will decide. If the judges' decision is that the match is a draw, a sudden-death contest is fought with only one point needed to win.

Two front kicks: taekwondo (top right) and karate (bottom left).

Taekwondo

Taekwondo has two distinct, but complementary elements, the physical and the mental. As the name attests: 'tae kwon' means 'kicking and punching' and 'do' ('tao' in Chinese) means 'path' or 'truth'. Students of taekwondo do indeed spend long hours practising the kicks, blocks, strikes and punches which make up the physical side of the sport, but equally important to compete successfully is the correct mental approach.

In competition athletes wear a loose-fitting uniform similar to those used for judo and karate, with head-guards and chest protectors. During the three, two-minute rounds of the contest, each competitor will look to score points by penetrating his opponent's defence and landing a successful attack on a legal part of his body. Flying kicks are a feature of the sport. Points are deducted if a competitor attacks a fallen opponent, injures the opponent's face with his fist or intentionally launches an attack after a 'break' order.

Contests are officiated by a jury of two, one referee and four corner judges, who sit outside the 8m (8³/₄yd) square contest area. These officials will disqualify any competitor who has had more than three points deducted in a match.

Sumo

The sight of two huge men exploding into action wearing little more than a loincloth is both thrilling and mystifying. Competition takes place on a dohyo, or raised clay mound, 6m (6½yd) square with a 5m (5½yd) diameter circle marked with rice straw. The loser is the first man to either touch the ground with any part of the body (except the feet) inside or outside the ring or to leave the ring itself. The contests rarely last longer than 10 seconds, but in that time, no strangling or eye-gouging, punching, kicking or hair-pulling is allowed to occur, while the loincloth that covers the genital area is always sacrosanct.

In a sport which has no weight divisions, size and speed are the key for the rikishi, or wrestler whose girth belies strength, agility and timing.

Most rikishi have a couple of dozen favourite kimarite, or techniques. These tend to be oshi zumo (pushing techniques) or yotsu zumo (holding techniques). Like a bull-fighter, agile opponents might sidestep an attack and then convert the aggressor's momentum into his downfall by deflecting his energy downwards or out of the ring.

More subtle, and therefore more appreciated by the connoisseur, are the yotsu, holds that are also familiar in other martial arts like judo. Some competitors aim to get a good grip on the mawashi or broad belt before trying to lift their opponent over and out of the ring for a carry out (okuri ashi). Or alternatively they just try to force them out (yorikiri).

When both men have good grips, the neck throws, hip throws and leg reaps, or trips, come into play. All, of course, have counter-moves but the speed of execution masks the skill to the novice viewer. The high-speed action is preceded by several minutes of ceremony. The presentation, complete with embroidered silk aprons, is all part of the show which includes ritual stamping to drive evil spirits from the ring, salt-throwing for purification, even spitting. The rikishi, eyeball to eyeball, are psyching themselves up for the moment of attack. Suddenly, both wrestlers touch the clay floor and the bout is on.

Great girth often conceals shrewd guile, massive strength and lightning speed.

Reorganization of the sport in 1992 resulted in increased TV coverage from circuits as far apart as Australia and the USA, Malaysia and South Africa, as well as the traditional base of Europe.

MOTORCYCLING

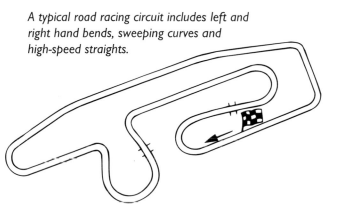

A typical road racing circuit includes left and right hand bends, sweeping curves and high-speed straights.

Road racing carries the greatest international prestige. It is highly commercialized and has a Grand Prix circuit similar to that of motor racing. Grand Prix meetings are held in many parts of the world and the cumulative results from the races lead each season to the naming of the 500cc World Champion.

World championship series are also held for machines of a smaller engine capacity (125cc and 250cc), as well as for sidecar combinations. The pressures of the grand prix circuit are now so intense that it is rare for a leading rider to compete in more than one category.

There is one annual race that is not part of any world championship series but, after more than 80 years, is the most famous single event in the motorcycling world. The Isle of Man TT (Tourist Trophy) takes place on the public highways of a small island off the west coast of England, which is virtually closed for the week-long meeting. It is the oldest motorcycle circuit in the world; each lap measures 60.6km (37 miles), takes in more than 200 bends and climbs from sea level to an altitude of 396m (1300ft).

Although the riders grab the headlines, it's the best machines that win the prizes.

THE CIRCUIT

The Isle of Man apart, most of the major racing circuits are now wholly artificial constructions, with each lap only a few kilometres long. Some are faithful replicas of a natural road (such as Brands Hatch in England); other are pure race tracks with no gradients (Monza in Italy and Daytona, Florida). The surfaces are of tarmac or concrete, with tight corners and sweeping bends to left and right linked by fast straights, to test the riders to the full.

EQUIPMENT

The motorbikes used in top-class racing are exclusively works machines, built, maintained and financed by the leading manufacturers of the day. They endeavour to sign up the outstanding riders, just as the Grand Prix motor racing manufacturers do; and those riders hope to sign contracts that enable them to ride the fastest machines. The huge noise produced by racing machines is caused by engines of very high performance relative to size, which means a very high rate of crankshaft rotation.

Tyres and their composition are a perpetual problem. 'Slicks' are used, with no tread pattern. These provide good adhesion for cornering on a dry track, but tend to aquaplane on water. A soft compound always provides the best traction, but will wear out sooner than a harder compound, which will not hold the bike on corners at as great a speed.

Riders are obliged to wear protective clothing, which is inspected before the start of a race. This includes a helmet and visor, one-piece racing leathers, gloves and boots. Their gear is streamlined to provide as little wind resistance as possible, but will usually include knee guards sewn into the overalls.

WINNING

The winner is the rider who completes the required number of circuits of the track before anyone else, and to achieve this he must keep lapping as fast as he can. Methods of starting vary. In a Grand Prix race the start is from a grid marked on the track. The fastest rider in practice is given the inside position on the front row of the grid, with the next fastest outside him and so on through the field.

Usually, the bikes are in position with dead engines, the riders beside them. When the flag falls, the riders push the bikes forward, the clutch lever pulled in against the handlebars. They drop the clutch to fire the engine as they leap on the machines.

In some international races, the riders are already in the saddle, engines running. When the flag falls, or when the traffic lights change from red to green, they increase the revs, drop the clutch and roar away. In a Le Mans start, riders have to run across the track to where the bikes are parked and kick-start them. With a rolling start, they begin to race at the moment they have completed a warm-up lap. Warm-ups, of one or two laps depending on the circuit, are intended not just to familiarize the rider with the track and its condition, but to warm the tyres, which do not work well when cold.

RULES

International meetings are held under the rules of the IRTA, the International Road Racing Teams Association, and each class of motorcycle has its own specifications that control, for instance, the size of the engine and of the tyres. Other restrictions on the machine are mostly for reasons of safety, such as ensuring clearance between the handlebars and the streamlining, and the covering of the drive chain or shaft by a guard. A false start by any rider may result in a one-minute penalty being added to his time for the race. The clerk of the course can disqualify any rider guilty of riding in a foul, unfair or dangerous manner. The rider will be shown a black flag and must then leave the track as soon as possible.

SKILLS & TACTICS

Starts and corners are where the skilful rider gains his ground. Down the straights the riders tuck the elbows and knees in, get the body behind the screen and let the bike do the work. Some go into a corner comparatively slowly, keeping the bike under control and upright, ready to accelerate out of the bend. Some go in alarmingly fast, brake late and hard, and power the machine in a controlled slide round the corner.

The classic way of cornering used to be to lean into the bend with the bike, banking it over at an incredible angle. More often now you will see the bike remaining more or less upright while the rider's body hangs over the side, like the passenger in a racing sidecar, to reduce the chance of the machine sliding away on the bend.

The early corners in a race are always potentially dangerous, with a bunch of riders attacking in different styles, at different speeds and on different lines. There are no mirrors on these machines, so the rider has no idea if another is trying to overtake him, on the outside or the inside.

As for the starts, precious seconds can be saved by the rider who gets this technique right. For push starts, long and strong legs give a clear advantage, and there is nothing those at the front of the grid want more than a fast start that gives them a clear run to the first corner.

Points scoring in Grand Prix events covers the top 15 finishes.
First   **25 points**
Second   **20 points**
Third   **16 points**
Fourth   **13 points**
Fifth   **11 points**
Sixth   **10 points**
Seventh **9 points**
and so on, down to
Fifteenth **1 point.**

WORDS

Earholing: cornering at top speed
On the limit: at maximum speed
Paddock: assembly area for bikes and transporters
Privateer: rider not sponsored by manufacturer
Shut the door: to prevent rider from overtaking
Slipstreaming: riding immediately behind another machine
Tear-offs: multi-layered visors that can be torn off when dirty
Wheelie: riding machine on back wheel only

SPEEDWAY AND MOTOCROSS

THESE TWO FORMS OF MOTORCYCLE RACING CAN BE COMPARED WITH
ATHLETICS. SPEEDWAY IS RACING ON A CIRCULAR TRACK; MOTOCROSS IS THE
EQUIVALENT OF CROSS-COUNTRY RUNNING

*B*oth these branches of motorcycle racing attract a tremendous
following. Speedway in particular, with its great inter-club rivalry, is
famous for the enthusiasm of its fans.

Both sports have high-profile professional performers (though
thousands of amateurs compete for fun at motocross), with world
championships hotly contested. Both have their eccentric versions as
well: those of motocross are exemplified by beach races in which
thousands of tons of sand are bulldozed into miniature mountains in
which the bikes often bury themselves; while speedway has versions
on sand, on grass and even on ice, with spiked tyres.

Speedway

Team racing is the backbone of this sport, which takes place on an oval track between 275 and 450m in length (300 and 500yd). It has a surface of cinders or shale, loose enough to enable the machines to broadside round the bends. It is sometimes called dirt-track racing and if you look at the riders at the end of a race you would know why. During the four-lap race around the track, which does not last much more than one minute, they and their bikes are absolutely covered with the dirt and grit thrown up by the wheels.

There are races for individuals in speedway, but it is the club element that rouses the fans. A meeting generally consists of 13 heats in which four riders race each other, two from each team. The winner gets three points, the second man two and the third man one. Each team has seven riders, who take turns to compete. At the end of the evening the points are totalled to find the team winner. The teams compete within domestic leagues.

Speedway motorbikes are purpose-built, very lightweight with coarse tyres and wide handlebars. They have 500cc engines with no gearbox, fuelled with methanol. Riders must hold their line on the track for the first 18m (20yd) of a race, before they break. If the man on the inside can get away really fast, he can dominate the race and block the efforts of those trying to pass him. Starting positions are changed with every heat.

Motocross

A British invention in 1927, motocross was for many years better known by its original and apt name of 'scrambling'. It was devised as an informal and entertaining kind of cross-country race on motorbikes, and it still attracts the more eccentric elements of the sport. At the same time, it has become a serious and rewarding business for the most determined riders, with a Grand Prix circuit that produces world champions in several different categories.

It takes place on a closed circuit, usually 3000–5000km long (about two or three miles), that comprises a wide variety of surfaces and any kind of natural obstacle that can be overcome on a motorbike. These include shallow streams, thick mud, rocky paths and appallingly steep hills. The tyres have knobbly treads and the suspension systems take a tremendous hammering.

So do the riders, who need to be seriously fit if they are to succeed in this sport. Their clothing is designed to offer the rider protection from the mud and pebbles with which he will soon be covered, and from the likelihood of his contacting the ground. Boots and a crash helmet with visor are essential, but keeping the visor clean is a constant problem.

Races may either be for a set number of laps, or for a set time, or for a combination of both; 40 minutes plus two laps, perhaps, with the total number of laps completed deciding the ultimate winner.

WORDS

Beach-bashing: *motocross on sandy beach course*
Broadsiding: *spectacular cornering method in speedway*
Diamond: *main frame of a* speedway bike
Gating: *the act of leaving a speedway starting gate*
Methanol: *alcohol-based, oxygen-bearing speedway fuel*
Scrambling: *former name of sport that became motocross*
Quad: *four-wheeled machine for motocross and trials*

For most of the world, Formula One Grand Prix racing is the best there is; in America, Indycar racing dominates: either way both provide highly entertaining competition.

MOTOR RACING

MOTOR RACING IS ABOUT THE MOST SPECTACULAR, EXCITING AND
MISUNDERSTOOD OF ALL SPORTS

To the uninitiated, racing cars look like over-powered monsters being thrown round a circuit at stupidly dangerous speeds by lunatic men bent on killing themselves, wrecking the car, or both. In fact, motor racing is about sophisticated engineering development sparked by immensely skilful and sympathetic driving. Designers and builders of cars must be inventive, dedicated, tireless and inexhaustibly competitive. Drivers must achieve extraordinary levels of fitness, perception, physical coordination and, of course, courage. Nothing less will bring success in a sport which is constantly growing throughout the world, with more classes, more meetings, more spectators, and more television coverage every season. It's not difficult to see why: to watch a gaggle of Grand Prix cars ripping around the tight bends, fierce gradients and disruptive cambers of a circuit such as the classic round-the-houses track at Monaco is to witness one of the greatest thrills in all sport.

The birth of motor racing was in France where a Panhard won a race from Paris to Rouen on 22nd June 1894 at an average speed of 16kmph (10mph). In the USA, Frank Duryea won a race in Chicago in 1895, averaging a mere 12kmph (7½ mph), but by 1898 Chasseloup-Laubat had set a world speed record of 63.1kmph (39.24mph) over a measured mile in France.

Formal races began at Le Mans in 1906 with a French Grand Prix. The Indianapolis 500 first took place at the specially-built oval on Memorial Day in 1911 . . . and has taken place on the same weekend ever since. The average speed of today's winners is over 209 kmph (130mph)!

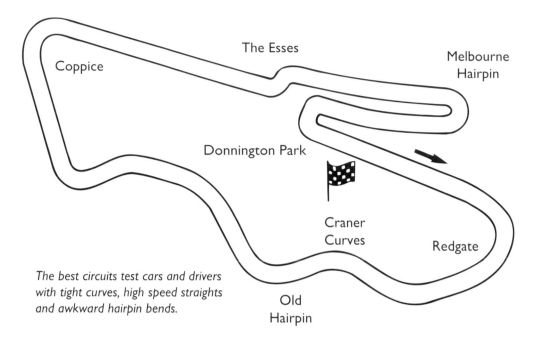

The best circuits test cars and drivers with tight curves, high speed straights and awkward hairpin bends.

THE TRACK

In the beginning, motor racing took place on open roads lined with spectators, and some of the most famous races are still run on public roads, albeit temporarily closed off. Le Mans, Adelaide and Monaco are obvious examples. But most races are now staged on special circuits, fully equipped with barriers, run-off areas, protected spectator facilities and instant access for fire and ambulance services if needed. The circuits are almost infinite in their variety, from the 5.2km (3.2 miles) of blindingly fast straights and tight corners of Britain's Silverstone – a former World War II fighter aerodrome – to the simple rectangle with rounded corners of Indianapolis in the United States.

Some circuits test outright speed – at Indianapolis the cars average around 350kmph (220mph). Others provide a severe and exhaustive punishment for the gearbox, suspension, or tyres. To get around the twists and turns of the 3.3km (2 mile) Monaco serpentine and undulating circuit at anything over 145kmph (90mph) means howling through the gearbox, snaking through vicious and narrow bends, ripping the engine up and down the rev range until it can stand no more. Whatever the course, along with all that the driver must be looking for places to pass, judging whether he needs to pull into the pits to sort out a handling problem, change a deflating tyre or adjust a displaced wing. The spectators can share in those trials and traumas by being positioned where they can see the key action. That could be opposite the pits, so that tyre changes can be timed, or perhaps on the long straight where there is the best opportunity for cars to pass. Maybe it will pay to be on a particularly demanding corner – that will show not only who is going fastest by skilful driving, but also who is trying to sneak past by very late braking into the corner. It is in watching these finer points that the sports enthusiast can derive the real interest and fascination of motor racing.

EQUIPMENT

A racing driver's greatest fear is fire. Although racing fuel is kept in special safety tanks, and cars must have extinguisher systems, there are still crashes which create fires. The driver's clothing is mainly designed to protect against fire. It starts with cotton briefs, then fire-resistant underwear of long johns, knee-socks and a long-sleeved polo-necked vest. That is covered by an outer fire suit, usually triple-layered. All this is designed to resist heat; even the fastenings and thread used to sew on sponsor's badges are of special materials.

Fire-resistant boots – light like a boxer's – are matched by multi-layered gloves (gauntlet style) and a woven balaclava which covers all but the driver's eyes.

The crash helmet is very sophisticated, with a shatterproof visor and a life support system which incorporates a tube feeding compressed air into the helmet to sustain the driver if he is in fire or smoke, as well as a tube through which he can have an energy-restoring drink. When he gets into the car, the driver is held snugly in by a six-point safety harness – two shoulder straps, two hip straps and two crotch straps – all linked to a central quick-release buckle. All that gear is very warm and it is not unknown for a man to be 4kg (10lb) lighter at the end of a Grand Prix in a hot country.

WINNING

Of course the point is to get the car across the line before all the others – but there is much more to it than that. Practice, also called qualifying, is the key to success. In almost all forms of motor sport there are official (timed) practice sessions in which drivers take their cars out on the circuit and try to establish as fast a practice lap as possible. This is crucial for two reasons. First it shows each team how they are doing compared to the opposition. Second, it establishes grid positions. As all the cars cannot line up at the start of a race, as in athletics, a grid is marked on the track. Two cars are in each staggered row with the fastest car in practice starting in the pole position – the place on the front row of the starting grid which gives the best chance of reaching the first corner ahead of the pack. That is clearly an enormous advantage, especially on a narrow and twisting circuit where overtaking is very hazardous.

RULES

The numbers and classes of motor racing are almost infinite, whether it is an old car having a last fling on a dirt oval to the the hugely expensive Formula One Grand Prix circus. These are some of the popular categories:

Formula One: the 'crème de la crème'. The formula by which the Driver's World Championship is decided, the sophisticated 3.5-litre cars develop around 750bhp (brake horse power). The deaths of two drivers at the Imola circuit early in 1994 (Ayrton Senna, Roland Ratzenberger) triggered moves by the sport's governing body to discuss ways to cut speed and increase safety: better head and neck protection, slower cornering, trackside barriers and better pitstop discipline. Restricting engine power and reducing the aerodynamic downforce are also among suggested changes.

Formula 3000: the stepping stone to Formula One, it is for cars with 500bhp 3-litre engines and a maximum of eight cylinders. The domestic series in Britain for Formula 3000 cars is known as Formula Two.

Formula Three: this is where the young talent emerges. They use 2-litre engines but with air box restrictors, which limit the drivers' power to about 200bhp which is still remarkably fast.

Touring Cars: these are standard-looking production saloons modified for circuit racing. Although each country has its own regulations, almost all have now adopted the British 2-litre rules. This means all are powered by 2-litre engines, tuned for racing to develop around 300bhp. The racing is always close and always dramatic.

Travelling at speed, drivers not only have to look out for other cars and fast bends . . . they watch for flags to warn them of danger.

Yellow flag:
danger ahead; do not overtake

Yellow flag with red stripes:
oil on track ahead

White flag:
service car on track

Green flag:
danger is now over

Red flag:
all cars must stop

Black and white checkered flag:
the finish

The spectators look for the car that takes the same line in and out of the bend, lap after lap. Consistency and smoothness are the signs of a good driver.

Formula Ford, Vauxhall Junior and Vauxhall Lotus: Starter formulae for drivers with top single-seater hopes and backed by major manufacturers. Ford and Vauxhall Junior racers have 1.6-litre engines developing around 125bhp, while Vauxhall Lotus uses a Lotus-tuned 2-litre Vauxhall engine with 160bhp. Vauxhall Junior and Lotus introduce drivers to slick tyres, while the Vauxhall Lotus cars also have wings to prepare drivers for Formula Three.

NASCAR: highly-modified production saloon cars are used for dramatic racing on the high speed ovals of North America. Capable of 320kmph (200mph) or more.

Indycars: all-out racing cars similar in looks to Grand Prix cars, but powered by turbocharged 2.65-litre engines. Most chassis and engines are UK-designed and built.

Sportscar: a type of racing in decline, but in recent years dominated by purpose-buillt sports racers by manufacturers such as Jaguar, Mercedes-Benz and Peugeot. The highlight of the sportscar year is the Le Mans 24-hour race in France.

IMSA: American endurance racing for purpose-built sports cars. Series highlight is another 24-hour race, at Daytona.

SKILLS

Motor racing is a team sport. Yes, it's the driver who gets all the limelight, but the most brilliant driver would be totally unsuccessful without the dedicated and efficient backing of his team manager, car designer, mechanics and back-up administrators. The manager must be the inspiration: he must raise the finance to support the whole operation; he must help the designer to develop a car which is better than all the rest; he must organize cooperation from suppliers of tyres, engines, suspension and other vital components; he must supervise the building of cars; he must integrate the schedule of practice sessions, travel to foreign circuits and so on; and he must encourage the whole team to bear defeats, disappointments, long hours, boring

WORDS

Aerofoils: also called wings: the aerodynamic surfaces at both ends of a racing car which push the car on to the track and so give maximum traction on the straights and adhesion through the corners

Aquaplaning: happens when a car is racing on a wet track, especially on slick tyres; the tyre treads become separated from the road surface and ride on a film of water, meaning the car loses virtually all braking effect and directional stability

Armco: steel crash barriers

Electrical cut-off: an automatic switch to cut out the electrical supply in the event of a crash and so minimize the chance of fire

Fire extinguisher system: another automatic system, which distributes extinguisher throughout the car on a crash impact, or can be operated by the driver manually

Grand Prix: the top motor racing events, usually Formula One

Ground effect: the aerodynamic effect obtained by the design of modern single-seater cars, where the bodywork between the wheels is shaped to make the whole of the centre of the car one big wing, using the speed through the air to produce negative lift and so keep the car glued to the track surface through corners

Intermediates: treaded tyres used when there is a possibility of rain or when the track is wet

Monocoque: the construction system used for most racing cars, where the central cell of sheet metal is the backbone of the car and the other components – engine, suspension, transmission are attached to it

Negative lift: the generation of a down-force to keep a car on the road by using wings or ground effect design

Open wheel: where the whole of the wheel can be seen, and is not covered in

Rip-offs: strips of plastic stuck across the driver's visor which he can rip off progressively as they become obscured by oil and dust thrown up by cars in front

Roll-over: a U-shaped tubular bar fitted to the back of the car's cockpit to protect the driver's head should the car roll over

Skirts: flexible sheets mounted along the side pods of a ground effect design car to enclose the central area beneath the car and enhance the ground effect of the air passing under it

Slicks: smooth racing tyres which have no tread pattern. They are used for dry circuit racing

Spaceframe: method of construction used for some sports cars, where a frame of welded lightweight tubes forms the main basis of the car, which is clad with light alloy or glass-fibre panels

Stickies: specially soft compound tyres used by drivers in practice sessions to set up particularly fast times. They are too soft to stand up to a full race

Turbo-charge: method of boosting engine power by using exhaust gases

The team work at a pit-stop is vital in a sport where races are won by fractions of a second.

travel, and inexplicable mechanical failures without complaint and still come up for the next race feeling as enthusiastic as ever.

The designer is vital. He must tread the tightrope between building a car heavy enough to last, but still light to make it fast, though possibly less reliable. He must be an expert in suspensions, braking systems, engine outputs, aerodynamics and exotic materials. And somehow he must blend them all together to make up a car which is as quick or quicker than anybody else's.

The mechanics are indispensable. They must be able to build a car, tune it to the limit, polish and prepare it lovingly and then bear up stoically when a split-second nudge at the start of a race can reduce it to a scrap-heap of battered metal and dusty debris. They must be able to work quickly but without overlooking a single detail – both for the safety of the driver and for the hope of victory. They must be able to work without rest, travel without complaint,

improvise without proper facilities.

The driver, of course, must be skilful, fit, competitive and brave. But he must also be a technician and tactician. In very few races are the options straightforward. Think of all the complications which affect the planning of a race: the tyres may be wearing too quickly, a vital gear starting to jam, a broken suspension arm causing the car to bottom on some corners; a threatening rain cloud making the need to change tyres a possibility; a flock of back markers causing him to lose time against the man in his mirrors; a pit signal indicating that the man ahead is in trouble and should be attacked now. After all the preparation it is the driver's choices that lead to victory or defeat.

TACTICS

In Formula One, the top level of the sport, there are usually two cars to a team. Both drivers help feed vital information to the designer and team manager to help prepare the cars for an event, while in the race itself one driver can defend his team mate's lead by racing – and hopefully distracting – a rival. Or one car can go all-out at the start of a race to lure the opposition into an engine-smashing duel while the team's potential winner is sitting back in the pack, waiting to ease through when the others have all been wheeled away to the dead car park. This happens more in endurance events such as the Le Mans 24-hour race, than in Grand Prix racing. Ultimately, though, a driver's biggest rival is his team mate . . . after all, with identical machinery it is easy to see which one is quicker!

How do you tell if a particular car is doing well when watching a race? Of course, the main way is to see if it leads the race. The car which goes to the front and then pulls away from the opposition must be the fastest, but in a long race like a Grand Prix relative speeds change, and it is often fascinating to watch a low-placed car carving through the pack to get among the leaders. The far-off observer can also tell a lot by the way the cars go through the corners. A car that slices round the bend on a neat line lap after lap indicates a driver well in control and perhaps saving a little for a late push if necessary. But a racer who drifts a long way sideways on the bend and puts wheels up the kerb where the others do not indicates a man trying desperately hard and probably very near the ragged edge.

A car that lags after a slow corner might have gearbox troubles – maybe selection difficulties or some gears defective – while a car that can be overtaken on the entry to the corner shows that it has brake troubles. Smoke rising from a car usually means an engine which is not long for this world, and a driver's arm raised high out of the cockpit signals 'avoid me at all costs, I'm about to stop'.

ALAIN PROST

Prost is known as the 'Professor' for the way he approaches motor sport. He is a tactician who analyzes every situation very carefully and is known for making few mistakes. He is the most successful racing driver, having already won three World Championships and is the first racing driver to win 50 Grand Prix events. He joined the Canon Williams team for the 1993 season. Alain is still the only Frenchman to have won the Drivers' title and is also the most prolific points scorer in the history of Formula One. His first interest in motor sport was at the age of 15 when he rented a kart during a family holiday in Antibes. Alain then bought his own kart for 700 FF and, after winning a national championship title, headed for the Winfield driving school at Paul Ricard. Alain could have had a career in professional football, as he played from the age of eight. He retired from Formula One at the end of 1993.

INDYCAR RACING

INDYCARS ARE SINGLE-SEATERS THAT RACE IN AMERICA ON ROAD RACE
CIRCUITS AND ON OVAL TRACKS, LIKE INDIANAPOLIS . . . THAT'S
HOW THE SPORT GOT ITS NAME

Although the cars look very similar to Formula One machines, there are many differences. The cars are heavier, longer, wider and taller, and are less sophisticated than Grand Prix cars. Power comes from a turbocharged 2.65-litre V8 engine developing around 750 bhp (about the same power output as a Formula One car) but Indycars have potentially much higher top speeds – 240mph (386kmph) against 210mph (338kmph). They use methanol fuel and refuelling pit stops are an important feature of Indycar races. Grand Prix sophistications such as semi-automatic gearboxes and hydraulic 'active' suspension systems are banned. A typical Indycar season has 16 rounds – including one which is in Australia – with six races held on the fearsome ovals.

THE RACE

Only two men in the history of motor racing have won their first ever Indycar race. And they've both been British and world champions. The first was Graham Hill, who won the 1966 Indianapolis 500, and the other was Nigel Mansell, who took up Indycar racing in 1993 after winning the world Formula One title in 1992.

But unlike Hill, who only drove in the Indy 500, Mansell's plan was to complete many seasons of Indycar racing. And although the cars look broadly similar to the Williams-Renault he was used to, the British 'Rookie' found he had a lot to learn . . .

SKILLS & TACTICS

One of the biggest differences between the two forms of racing is that a typical Indycar race is run over a far greater distance than a Grand Prix. Pit stops for fuel and tyres thus play an important part in the race, as does the 'yellow flag'. After an accident, yellow flags are shown to indicate that overtaking is not permitted and the cars line up behind a pace car while the wreckage is cleared. This enables the drivers to bunch up and it is not unknown for substantial leads to be cut to nothing. Once the wreckage has been cleared, the pace car peels off into the pit lane, the green flag is shown and then racing begins again. Many drivers attempt to time their stops for these 'yellows' as their rivals are not at full racing speeds while they are in the pits.

Accidents are common in Indycar racing, especially on the ovals. These tracks, often no more than just a mile (1.6km) long, have little or no run-off areas and are next to solid concrete walls. Contact with a wall will bring instant retirement as the Indycar's wheels and wings are ripped off.

NIGEL MANSELL
In 1992 Nigel Mansell became the first British driver for 16 years to win the Formula One World Championship. Starting with a record five successive wins, he went on to notch up another record, nine victories during the season. Mansell began his Formula One career in 1980 when he competed for the Lotus Ford team in the Austrian and Dutch Grand Prix. Despite his low-key personality in this glamorous sport, Mansell was idolized by British fans for his daring charges in races. After a career in which he competed in 181 Grand Prix (winning 30), he shocked the Formula One world by joining the American Indycar circuit in 1993 . . . and promptly won the Championship!

MOTOR RALLYING

TIME WAS WHEN THE RACING DRIVERS WHO COMPETED IN TRACK EVENTS
ALSO ENTERED FOR RALLIES. NOW THE TWO SPORTS ARE ALMOST SEPARATE,
WITH THEIR OWN DRIVING SKILLS AND STAR DRIVERS

In rallying, cars based on standard production saloons compete over every conceivable kind of surface and in every kind of weather condition. So a typical rally would have open road sections, which the cars cover at normal (legal) speeds, linking up special stages where the aim is to cover the length of the stage in the shortest possible time. There is no car-for-car racing; every driver is racing against the clock, on stages which can be over closed public roads (mainly in Europe) or even on private land, such as forest tracks. Many a car rally is won, or lost, by seconds on the last special stage of the race. Crowds identify with rally drivers, as the cars they drive and even the roads that they drive on are more familiar than the Grand Prix variety.

THE ROUTE

Rallies are staged anywhere in the world and the harder the going, the better for the competitors. In Finland's Thousand Lakes Rally, the most skilful drivers manage to produce incredibly fast times on farm tracks covered up with small stones that roll around like ball bearings, while even the solid ice of a frozen lake is used as a special stage in the rally.

At the other extreme, the Safari Rally in Kenya includes long high-speed sections on baked mud roads where the huge cloud of dust kicked up by a speeding competitor can hang in the air for an hour, or a sudden tropical squall can reduce the section to a virtually unnavigable quagmire in seconds. Most European rallies are either tarmac events – using closed stretches of public road for the event – or run over special forest tracks.

EQUIPMENT

Rally drivers use much the same equipment as their track racing colleagues, though the main difference is the helmet which is 'wired for sound'. Rally co-drivers using pace notes tell the driver what to expect up ahead by radio because the noise of the engine and stones thrown up in the rough going drown out the human voice.

WINNING

The winner of a rally is the car which has the fastest time over all the stages – and manages to avoid any penalties (time added on) for being late on the open road sections. Success or failure depends on both members of the crew working together – the driver has to be very quick and positive on the special stages of the race while the navigator must be immaculate in his route-finding skills and reading of pace notes based on his earlier reconnaissance of the particular stage in question.

RULES

Rallying is a very complicated sport with many classes and regulations, manufacturers often creating special versions of their road cars – the Ford Escort Cosworth and Lancia Delta Integrate – specifically for rallying. All a casual observer needs to be aware of is the fantastic skill and bravery of men who hurl 300bhp machines down narrow forestry tracks between rocks and trees and slither skilfully over surfaces where even special chunky tyres provide only the minimum grip for their cars.

SKILLS & TACTICS

Many of the top rallies are week-long events, where stamina and a good back-up service are just as important as excellent driving skills and faultless navigation. The crews must know how to conserve their strength, how to take it in turns to sleep on the move and how to arrange their meetings with service vehicles to keep their cars in peak order. They also need to know when to drive all out and when to keep a little in reserve so as not to seriously damage or wreck their car.

Tiny Finland's national sport could well be rallying. Drivers like Hanu Mikkola, Timo Makinen, Pentti Arikkala, Juha Kankkunen and Markku Alen are national heroes and dominate the world stage, whether they are swerving their way along English country lanes on the RAC Rally, through clouds of dust in Kenya in the Safari Rally or past forests of pine trees in Finland's own Thousand Lakes Rally, based round the town of Jyvaskyla in the centre of the country. The fiercest rivalry is with the neighbouring Swedes who are equally talented and enthusiastic.

WORDS

Chunky studs: to give extra grip to tyres on loose surfaces

Co-driver: second driver

Drift: controlled four-wheel slide round corner, using throttle

Pace notes: used by navigator to guide driver along route at top speed

Spikes: tyres with very long studs to dig in to ice and snow

Yump: when car is airborne after bump; from Scandinavian pronunciation of 'jump'

OTHER MOTORSPORTS
DRAG RACING DEVELOPED IN THE USA FROM HOT ROD RACING, WHERE ORDINARY CARS WERE FITTED WITH MORE POWERFUL ENGINES TO GIVE THEM GREATER SPEED

After World War II would-be racers who could not get to official tracks began to race on the main streets (or 'drags') of towns, using traffic lights as starting lines. Citizens' complaints and police disapproval led to the formalization of this sport. Today, drag racers use a quarter of a mile (0.4km) 'strip' with electronic eyes to record elapsed time and terminal speed. The classes of vehicles range from everyday mass-produced cars to highly specialized racing dragsters called 'rails'. Some classes even need parachutes as part of the braking system.

Drag Racing

Most cars are rear-engined and these may be supercharged, turbocharged or run on nitromethane. The most obvious features of these cars are the enormous slick rear tyres.

In each race there are only two cars and the first across the line is the winner. A series of eliminating heats leads to a final and handicapping is used if cars of different classes are competing together. The other thing about drag racing is that it's all over in a matter of seconds.

Truck Racing

People have raced all sorts of odd things over the years, but one of the strangest forms of the sport is truck racing. Although it started as something of a joke – an alternative form of entertainment at a conventional motor race – truck racing quickly became popular with drivers and crowds alike. Only the chassis cabs of articulated rigs are used and all have a top speed limiter to ensure the racing is close. It's certainly dramatic and seeing dozens of gaudy trucks, belching out fumes and aiming for the same spot, is not for the faint-hearted.

Not being purpose designed for racing means that trucks look particularly unwieldy when being hurled into a bend. They lean and lurch and the very short wheelbases means they are more likely to spin if inadvertently nudged from behind.

Monster Trucks

An American invention, monster trucks offer a cross between motor sport and pure entertainment. The pick-up trucks, sometimes with bizarre custom bodies, sit perched 12ft (3.6m) above four wheels and tyres stolen from massive earth-moving machinery.

Racing takes place on mud-covered arenas and, amid laser lights and stage-managed pyrotechnics, trucks bounce their way from one end of the arena to the other and back again, racing two by two against the clock.

Karts

Karting is a fast form of motor sport where many top champions have learnt their skill, and it's open to anyone from seven to 70. The karts are tiny, but powerful and the international machines have highly tuned racing engines and gearboxes.

Karts can race on full-sized car racing circuits, but much of the best racing is on kart tracks with complex, small circuits. Engines vary in size from 50cc up to 250cc. For Grand Prix racing, all use grooved, dry or wet weather tyres.

WORDS

Burn-out: spinning the wheels in the burn-out pits or bleach box
Elapsed time (E.T.): the electronically measured time between start and finish
Fire-up road: side road where vehicles are started
Shut-down area: braking distance, usually ¼–½ mile (about 400–800m) beyond finish line
Terminal speed (T.S.): electronically clocked speed as car crosses finish line
Wheelie: lifting front wheels off the ground, so car is only balanced on the rear wheels

NETBALL

PLAYED ALMOST EXCLUSIVELY BY WOMEN AND DEVELOPED FROM BASKETBALL,
NETBALL COMBINES INDIVIDUAL SKILLS OF THROWING, CATCHING,
RUNNING, JUMPING, TURNING AND SHOOTING

Unlike basketball, players are restricted to various areas of the netball court which they must not leave. The ball can only be passed, rather than carried, forward.

New Zealand created the first national association in 1924 followed by England in 1926. In 1960, a world body was formed (the International Federation of Women's Basketball and Netball Associations) followed three years later by the first World Championship. Although this seven-a-side game was invented in the USA in 1891, Australia has dominated the World Championship, winning it outright on five occasions.

Netball is a non-contact sport controlled by two umpires. Rough play, obstruction, intimidation and personal contact are all fouls.

THE COURT

Netball is played on a hard surface 30.50m by 15.25 (100ft by 50) which is divided into three equal areas. The goal is a ring 38cm (15in) in diameter which is positioned at the top of a 3.05m (10ft) high goal post. Unlike basketball, there is no backboard.

EQUIPMENT

Players wear rubber-soled shoes and a skirt or pair of shorts with a plain shirt usually in team colours. A bib with letters indicating a player's position is worn over the shirt.

The ball should weigh between 397 and 453g (14–16oz) and measure between 68 and 71cm (27–28in) in diameter.

WINNING

The winning team is the one that scores the most goals. A goal is scored when the ball is tossed through the ring; however, only two players, the goal shooter (GS) and goal attack (GA), are allowed to shoot for goal. Even then, they must be inside the shooting circle.

RULES

The seven players on each team are easily identified by the bibs they wear. There are three attackers – goal shooter (GS), goal attack (GA), and wing attack (WA); three defenders – goalkeeper (GK), goal defence (GD), and wing defence (WD) as well as a centre (C) who links defence and attack.

Each player is limited solely to her particular area of pitch. She is offside if she enters another area.

The game lasts for an hour and is divided into 15-minute quarters. Players can only hold possession of the ball for three seconds and are not allowed to dribble the ball.

Fouls are penalized by the award of a penalty pass. If a foul is committed right in the shooting circle, a penalty shot at goal is awarded for the other team.

SKILLS & TACTICS

Netball players need good speed and the ability to pass rapidly and accurately. Two main options are open to defenders: a zone defence, in which each defender marks an area and tries to prevent a pass being made or received in that area; and one-on-one marking in which each defender closely marks one specific opponent.

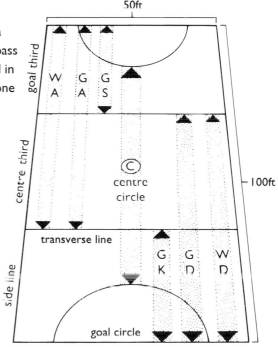

WORDS

Blocking: defending against a player who does not have the ball

Circle: the semi-circle at the foot of each goal post

Dragging: illegal; as one foot must be still when a

player has the ball before passing or shooting

Obstruction: illegal; standing closer than one yard to an opponent

Travelling: illegal; if a player catches the ball in

midair outside the circle, lands in circle and attempts a shot at goal

Two-lines: illegal; if the ball crosses one-third of the playing field without touching another player

A rowing eight is coordinated by a cox who, nowadays, passes instructions via a microphone linked to tiny loudspeakers all along the slender craft.

ROWING

TODAY'S NEEDLE-LIKE AERODYNAMIC CRAFT BEAR LITTLE RESEMBLANCE TO
THE ROWING BOATS THAT WERE RACED BY SAILORS AND WATERMEN
CENTURIES AGO

The fastest and most prestigious of the various craft is the Eight, with eight oarsmen, each pulling one oar, and a cox who steers. Then there are the Fours. There are two types: both have four oarsmen, each with one oar, but one is coxed and the other is coxless. In the coxless four, the boat is steered by one of the oarsmen, usually the bowman, using steering lines attached to his shoes. The Pairs, two-man craft, are both coxed and coxless.

Another discipline is sculling, where the oarsmen (or scullers) have two oars (sculls), one in each hand. The individual event is the Single Sculls, with just one sculler in the boat and no cox. Double Sculls features two rowers each with two sculls while Quadruple Sculls with four rowers is probably the most sleek of all the boats to watch, but also one of the most difficult to row well. Only in women's rowing does the quad-scull carry a cox. An eight-man sculling boat is gaining in popularity for training and competition.

Most international and Olympic courses are artificial, rather like a large, shallow swimming pool, so there is no distorting current in the water. Therefore, no one lane is better or worse than any other.

One of the world's oldest sporting encounters is between the oarsmen of Oxford and Cambridge Universities. Called simply the Boat Race since its inception in 1829 it has become a major spring event in the British calendar of 'things to see'. Despite getting little more than a fleeting glimpse of the passing crews, crowds line the banks of the River Thames between Putney and Mortlake in West London. However, the 7km (4¼ mile) long Boat Race should not be written off as an irrelevant students' race. In recent years, student rowers from Germany and the USA, Australia and Britain have gone on to win World and Olympic titles.

THE COURSE

At full international and Olympic level the standard course is dead straight and 2000m (about 2200yd) long for men. Women row 1000m (1100yd), Juniors 1500m (1640yd). The boats row six abreast in lanes which are clearly marked by buoys.

EQUIPMENT

Oars and boats are reinforced with carbon fibre to make them light, strong, and inflexible under pressure. Everything adjusts to suit the individual, so each oarsman has a seat which runs up and down a slide and feet go into training shoes on a rack called a stretcher. On the outside of the boat, an adjustable metal rigger has a gate for the oar.

WINNING

International and Olympic rowing is divided into various classes and categories, both of competitors and boats, who race against each other.

Men's Heavyweight: men of any weight can take part, but, in effect it means the fastest and most prestigious crews, because in rowing bigger means stronger.

Men's Lightweight: which is for crews of an average weight of 70kg (154lb or under) and where no individual in the crews weighs more than 72.5kg (159lb).

RULES

Championship regattas commence with heats in which some crews qualify direct for the semi-finals or finals. For those beaten in the heats there is another chance to qualify when they race in repechage. This is to ensure that a possible medallist is not knocked out in the first round. The finals are always contested by six crews. The umpire follows in a launch, checking that boats stay in their own lane.

SKILLS

The power comes from the whole of the body, the legs doing as much as the arms and the torso. Each oarsman's seat is on small wheels and runs on a pair of tracks, called a slide, which helps to lengthen the sweep of the oar in the water. Look to see whether the timing is good; whether all the oars are going into and out of water at precisely the same time. If the timing starts to get ragged in top-class rowing it means competitors are tiring and starting to row badly. Usually this only happens towards the end of the race and it's always in this last 500m (547yd) that

WORDS

Bow: front of the boat – also the oarsman nearest the front of the boat

Button: the part of the oar that fits in the gate and holds it steady

Cover: distance between two sets of puddles

Cox: coordinates the efforts of the crew, steers the boat

Puddle: the whirlpool made by the oar as it leaves the water – a guide to the distance a boat travels before the next stroke

Repechage: the race for crews losing in the first round of a regatta so that they can still reach the final

Shortening up: rowing too fast, at too high a rating,

and not pulling the oar right through the water

Stroke: the oarsman nearest the back (stern) of the boat who sets the pace which everyone follows

Stroke side: the side of the boat on which the stroke's oar is, as opposed to bowside; in the USA, port and starboard respectively.

mistakes start to appear. The cox, often female, shouts commands via a microphone and loudspeakers and usually sits in the back but often is supine in the bow (front) with just her head visible.

TACTICS

The opening strokes should be rather short as the oars dig into the water to get the boat up to full speed. Some crews might take about half a minute to achieve this. When the boat is running well, after about 250m, (273yd), the cox and stroke together try to settle the crew down to a steady rowing rhythm by lengthening the stroke out. They maintain this for the next 1250m (1367yd), then with some 500m (546yd) to go they sprint for the finishing line. At a point picked out by the coach in the middle of a race, crews often put in a burn, either to test their opponents' skills or to catch up if they are falling behind.

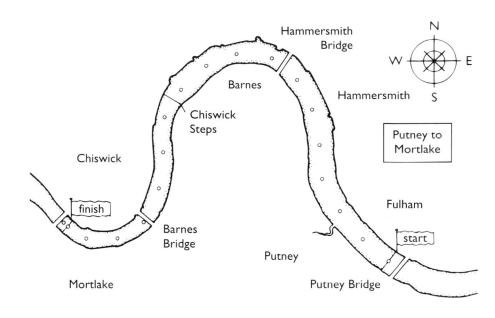

The course on London's Thames for the most famous rowing challenge in the world – the Oxford and Cambridge Boat Race, raced over 7km (4¼ miles).

STEVE REDGRAVE Britain's most successful Olympian of modern times is a towering oarsman from Marlow in Buckinghamshire who has dominated international rowing since 1984 when he picked up his first Olympic gold in the coxed four. In 1986 at the Commonwealth Games he managed to collect an astonishing hat trick of wins in the single scull, coxed pairs and fours. If you then add more gold medals that he obtained at the world championships it is easy to see why Redgrave is considered one of the all-time greats of the sport. At the 1988 Olympics, he partnered Andy Holmes to win the coxless pairs; in 1992, with Matthew Pinsent, eight years his junior, Redgrave collected his third Olympic gold, again in the coxless pairs event. The last Briton to win three Olympic golds was way back in 1920!

Redgrave has recently acquired the sponsorship necessary to enable him to try for yet another Olympic Games in Atlanta, USA in 1996.

Possession is the name of the game in rugby league, so players must keep a tight hold on the ball while their opponents try to jar it loose from them with crushing tackles.

RUGBY LEAGUE

RUGBY LEAGUE FOOTBALL IS A 13-A-SIDE ADAPTATION
OF THE 15-A-SIDE RUGBY UNION GAME

It was born in England in 1895, when 21 northern clubs broke away from the rugby union in protest at that governing body's refusal to let them compensate players for money lost when they took time off work to play football. Soon the rugby league accepted the principle of part-time professionalism for players, which has ever since been the insurmountable barrier preventing cooperation between the two codes.

There are many amateur teams playing rugby league football, but it is the professionals of Australia and Britain who tend to dominate the game, usually beating those of New Zealand and France.

The ultimate objective is the same in the two codes: to score points by running the ball over the opponents' try line, and by kicking the ball between their goal posts. Rugby league is an uncompromisingly hard game, and a more open and faster one than rugby union.

This is not just because there are only six forwards in the scrum rather than eight, but because the game's rules encourage a running game and the elimination of close-quarter mauling of union scrums.

THE FIELD

Rugby league is played on grass pitches with a maximum length the same as those of rugby union, 100m (110yd), but league pitches are often significantly narrower. A minimum width of 55m (about 60yd) is stipulated, compared to union's maximum of 69m (75yd). The goal posts are exactly the same, with a crossbar 3.05m high (10ft) between posts 5.6m apart (18ft 6in).

EQUIPMENT

The inflated oval ball is slightly smaller than that used in rugby union. Shirts, shorts, stockings and boots are the standard personal equipment, but league players are also encouraged to wear some protective shoulder padding.

WINNING

Grounding the ball over the opponents' try line scores four points, and gives the team the chance to add two more with a conversion kick at goal. This is taken from a point in line with (but at any distance from) the place where the try was scored. The ball is placed upright on the ground and, to be successful, the kick must pass over the crossbar and between the posts. In exceptional circumstances, the referee may award four points automatically if he thinks that a certain try has been prevented by foul play. The conversion kick for this 'penalty try' is taken from in front of the posts.

Possession of the ball is obviously the essential ingredient for scoring tries. The team with the ball attempts to run with it towards the opposing try line, passing the ball from one to another as they go in an attempt to elude the defenders. The team not in possession tries to stop the attackers by tackling them to the ground.

A penalty kick may be awarded against a team committing a foul during play, and this is taken from the spot where the offence took place. If a goal is then kicked, it is worth two points. At any time during play, a player may attempt a 'drop goal', by bouncing the ball on the ground and kicking it on the half-volley over the bar. By international rules, this scores one point, and is a specialist skill.

RULES

The game is played in two halves of 40 minutes each. A team may use two substitutes at any stage of the game.

The principal rule of play is, as in rugby union, that the ball must never be passed forward, but only behind or to the side. (It can be kicked forward, but that may lead to the other team gaining possession.) The most influential difference between the two codes of rugby occurs when a player with the ball is effectively tackled. In league, play is immediately and briefly stopped while he gets up and plays the ball with his foot to a player behind him; he may also play it forward and pick it up himself. His team thus retains possession and all of the players are, usually, ranged across the field ready to receive the ball and run.

Each team is allowed to retain the ball for only five consecutive tackles. On the sixth, possession goes to the opposition, so a deep kick is the usual tactic to reduce the opponents' advantage. A scrum is formed when a player takes the ball out of play over the side lines (touch lines), when a scrum is held opposite the point at which the ball went out of play; when a kick sends the ball directly out of play over the side lines without touching the ground in the field of play first, in which case the scrum is held at the point at which the kick was taken; when a player 'knocks on' – fails to catch the ball cleanly from a pass or kick and fumbles it forward; and for other minor offences against the rules not serious enough to warrant a penalty kick. Dangerous or violent play may be penalized by the referee sending

Rugby league had a major shake-up of the rules for the 1983–4 season when the value of a try was upped from three to four points. The other change, also aimed at increasing the appeal of the game by making it flow more easily and quickly, was to abolish the scrum after the sixth tackle. As England's rugby union fortunes improved and attracted far more public attention to that game, so the rival code became more innovative and colourful, pledged to entertain both on and off the field.

the player off the field.

When the ball is behind the goal line and a defender manages to touch it down before an attacker can, play is re-started by a drop kick from the defenders' 20m (22yd) line.

SKILLS

Speed, strength and stamina are vital ingredients in the all-round rugby league footballer. For the two second-row forwards, who supply most of the push in the scrums, strength may be more important than speed; for the two half backs, the reverse applies. In addition these two, the playmakers of the team, need agility, good acceleration from a standing start, and an acute tactical awareness. All the runners in the team, but particularly the three-quarters, need the ability to deceive by swerve and sidestep as well as to beat by sheer speed.

The full back, the last line of defence as well as a frequent surprise attacker, needs all the basic qualities plus good positional sense, the ability to catch a high ball with the opposition thundering towards him, and the timing and courage to bring off some try-saving tackles.

Of all the team, the fly half is the man most likely to have the opportunity to kick a drop goal, which is a skill on its own. And

someone in the side must be a reliable place kicker, to make the most of penalty and conversion kicks.

TACTICS

As in any form of football, a rugby league team plays to its strengths. The best spectacle in the game is a team with strong and lively forwards, astute half backs with great handling skills, and searing three-quarters who can run past or through the opposition. They will almost certainly play an open, running game that will thrill the viewer.

But there are many less spectacular sides whose success is built on a relentless defence. All the speed and craft in the world ranged against them will founder if the tackles just keep coming, hard and fast. The variations to the original game that have been introduced to rugby league over the past century have all been designed to attract spectators by attaching greater rewards to the skills of running and passing. The urge to win, by the players and their coach, is much greater than the urge to entertain, and at least as much thought is given to stifling the attacking moves of the opponents as to exploiting all of their defensive weaknesses.

Some of the referee's signals: 1, penalty; 2, obstruction; 3, foot up in the scrum; 4, verbal dissent.

1   2   3   4

WORDS

Conversion: place kick with which the attacking team endeavour to convert a four-point try into a six-point goal

Dead ball line: absolute limit of play, some metres behind the goal line

Drop out: method of re-starting play by a drop kick from the defenders' 20m line

Early bath: jocular reference to a player who is sent off and heads for the dressing room

Hooker: front-row forward whose job it is to hook the ball back to his own side at a scrum

Knock-on: to propel the ball forwards with hand or forearm, often by fumbling a pass; illegal

Obstruction: illegal impeding of opponent who does not have the ball

Play-the-ball: action in which an attacking player, having just been tackled, foots the ball behind him to a colleague; or forward, to pick it up himself

Scissors: three-quarter movement in which two players run forward on opposite diagonal paths; the one with the ball passes to the other as they cross

Scrum: set play in which both sets of forwards bind together in opposing packs and try to win the ball

Selling a dummy: deceiving an opponent by pretending to pass the ball; also used in 'dummy scissors'

Stiff-arm tackle: made with the forearm, usually aimed at the neck or head of an opponent; dangerous and illegal

Touch: out-of-play area beyond the sidelines

Touchdown: grounding of the ball beyond the goal line

Up-and-under: high kick ahead made to put the defence under pressure; the kicker follows up to try to regain possession

FRANO BOTICA

This New Zealander could well be the greatest goal kicker the game has ever seen. The man from North Harbour in Auckland won a handful of caps for the All Blacks Rugby Union side and was a member of the 1987 World Cup winning squad, but was always in Grant Fox's shadow. After a spell playing in Italy, Frano turned professional with Wigan in 1990. Coach John Monie eased him in to the new code.

Botica played wing, full back and scrum half before settling in to the pivotal stand-off position. But it's his kicking that has re-written the record books – the fastest scorer of 1000 points in the game's history, Botica converted an astonishing 10 out of 10 against St Helens in 1992 in the Premiership Trophy.

Using the round-the-corner style, Botica's accuracy helps him play a major role in his club's success.

Players of all shapes and sizes play rugby, from the tall men who jump to catch the ball in a line-out to the small, agile scrum half; burly props are as important as a speedy wing.

RUGBY UNION

LEGEND SAYS THAT IN 1823 WILLIAM WEBB ELLIS, A PUPIL AT RUGBY SCHOOL,

ORIGINATED THE GAME WHEN HE PICKED UP A FOOTBALL

AND STARTED RUNNING WITH IT

In 1987 the inaugural Rugby World Cup was staged in Australasia, confirming that rugby had reached international status.

Rugby union is an amateur game played with 15 players a side. Players run, pass and kick the ball in an attempt to score by grounding the ball right behind their opponents' goal line or by kicking the ball between the posts at the opposition's end of the field.

The side without the ball attempts to obtain possession of it by tackling an opposing ball carrier, catching the ball when it is kicked forward by the opposition or by winning the ball in the various methods of re-starting the game.

The eight forwards are the men whose main job it is to win possession of the ball. They are normally the biggest and strongest members of the team. The seven backs are the runners and handlers who are expected to use the possession won by the forwards either by running with the ball towards the opposition's end of the field or by cleverly kicking the ball into their opponents' territory in the hope that their forwards can once again win possession.

Which country is the reigning Olympic rugby union champion? Rugby featured in four games before being abandoned after the 1924 Olympics. In 1900 France beat Germany into second place with Britain a surprising third. Eight years later in London, the British were again beaten, thrashed 32–3 by Australia in the final. In 1920, the USA were the champions, defeating France 8–0. Four years later, Parisian crowds were shocked to see their heroes beaten yet again by the Americans. Robert Doe, John O'Neill, John Patrick and Colby Slater played on both teams, while Daniel Carrol also won two golds – for Australia in 1908 and the USA in 1920! So the USA are still the Olympic champions!

THE PITCH

The pitch can vary in size, but from goal line to goal must not exceed 100m (110yd) and must not be wider than 69m (75yd). Like the pitch the H shaped posts can come in many sizes. The surface is always grass.

EQUIPMENT

Shirts and shorts must be strong. Some forwards protect their ears from damage by wearing either a head band or bandaging.

Players, especially forwards, tend to wear strong ankle-supporting boots to prevent injury. The studs though must conform to strict regulations.

The ball is oval, weighing 380–430g (13–15oz) and conforms to rigid dimensions.

WINNING

There are two methods of scoring points – the try and the goal. A try is worth five points and is scored when the ball is carried or chased over the opponents' goal line and grounded between the goal line and the dead ball line. The scoring team can then attempt to convert the try by means of a place kick or drop kick in line with the place where the ball was touched down. A successful kick at goal must pass above the cross-bar and within a line formed by the posts. The conversion is worth an extra two points. There are two other methods of scoring a goal. Both are worth three points. For some offences the referee can award a penalty and a kick at goal can be taken. When a player kicks the ball on the half-volley, after bouncing on the ground, this is a drop kick. A dropped goal can be attempted by any player during open play. A penalty try can be awarded if the referee feels that a certain try has been prevented through foul play by the defending side.

Opponents can only tackle the man with the ball.

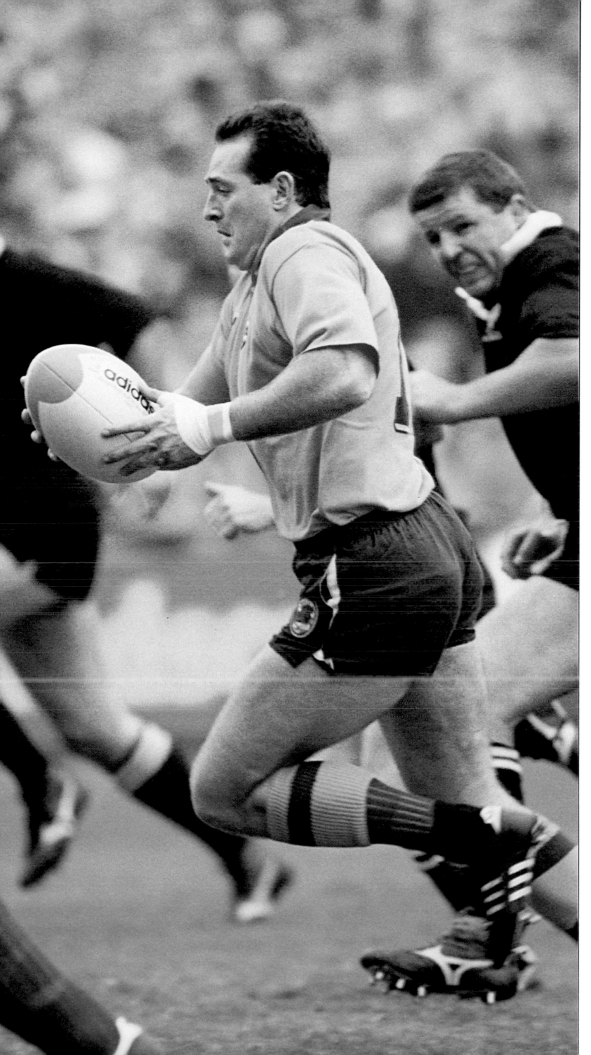

Rugby union is at its best when the ball is passed from hand to hand by speedy, elusive runners. While plenty of tactical ploys have been devised to grind down opponents by maintaining possession through powerful forwards, the simplest tactic is still often the most effective – the ball is heeled rapidly from a scrum, passed rapidly along the three-quarter line to release the winger, who runs at his opposite number. Great wingers have to have natural acceleration, a deceptive side step and the strength to shrug off any crashing tackles occurring on their way to the try line.

LAWS

When tackled the ball carrier must release the ball immediately after the tackle. Frequently both sets of forwards will form a ruck (with the ball on the ground) or a maul (when the ball is held) in an attempt to regain possession. Often these prove inconclusive in which case a set scrum is formed by the forwards.

The ball is often kicked out of play. From within his own 22m (24yd) line a player can kick directly into touch. Elsewhere he must bounce the ball in play before it crosses the line. A line-out takes place where the ball went into touch, the ball being thrown between the two lines of forwards to re-start the game. If a player (illegally) kicks the ball directly into touch outside his 22m line, the line-out is awarded level with the spot where the kick was made.

A player is offside when he is in front of the ball and attempts to play it after it has been played by a team mate. At scrum and line-out, though, more specific laws are used to keep the two teams apart.

Minor infringements are penalized by the awarding of a set scrum. More serious ones either by a free kick or a penalty.

SKILLS

The front row: the props and hooker are the foundation of the scrummage. Ideally strong and stocky, their main job is to overcome the opposing front row at the scrum. More and more the hooker has to be mobile, and act defensively in open play.
The locks: the biggest men in the side. They have to use their power at the scrum, their height at the line-out.
The back row: two flankers and the number 8. Their role is to support the ball carrier in attack and to be the first to a ruck or maul.
Scrum half: the link between forwards and backs. From set pieces and loose play he will decide whether to pass, kick or run.
Outside half: he is the pivot of the back division. He controls the tempo of the game and must be able to pass well and be a reliable tactical kicker.
Centre three-quarters: in attack they pass to their wings or attempt to break through the opposition. In defence they must tackle well and often.
Wing: like centres, they should have a good turn of speed. Additionally the skills of sidestep, swerve, and change of pace are of great value. Normally the fastest players.
Full back: the last line of defence. Ideally with a cool temperament, he must be a good kicker both to touch, and often at goal, with the ability to help his three-quarters in attack.

TACTICS

If a team has a strong set of forwards, play often revolves around them – at a scrum the number 8 may pick up the ball himself and then link up with his flankers or scrum half. The forwards may interpass and in a succession of mauls take the game upfield. Alternatively the scrum half or outside half may kick ahead for their forwards to follow up and gain possession. From a line-out the forwards may hold the ball amongst themselves rather than releasing it for the backs. In addition, the half backs may consistently kick for touch allowing the forwards to attempt to gain the possession from a succession of line-outs. On the other hand if the strength lies with the backs then the forwards will be keen to transfer the ball as quickly as possible to half backs and backs. There is an armoury of moves available to a back in an attempt to outwit his opponent; missing out a centre with a long pass, bringing the full back into the line, working dummy moves. Finally, though, there is no real substitute for good pace and acceleration to take a back past his opponent.

AUSSIE RULES

The world's leading try scorer at international level only took up rugby union when he was 17. In fact, David Campese grew up near Canberra on rugby league territory and played that code as a youngster. He then tried his hand at golf for a year before dabbling in union. Within two years he had made the Australian test team against New Zealand, aged 19! 'Campo' scored his 50th try in 1992 and has played in over 70 international matches.

WORDS

Advantage: if after an infringement by one side the other side gains some advantage the referee may allow play to continue

Blind side: also called the narrow side. When play is on the left hand side, for example, the smaller area between the ball and right hand touch line comprises the blind side

Dummy: when a player feints to pass, but in fact holds onto the ball

Knock on: when a player drops the ball or propels it forward and it subsequently hits the ground; a scrum is awarded to the opposition

Lifting at the line-out: an illegal move – when one player attempts to lift or keep in the air a team mate to help him reach the ball

Loose forwards: the two flankers and the number 8.

Loose head prop: the prop standing to the left of the hooker

Open side: the opposite of the blind side

Punt: allowing the ball to fall from hands and kicking it before it touches the ground

Scrum five: if the defending side carries the ball over its own goal line and grounds it, a scrum is awarded to the opposition 5m (5½yd) from the goal line

Strike: the act of hooking the ball in the front row

Strike against the head: when the opposition wins the ball from the other side's put-in at the scrum

Tight head prop: the prop who stands on the right of the hooker

WILL CARLING

Carling is one of rugby union's most instantly recognizable players. A strong running and fierce tackling centre, he led England to the final of the 1991 rugby World Cup and to two Grand Slam victories in 1991 and 1992. He became England's youngest captain for 57 years when he led the team to victory over Australia at the age of 22 in 1988. Consistent selection has ensured a strong England squad, with Carling now England's most capped centre as well as holding the current world record for the most international wins as the team's captain. Carling is a strong believer that all rugby players should be allowed to benefit financially from any rugby-related activities.

The great appeal of sailing is that it accommodates both the rich and the relatively poor, and everyone in between. On sea, lakes or reservoirs, sailors delight in using a free source of energy – the wind.

SAILING

SAILING IS AN INCREDIBLY WIDE-RANGING SPORT. IT CAN MEAN TINY
OPTIMIST DINGHIES ON A SMALL BOATING LAKE OR THE 72M (236FT)
FOUR-MASTED SCHOONER 'CLUB MEDITERRANEE', WHICH COMPETED IN THE
1976 OBSERVER SINGLEHANDED TRANSATLANTIC RACE

There are hundreds of classes, types of dinghies and small keel boats, thousands of fully-crewed off-shore yachts which may race over courses of a few dozen or several hundred miles, and strong but sleek racing craft which battle over huge distances – even round the globe in the 'Whitbread Round the World Race'. Perhaps the most active class in the world is the Laser, with over 150,000 built and sailed in more than 80 countries.

The idea of competitive sailing is to test a sailor's ability to get the most out of the boat as well as the wind. It is all a matter of angles, rather like snooker. A good sailor will be able to appreciate at which angle to sail in order to get the most wind to blow the boat along. When the wind is behind, the boat is running, wind aft. Since a boat can't sail straight into the wind, the sailor has to zig-zag or tack at a 45 degree angle to the wind, from left to right or port to starboard with the sails close-hauled. The closer to the wind a helmsman can make his boat sail, the faster he gets to the windward mark, so the beat is the main test of skill.

THE COURSE

The 'Olympic course' is the favourite triangular configuration for all boats racing in open water and is invariably used in the Olympic yachting competition because it provides a thorough test. The course is laid according to the direction of the wind so the fleet starts with a beat to windward, sailing into the wind, then turns the weather mark (the marker nearest the wind) before going off at an angle to a wing mark that is usually on the port side of the triangle. From the wing mark the boats return to the starting mark (the leeward mark). A second beat up to the weather mark is followed by a dead run (with the wind behind the boats) from the weather mark to the start point before a final beat to the finishing line, laid by the weather mark.

Sailors usually talk of these courses as consisting of triangles and sausages, so the standard Olympic course is a triangle, a sausage and a final beat. Occasionally, the triangle is left out altogether – making a string of sausages!

EQUIPMENT

A yachtsman's main need is protection against wet and cold. For the off-shore sailor this will often mean tough oilskins with welded seams and adjustable cuffs and hood, over a suit of woolly polar wear. A wet-suit underneath the outer layer of protection keeps the body warm even after a capsize. Boots vary according to the type of boat being sailed – heavy ones with lace-up tops for the off-shore yachtsman, light and flexible ones for the dinghy sailor, with ribbing across the instep to prevent chafing from the toe-straps. Dinghy sailors also use buoyancy aids which are lighter than a life-jacket but able to support a waterlogged sailor after a capsize.

Off-shore sailors often use a safety harness for extra safety in heavy weather conditions. It consists of a harness which fits around the body with a line that can be attached to a strong part of the yacht so that if a big wave comes over the top or the boat keels suddenly, the sailor is secure and cannot be swept overboard.

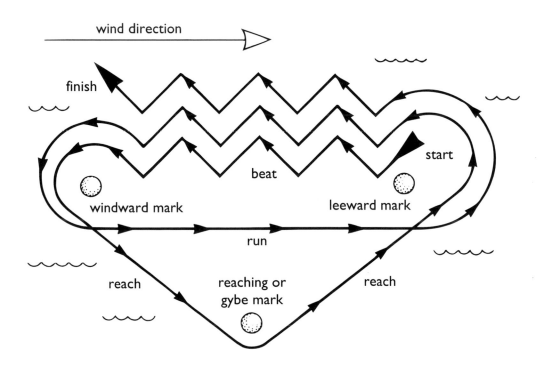

The Olympic course: first leg is a beat to windward followed by two reaches, then a beat and a run; finally a beat to the finish.

wind direction

finish

beat

start

windward mark

leeward mark

run

reach

reaching or gybe mark

reach

Just as skiers have developed freestyle skiing, so boardsailing enthusiasts have invented tricks on the water. Back at the 1976 World Championships in Nassau, Americans really astonished all the crowds by railriding, riding their boards right on the edge! Nowadays, all competitors demonstrate an array of difficult stunts. Some sit or lie on their boards, while others do some spectacular somersaults through the boom! Expert board sailors mimic motorcyclists by doing a wheelie, jumping on the tail of the board to make the bow leap out of the water. Whether the move is Rock 'n' Roll or a Body Dip, it takes hours of practice to execute a trick without falling off!

WINNING

In one-design boat classes, the first over the winning line takes the honours. At the Olympics, the winner is the boat with the best results over six races. Seven races take place, but the worst result can be discarded and a points system then decides on the overall winner.

The many parts of a simple sailing dinghy.

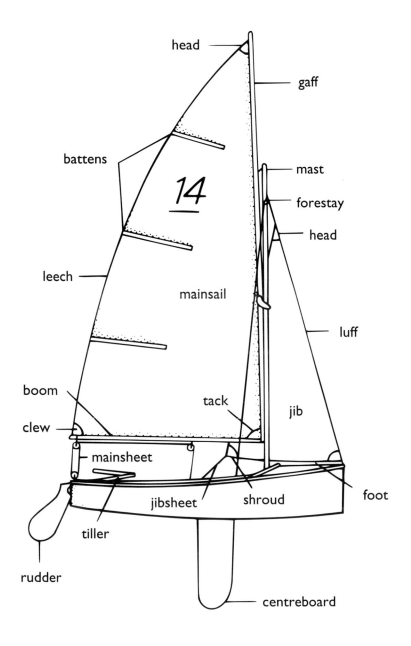

Off-shore boats are built either to the International Off-Shore Rule (IOR) or, more often in the UK, to the Channel Handicap System (CHS). This is a rating formula from which a series of complicated calculations will produce a rating for the boat in feet. This is usually fairly close to the length of the boat measured along the waterline. When boats of different sizes are taking part in a race, this rating is used as a handicap figure and computed with the elapsed time, the time that a boat has taken to cover the course of a race. From that computation comes the corrected time – and the boat with the best corrected time is the winner. In practice this means that the first yacht home (usually called the boat taking line honours) is seldom the actual winner of the race. Indeed, on a long race, such as the 1000km (600 mile) Fastnet classic which rounds off the Admiral's Cup series, it is quite possible for a smaller yacht which crosses the line many hours after the leader to emerge as the overall winner.

RULES

Once the boats are racing, the main rules cover which boat has right of way going round buoys and markers. Basically, a boat with the wind on the port (left-hand) side must give way to one with the wind on the starboard (right-hand) side.

SKILLS

The best sailors know how to make boats go as quickly as possible on every point of sailing – that is, no matter from which direction the wind is coming. Sailing into the wind – beating – the skipper must sense how close he can sail to the wind, how to adjust for wind shifts, how to sail the close-hauled course without pinching and so losing power, and how to use his own and the crew's body weight to keep the boat sailing as near upright as possible and thus keep the boat's sails full.

WORDS

About: a boat goes about when her bows pass through the wind

Bear away: alter course away from the wind

Beat: a course which requires the yacht to sail close-hauled and tack

Boom: the horizontal spar at the foot of a sail

Close-hauled: a boat is close-hauled when her sails are sheeted in tight and she is sailing as close to the wind as possible

Ease: slacken a rope

Genoa: a large triangular foresail

Gybe: to bring the wind through the stern so that the boom swings to the other side

Helmsman: the man at the tiller or wheel

Leeward: the side of a boat furthest away from the wind

Mainsail: the sail aft of the mast

Port tack: a boat is on port tack when the wind is blowing on her left side

Reef: to reduce sail area

Run: to sail before the wind – also called sailing downwind

Spinnaker: a full-bellied triangular sail set when reaching or running to take advantage of good wind

Starboard tack: a boat is said to be on starboard tack when the wind is blowing on her right side

Tack: to beat to windward on a zig-zag course

Tiller: the handle for the rudder, like the steering wheel of a car

Trapeze: where a crewman wears a harness attached to a wire and hangs over the side of the boat to try to balance it

Windward: the side of the boat against which the prevailing wind blows

Each class of boat has its own logo on the sail. Below: J24, Mistral and Laser.

Sailing with the wind on the beam, he must know how to balance the boat properly, how to use the crew's weight to induce the hull of a dinghy to rise on the plane (to skim along the surface), how to set and control a spinnaker for maximum speed and how to balance his other sails to keep the spinnaker drawing at its best.

TACTICS

A good start is essential for success but unlike athletics or motor racing, boats cannot line up at a starting line. They have to be moving so, by manoeuvring, they try to cross the starting line as soon as possible after the gun goes off. A good start gives the advantage of sailing into clean air – not disturbed by boats ahead.

In match racing events such as the America's Cup, where there are just two boats and each tries to cover the other, the yachts may manoeuvre warily in circles behind the start line for some minutes before the gun. But in fleet racing you will see 20 or 30 boats coming up to the line, all on starboard tack, all battling for that extra ounce of speed.

Then the sailors must choose the correct side of the course to get the best wind or avoid the adverse tidal flow. They must calculate the approach to the next mark to have the tactical advantage of being on starboard tack (with right of way). They cover close rivals to blanket the wind and prevent other boats getting away on a sudden lift or gust of wind.

Recreational skiers find it hard to appreciate the speed and control of top-class competitors. Men touch 100 kmph as they drop 900m during a 3000m run which has a 35 per cent slope!

SKIING

In addition to the downhill events, Alpine skiing also includes the slalom and the giant slalom, where skiers swerve in and out of obstacles.

There are two other branches of the sport which were not born in the Alps: Nordic skiing and freestyle skiing, both of them on the Olympic programme. At the heart of Nordic skiing is cross-country skiing, which arose as a matter of practicality in the Scandinavian countries. Then there is the biathlon, a combination of cross-country racing and rifle shooting; and ski jumping, another Nordic creation that now takes place from huge towers and has become an exciting element of competition.

Freestyle skiing is a comparatively new and more acrobatic sport which has little in common with the others. Created in the United States as 'hot-dogging', it has since been internationally organized with safety in mind. There are three separate categories, one of which – moguls – was a medal event at the 1992 Winter Olympics. The other two – ballet and aerials – were demonstration events there.

Alpine Skiing

THE COURSE

Downhill skiing courses challenge the courage and daring of the competitor as much as his speed. They may be as much as 4500km long (nearly 3 miles) for men, with a vertical drop of up to 900m (2950ft). Sharp bends are not included, but there are many bumps and gullies.

Slalom courses are shorter but include between 50 and 75 'gates' through which the skier must pass. They are flexible poles set into the snow in pairs, about 5m (5.5yd) apart. The giant slalom is a longer version with wider gates and Super-G is a cross between slalom and downhill skiing. In every category, the women's races are shorter and are usually less steep.

Because, more often than not, all course conditions deteriorate during the race, early runners have the advantage. This is always given to the most highly-ranked skiers.

EQUIPMENT

There is no end to this, as skiers become more specialized and manufacturers respond by offering a staggering choice of skis, sticks, boots, release gadgets and clothing of all kinds. There is no sport in which the competition between manufacturers is more fierce, and they go to amazing lengths to get the best-known skiers under contract. Time was when a skier would use the same pair of skis whatever the event, but that is long past. High technology has taken over.

Downhill skis are usually wider and longer than slalom skis (slightly longer than the height of the wearer), and need to be stiffer at the tail and more flexible at the tip, in order to negotiate bumps more easily at high speeds. With these qualities, they are less manoeuvrable in turns. With turning and twisting paramount, the slalom ski is shorter. Nearly all skis are now made of fibre-reinforced plastic.

A crucial accessory for the star performer is ski wax, applied to the soles of the ski to help speed and control. A wide variety of waxes is available, for use according to the conditions of the day. Lightweight ski sticks now have kinks in the shaft, and serious racers have discarded stretch trousers and anoraks in favour of close-fitting ski suits that offer less wind resistance. Gloves, a helmet and goggles complete the kit.

WINNING

With the exception of the parallel slalom, which is not often seen at top level, all Alpine events are raced by one competitor at a time, against the clock. The downhill

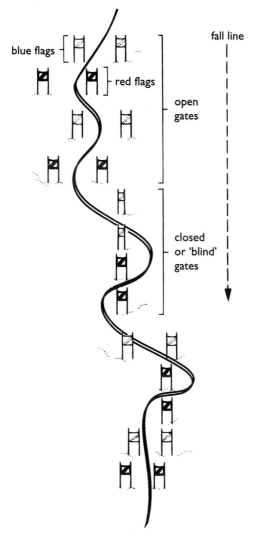

A giant slalom course, starting and finishing with pairs of 'open' gates. The single gates are 'closed', or 'blind'. Skiers have a split-second in which to decide the quickest line. Open gates have flags or banners side by side; closed or blind gates have flags set below one another.

event is won by whoever completes his single run down the course legally in the fastest time.

Slalom competitors are not allowed to practise on the course, so must memorize the gate positions on their way up to the start. They are allowed two runs, the fastest aggregate winning.

RULES

All competitors must keep to the marked course. A slalom skier who misses a gate will be disqualified unless he goes back to take it. A competitor losing both skis is, naturally, eliminated; but a racer losing only one is not automatically disqualified, though his chances of winning would be negligible.

The rules governing the starting order draw remain controversial. The International Ski Federation (FIS) has devised a system of points which racers earn at stipulated international meetings, according to the position in which they finish. The number of points a racer collects determines his

qualification to enter an international event, and the level of group in which he starts.

The 15 or so most highly-ranked skiers form the first group to start, and thus enjoy the best conditions on the course. Within each group, they draw for starting order, and when there are two runs, the order within each group is reversed for the second run.

SKILLS & TACTICS

Downhill skiers crouch in the familiar 'egg' position, head forward and sticks tucked back. On the fast icy runs, the weight will be thrown forward, but soft, powdery snow slows the pace and will cause the skier to straighten his posture and put more body weight to the rear of the skis. The upper body moves as little as possible. Turns are achieved by transfer of weight to one side or the other.

Slalom skiing requires a different technique; a more upright body in the gate areas and a graceful, hip-swinging style – a delight to watch when expertly performed.

Although it looks spectacular to fly through the air, it actually slows a skier down!

WORDS

Basket: circular attachment near the point of ski stick to prevent excessive penetration into the snow

Camber: the arch of the ski from tip to tail

Christie (or Christiana): a medium to fast swing turn with skis parallel

Edging: tilting the skis so that the edges dig into the snow to gain a firm grip

Egg position: crouching, compact stance for downhill racing

Fall-line: direction of steepest descent

Gate: two flagged poles in matching colours between which slalom skiers must always pass

Hairpin: sharp turn in slalom course

Herringboning: method of climbing with tips of skis turned outwards

Mogul: pronounced bump in course created by constant use (also, discipline of freestyle skiing)

Piste: prepared and firm downhill trail

Pre-jumping: technique used to clear bumps or sudden changes in gradient

Safety bindings: accident-prevention devices that automatically release the foot from the ski when falling over

Schuss: a straight downhill run at speed without turning

Schussboomer: a racer who skis out of control

Seelos: series of three slalom gates with the middle one at right angles to the other two

Shovel: the upturn of the forward tip of the ski

Sideslipping: method of controlled sideways or diagonal sliding by raising the ski edges

Sitzmark: depression in snow made by falling skier

Stem-christie: turn initiated by stemming and ended by a Christie

Stemming: pushing out the heel of one or both skis to achieve an angle to the direction of movement

Swing: high-speed turn with skis parallel

KJETIL ANDRE AAMODT

The combination of gymnastic agility and an uncanny touch on skis makes this young Norwegian from Oslo a strong contender for the world's best skier. His fellow countrymen have traditionally preferred cross-country skiing, but when the small town of Lillehammer was awarded the 1994 Olympic Games in 1986, alpine skiing was given a huge boost. Aamodt responded by winning a World Championship silver medal at Saalbach, a gold medal at the Albertville Olympics and helped the Norwegian 'Vikings' to dominate the 1993 World Championships when he contributed two golds in slalom and giant slalom. Racing on his home territory, Aamodt won silver and bronze medals at the 1994 Games.

Freestyle Skiing

Originally an exhibition of American agility and daring, freestyle skiing has now become a full international sport with a World Cup circuit. It is comprised of three completely separate disciplines, each producing a champion, with an overall championship for those who compete in them all.

Aerials are the most dynamic and acrobatic element. Skiers use snow ramps or 'kickers' to launch themselves into a series of turns, tucks and twists in mid-air.

Ballet allows the competitor a seven-minute routine of spectacular spins, jumps and pole flips to music – a kind of ice skating on snow.

Moguls, which was a part of the 1992 Olympics, sees the racers descending a steeply-bumped 200m (220yd) course in the fastest possible time.

SPEED SKIING

Speed skiing has to be the easiest winter sport to understand. Quite simply, competitors hurtle straight down a slope with a 70 per cent gradient trying to go as fast as possible over a timed kilometre. No wonder it's often called 'white fear'. In order to qualify for the 1992 Olympics, where it was a demonstration sport, men had to have clocked a minimum of 150kmph (nearly 100mph) and the women 140kmph (nearly 90mph). An internationally-recognized sport for less than a decade, competitors wear space-age, friction-resistant, all-in-one suits, aerodynamic helmets and throw themselves down the side of a mountain. Philippe Goitschel of France set the world record of 233.615 kmph (145.168 mph) at Les Arcs in France in April 1993.

What started out as high-spirited exhibitionism is now a world championship sport.

Cross-country Skiing

There is a great difference between pursuing this Nordic activity for pleasure and competing at it, when it becomes the most physically demanding of all forms of skiing. Men compete at distances of up to 50km (31 miles) and women at up to 15km (9 miles). The skis are longer, narrower and lighter than the Alpine kind, with the shoe only bound to the ski at the toe, so that the heel moves freely up and down. The sticks are longer to help push the skier forward faster.

Competitors start at half-minute intervals over a course that is roughly circular, and so arranged that they do not use any part of it more than twice. With a long, rhythmic stride not unlike that of the speed skater, a good racer can average more than 16kmph (10mph) when the going is favourable. Nevertheless, the 50km (31 mile) race will take about two hours, during which food and non-alcoholic drinks are allowed.

The course should be ever-varying – uphill, downhill and level. Climbs should not be too long or steep, and downhill sections neither difficult nor hazardous. The strenuous part of the course is generally in the second half, minimizing early strain. Turns are achieved by the skier using a diagonal stride, and climbing a gradient by the herringbone technique, the ski tips turned outwards and the heels together. When climbing or turning, both sticks are planted in the snow at the same time to give extra propulsion.

As in long-distance running, the slightly older competitor often proves the most effective, stamina being more important than explosive power. Rhythm, harmony of all movements, deep and steady breathing, and everlasting determination are all the necessary assets.

Biathlon

A unique test of cross-country skiing and marksmanship, in which three separate races are usually featured. In the 20km (12½ mile) individual race, competitors have to fire five shots at each of four 50m (55yd) ranges on the route, alternately lying and standing. A shot in the bull incurs no penalties; every time the bull is missed, one minute is added to the time taken to complete the course.

The 10km (6¼ mile) race is called a sprint. There are only two stops for shooting, but this time the targets are of the breakable or falling type. For each one still standing after five shots, the competitor must run a penalty loop of 150m (165yd). There is a similar penalty in the relay race, when each of four men in a team skis 7.5km (4¾ miles) and then shoots eight rounds on two different ranges.

CATCHING UP WITH THE MEN

The gap between the best men's and the best women's performances is closing in cross-country skiing. At the 1992 Olympics, Lyubov Egorova's winning time in the 15km (9 mile) event would have won every men's event up to 1976! However, Stefania Belmondo's time in the 30km (19 mile) is misleading. Fractionally slower than the men's 30km winning time, the Italian woman was using the modern skating technique while Norway's male gold medallist used the traditional, classical style. Skating may be 12–15 per cent faster . . . but the women are still catching up fast!

The new skating style here contrasts with the traditional style in the picture opposite.

Many sports can claim to be the most demanding in the world, but sports physiologists are always impressed by the men and women who compete in the biathlon. Imagine racing flat out on cross-country skis, heart pumping, gasping for air . . . and then having to stop, calm the pulse and shoot accurately at a target. The contrast between the two physical conditions has no parallel in sport and is a real test of self-control.

Ski Jumping

This is the most spectacular and awe-inspiring event in the skiing calendar, and one which makes magnificent viewing not only on television, but for the thousands of spectators massed around the area at the bottom of the jump. It originated in Norway, which still has the world's most famous jumping site – the Holmenkollen Hill outside Oslo. Every March they stage there the highlight of the Scandinavian winter sports season, with a finale attended by crowds of more than 100,000. Most of the other main jumping hills were built for various Winter Olympics since the sport came into the Games in 1924.

In world and Olympic championships there are two categories of competition – 90 and 70m (about 100 and 80yd). This does not denote the height of the jump towers – which can be an ugly blot on the landscape – but the calculated length that can be jumped from them. Competitors ascend in a lift to the start point and ski down the artificial slope (known as the in-run) to the take-off point at its lip.

The distance from there to the middle point where the jumper's feet touch the snow on landing is automatically measured to an accuracy of 0.5m (20in), but it is not necessarily the longest jumper who wins the competition. The best jump in each round will receive 60 points for distance, with lesser jumps marked proportionately lower; but a panel of judges are also marking each jump for style, from a possible 20 points.

Deductions are made for untidiness in the air, lack of control, poor style and faulty landing. However good the jump, a fall will cost the competitor 10 points on every scorecard. He is expected to land without stumbling and move into the telemark stance, one foot in front of the other, arms at the sides and knees slightly bent. Spreading his arms to aid balance, he then skis along the level out-run area and skids to an abrupt halt.

The classic style that all jumpers once tried to reach in mid-air required skis to be together and parallel, inclined slightly upwards; arms straight and close to the sides; knees and hips almost straight, with the whole body in a pronounced forward lean from the ankles. Just before the landing impact, the body would flex. Lately a new style has become accepted, which appears to give greater distance to the jump, in which the long skis are held in a motionless V position, the heels together.

Ski jumping can be dangerous on mountains, where wind can unbalance competitors. Contests can be postponed, but some competitions are decided by the ability of a jumper to handle a side wind.

WORDS

Critical point: point on landing hill beyond which it is dangerous to land
Inrun: downhill run at start of ski jump
Judges' tower: at side of ski jump
K: critical point (see above), marked in red on landing hill
Nordic combination: test of both ski jumping and cross-country skiing; scored on points basis
Outrun: flat area at bottom of hill for stopping
P: expected landing point, marked in blue on landing hill
Telemark: style of skiing, used by jumper on landing, down on one knee
Vorlage: exaggerated forward lean used in mid-air, arms at side, legs straight

Ski jumping made front page news in 1988 when a no-hoper from Britain charmed television viewers around the world. At the Calgary Olympics, Eddie 'The Eagle' Edwards came last by a long, long way but gave the sport more publicity than it had ever enjoyed since the first competitions in Norway back in 1862. Norwegians won every gold medal between 1924 and 1952, but more people recognize the bespectacled plasterer from Cheltenham than any Olympic champion, past or present. Today's young stars use the unorthodox 'V' position for greater distance.

At the highest level, all snooker players have amazing skills. However, the ability to perform under severe pressure over long periods separates the champions from the also-rans.

SNOOKER

SNOOKER WAS INVENTED BY BRITISH OFFICERS IN INDIA IN 1875; IT IS
NOW PLAYED IN THE BRITISH ISLES, THE COMMONWEALTH AND THAILAND,
AND IS GROWING IN EUROPE

The English Amateur Championships were first played in 1919 and the World Professional Championships followed in 1926. Joe Davis, the dominant figure in the sport from the 1920s to the 1960s, was still playing when the advent of colour television greatly increased the game's popularity in the 1970s and 1980s. With the likes of Alex Higgins, Steve Davis and Stephen Hendry a new generation of players emerged and although its attraction as a television sport may have reached a plateau, snooker still holds its place as one of the most-watched of all sports.

Snooker has similarities with both billiards and pool. In billiards each player has his own cue ball and there is only one red. The aim of the game is to strike the cue ball so the other balls cannon into one another or to pocket either your own cue ball or the red. In Britain, pool is dominated by the eight-ball version, one player attempting to pocket balls numbered one to seven whilst his opponent goes for numbers nine to 15. When a player has completed his sequence, he pockets the eight ball to win the game.

Snooker table at start of play.

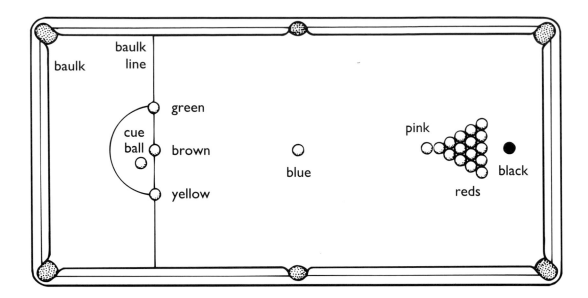

THE TABLE

The table is level and solid, with a bed of slate surrounded by hard rubber cushions which edge the playing area. The whole is covered with a green baize cloth.

At televised competitions, special lighting is used to illuminate the table. The heat of these lights can affect the 'speed' of the table; alternatively, a heater can be placed under the table which also ensures that the balls are 'lively'. As the game is decided by the smallest of angles and distances, the speed of the balls across the cloth is vital for top-class players who have to adjust to the slightest variations from venue to venue.

EQUIPMENT

The cue is made of wood – the shaft is ash, the butt often of ebony which gives it its weight and rigidity. The cue normally weighs about 500g (18oz) and is about shoulder high. The end of the cue has a small leather-covered tip which is rubbed with chalk to give a slight grip on the ball when struck. The balls are now made of a dense substance called crystallate.

WINNING

Success at snooker calls for a combination of both mental and physical ability with a high degree of concentration needed for matches played over several hours in tournaments lasting several days.

A game of snooker, called a frame, is won by the player who scores the most points. A match is decided over a specified number of frames, the winner needing to win more than half that number. Points are scored by potting (knocking the balls into one of six pockets around the table) or by acquiring penalty points from the opponent. At the start of the frame, 22 balls are on the table with the 15 reds arranged in a triangle and six so-called colours – yellow, green, brown, blue, pink and black – on allotted spots. The white or cue ball (the only one the cue may hit) is used to knock the other balls either into the pockets or to different positions on the table. Each ball has a value when pocketed – red (1), yellow (2), green (3), brown (4), blue (5), pink (6) and black (7). Initially, a red ball must be potted first before a player can hit a nominated colour. If that is potted, the player continues the red/colour sequence. Although the reds remain pocketed, the colours are replaced on their spots until all the reds are sunk. The player then attempts to go for the colours in ascending points value. The frame ends when the black is pocketed or one of the players decides to concede.

RULES

The cue ball is placed inside the 'D' for the first shot of each frame, but after that it is played from wherever it comes to rest. If it falls into a pocket, it is returned to the 'D'. A sequence of scoring points known as a break is a simple matter of addition but penalty points after a foul are more complex. The minimum penalty received is four points but if blue, pink or black colours are involved, then the penalty equals the value of that colour. This penalty is added on to the opponent's score.

A foul is committed when:
– *a player, going for a red, misses completely, or hits a colour*
– *a player, going for a nominated colour, misses completely, or hits another colour*

– *a player pockets the cue ball*

These fouls can be forced by a snooker. Top-class players manipulate the cue ball into difficult positions, tucking it, perhaps, behind a colour when the opponent's next shot has to be at a red. Since the cue ball cannot hit the object ball directly, the opponent is 'snookered' and has to use swerve or bounce the ball off a cushion to extricate himself from this trap.

A good snooker player will induce a foul. If, after the foul, a player is still snookered, he has two choices: he may ask his opponent to play again or he can choose to take a free ball. This means that he can nominate any colour and count it as a red (or a colour if no red remains on the table). This ball has the value of the ball which would normally have been hit. If a colour is potted, it is then replaced on its spot.

If the scores are level at the end of the frame, the black ball is put back on its spot and the players toss a coin to see who has first shot from the 'D'. The winner is the first player who manages to pot the black or who is awarded penalty points as a result of his opponent's foul.

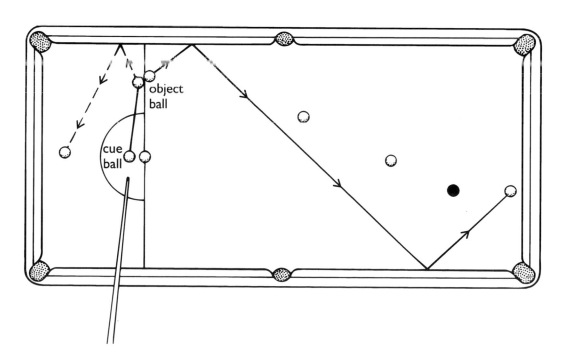

The player tries to lay a snooker by leaving the cue ball in such a position that it cannot directly strike the object ball. The cue ball rolls into baulk while the object ball bounces off two cushions on its way to the far end of the table.

RECORD BREAK

It must be the highest score ever recorded in any sport, anywhere. Playing billiards in 1907, Tom Reece built a break of 499,135! Although Reece did not play continuously his monstrous score took over 85 hours to compile and included 249,152 'cradle cannons'. You have to feel sorry for his opponent, one Joe Chapman. He did not manage to get a turn at the table between 3rd June and 6th July 1907 and, when the match at Burroughes' Hall in Soho, London was abandoned, the break was still unfinished. The rules have since changed, and billiards today is an altogether sharper and less tedious game.

SKILLS

The assessment of angles is of great importance. By hitting the cue ball a little off centre the player can make it spin, swerve to the right or left, or stun it so that it stops dead after hitting the object ball. He can even, by employing a deep screw, cause the cue ball to spin backwards after hitting the object ball. This is achieved by hitting the cue ball low down to produce reverse spin.

The idea behind these special shots is not only to pot the object ball, but also to ensure the cue ball is in a good position for the next shot. A good player is always thinking several shots (moves) ahead just like a chess player. At the highest level the element of chance is cut to a minimum; the players decide where the balls will roll. In the professional game, playing one-on-one, snooker needs tremendous mental strength.

TACTICS

The opening break is invariably a safety shot, in order to leave the opponent with no opportunity to pot a ball. After glancing against the triangle of reds, the cue ball often returns to rest at the bottom of the table, behind the green, brown or yellow. In reply, the second player may also play a safety shot. These exchanges continue until one player sees a chance to pot a red and build a break. At this early stage the importance of snookering is primarily tactical; its object being to force the opponent into leaving an opening. Pure potting ability is vitally important but every player has to weigh up the benefits that a successful pot would bring against the consequences of missing it and allowing the opponent to get into the frame.

Some frames are decided by a single large break but some combine a series of smaller ones with safety shots and snookers. The closing stages of a frame produce many absorbing tactical battles, either when the scores are close or when one player trails by a greater margin than the combined values of the balls remaining on the table. If, for instance, a player is 30 behind with only six colours remaining (value: 27 points) he is said to need a snooker. By laying a snooker and forcing a foul (four points or more) by his opponent, he would reduce the points margin to 26, giving him a chance of winning by potting the remaining colours.

WORDS

Break: a sequence of scoring shots

Break-off: the first shot of a frame

Clearance/Clear the table: when a player wins by potting all the balls left on the table

Cue ball: the white ball

Double: when a ball enters a pocket after bouncing off a cushion

Free ball: if a player is snookered after a foul by his opponent, he may nominate any colour in place of the snookered ball

In-off: when the cue ball enters a pocket after striking another ball

Maximum: when a player pots all 15 reds with 15 blacks, then all the colours; total 147

Plant: when one ball is played onto another to make the second ball enter the pocket

Safety shot: a defensive shot; a player leaves his opponent no opening to score

Screw: backspin; striking the cue-ball either to the right or left of centre to make it swerve

Stun: making the cue ball stop dead when it hits the object ball

Pool

Pool is a generic term which covers all games played on pool tables. There are many such games and standardization of rules, particularly internationally, is incomplete. Table sizes vary. In America, though, the championships organized in the '14.1' version of the game carry the most prestige. The object of the game is to reach an agreed points target, usually 150. Fifteen balls are initially racked in a triangle. A player scores one point for each ball he pockets. He must call each ball and pocket in advance.

When 14 balls have been pocketed they are replaced in the triangular shape without the apex ball. As he takes the 15th ball, the player attempts to send the cue ball into the triangle to scatter the balls and leave an opportunity to continue scoring.

There is a penalty of two points for failing to break properly and of one point if the cue ball enters a pocket. Safety shots are permissible if the player calls safe prior to striking and causes an object ball to hit a cushion. Breach of this rule involves a one-point penalty.

Billiards

Billiards is played with three balls, two whites and a red. One white, with two black spots, is called spot and the other plain.

The first player must play away from the 'D' and hit the red with his opening shot. If he pots the red or if his white goes into the pocket (in-off) the red, he scores three points. If he misses the red, his opponent is awarded one point, but if he misses the red and the white goes into a pocket his opponent gets three points. The break ends when the first fouls or fails to score. The second player then places his ball anywhere within the 'D' and can aim at either the red or his opponent's white, if it is not in baulk (between the baulk line and baulk cushion).

A player can drive his opponent's white into a pocket (pot white), cause his own white to enter a pocket after striking his opponent's white (in-off white), or cause his own white to strike both the red and his opponent's white (a cannon). If successful, these shots are valued at two points. The game proceeds until one player reaches a points target of 100 or 1000, for example.

STEPHEN HENDRY
Hendry is the youngest player ever to win the World Professional Snooker Championship. This Scot turned professional at just 16 and then won his first title, the Scottish Championship, the following year. He was World Champion at the age of just 21 in 1990 and won the title again in 1992, 1993 and 1994. He has also made more than 200 century breaks during his snooker career, a record, and has already accumulated over £3 million in prize money. The hallmarks of his game are a superb, steady temperament, brilliant long-potting and a consistent ability to build up large breaks.

SQUASH

PROPERLY CALLED SQUASH RACKETS, THE GAME OF SQUASH IS AN OFFSPRING
OF THE ANCIENT GAME OF RACKETS

Both squash and rackets are played in a completely enclosed court, squash with a very soft ball that rebounds slowly, rackets with a hard ball that travels at very high speed in a court nearly three times the size of a squash court.

Not an easy game to televise, despite the introduction of the transparent court, squash is an extremely popular participant sport that has a small band of international professional stars. The nations of Pakistan (particularly) and Australia have dominated the game for the past 50 years. A different form of the game is also played in North America and Mexico, with a narrower court, a harder ball and another type of scoring system.

THE COURT

At 32ft long and 21ft wide (9.75m by 6.4), a squash court is not as big as one half of a singles tennis court. Players stand side by side, hitting the ball alternately against the front wall, 15ft high (4.57m). There are side walls and a 7ft (2.13m) back wall. The floor is wood, the walls smooth and hard, and a door is set flush in the back wall. A strip of resonant material 48cm (19in) high, runs along the foot of the front wall. Balls hitting this tin or board are considered 'out'.

EQUIPMENT

The racket is a smaller, lighter version of a tennis racket, with a round head. The ball is rubbery, black and squashy, with a diameter of about 1¹/₂in (40mm). It weighs less than an ounce (24g).

WINNING

A game is won by the first to reach nine points, and a match is usually the best of five games. Points can only be won by the server. When he loses a rally, the service passes to his opponent. If the score reaches 8–8, the non-server can take the game to 10 points.

RULES

The server starts from the right-hand back quarter of the court and hits the ball directly

against the front wall so that it lands inside the left-hand back quarter. It can be returned by the receiver before it hits the ground. If the server wins the rally, he next serves from the left, and so on.

If a fault is called, the receiver can play it if he wants to. If he does not, there is a second service. A second fault loses the rally, as does any service that is out of the court.

As soon as a shot has been played, the player must make every effort to give his opponent room to see the ball and to hit it. If he does not, the referee can award the rally to his opponent. If he tries but fails to get out of the way, the rally will probably be played again.

SKILLS & TACTICS

Players try to get back to the centre of the court after shots as it is from here that they can dictate play. They often do this by playing the ball down the side walls to the back corners, drawing the opponent out; or by playing drop shots to a front corner. At the top level of the game, rallies may continue in play for a very long time before there is a winning shot scored.

The canny player stays right in the centre of the squash court, forcing his opponent to run back and forth for the ball.

WORDS

Boast: shot played hard into a back corner that reaches the front wall
Drop shot: softly played to touch the front wall just above the tin
Nick: the angle between two walls, or between a wall and the floor
Tin: the out-of-court strip at the base of the front wall; makes a noise when the ball hits it

Swimming races are contested in four different styles: top left, backstroke; top right, breaststroke; bottom left, freestyle or front crawl; bottom right, butterfly.

SWIMMING

DESPITE THE POPULARITY OF SWIMMING, THERE IS NO REAL
PROFESSIONAL CIRCUIT

Tremendous crowds are attracted to world and Olympic competitions to see this sport. Spectators have an uninterrupted view of the whole of every race; the finishes of all but the long races are invariably exciting; and there is a variety of strokes on display.

Both men and women race at freestyle (which in effect means front crawl), backstroke, breaststroke and butterfly. In addition, there are individual medley races in which each swimmer has to use all four strokes, as well as team relays.

The sport at its highest level was dominated for many years by the men of the United States and Australia, and the women of East Germany. Recent Olympics have shown how the talent is spreading: in the 1992 Games the women of China won four gold and three silver medals in the pool, more than any other nation.

Under the swimming umbrella there are now another three international sports. There is diving from both springboard and high board, at which China won three of the four gold medals in Barcelona. There is fast and particularly furious competition at water polo, now played by women as well, though not at the Olympics. And there is synchronized swimming, a kind of competitive water ballet that was introduced to a largely amazed world at the Los Angeles Olympics.

THE POOL

There are some short-course championships held in a 25m (27yd) pool, but major events take place in a pool exactly 50m long (55yd) and at least 21m wide (23yd). This gives room for eight lanes, separated by floating lane dividers that absorb the waves as well as confining the swimmers. On the floor of the pool a bold line down the centre of each lane guides most competitors. For the backstrokers, a line of flags is strung across the pool 5m (5yd) from each end to let them know when a turn is coming up. And the water? Just 1.8m deep (6ft) and at a constant temperature of 24 degrees Celsius (75 degrees Fahrenheit).

EQUIPMENT

There is nothing to hide: a swimsuit (even a woman's weighs just 30g [1oz]) and if you want to use them, a hat and goggles.

WINNING

The first to complete the race without infringing the rules is the winner. All major championships operate a system of seeding that benefits the fastest swimmers. Official best times of each competitor are submitted in advance. If there are, say, six heats, the six fastest swimmers will each be placed in a different heat; so will the next fastest six, and so on for all the competitors.

For each heat, right through to the final, there is a spearhead system of seeding: in an eight-lane pool, the fastest swimmer will be in lane four, the second fastest in lane five, the third in lane three, the fourth in lane six and so on. The swimmers in the centre of the course, who are expected to lead the race, are in a better position to see their rivals and are also swimming in marginally less turbulence than those on the outside.

Swimmers are timed electronically (there are starting blocks, and touch pads at each end of the pool) and the race placings appear on the scoreboard instantly. Only two decimal points are considered. Two competitors who recorded 48.841 and 48.845 for the 50m would be listed at 48.84 and would share the world record.

RULES

Apart from the freestyle events, for which any kind of stroke can be used, each stroke carries its own technical requirements. Backstrokers are allowed off their backs only during turns, for the brief moment between touching the end with their hands and pushing off with their feet. In the weird butterfly stroke, the legs may not be kicked

---

GOLDEN TOUCH

Mark Spitz set a swimming record that is unlikely ever to be beaten. The American swimmer won a mere two relay golds in a very disappointing 1968 Olympic Games. In Munich, four years later, the Californian not only won seven gold medals . . . the world record was also broken in every event!

100m freestyle
51.22 sec
200m freestyle
1 min 52.78 sec
100m butterfly
54.27 sec
200m butterfly
2 min 00.70 sec
4 x 100m medley
relay (USA)
3 min 48.16 sec
4 x 100m freestyle
relay (USA)
3 min 26.42 sec
4 x 200m freestyle
relay (USA)
7 min 35.78 sec

WORDS

Negative splits: the second half of a race being swum at a subsequent faster speed than the first half
Shave-down: the removal of all body hair (even from the head in some cases) before a big race to try to increase speed
Split times: the times taken for each length in a race; the times achieved by each individual in a relay
Stroke-shortening: the loss of optimum efficiency from each stroke as the swimmer tires; he compensates by raising the rate, but without increasing the speed
Taper: that part of the preparation for a big event during which the workload is decreased so that the swimmer is sharp for a particular day
Tying up: indication of race fatigue, when the muscles start to lose their efficiency because they are not getting enough oxygen

independently (as in the front crawl). Most performers use the fish-tail kick, with the legs lashing up and down like the bottom half of a mermaid.

Breaststroke rules are the trickiest. Both hands must touch the end of the pool together and they must always be at or under the surface of the water. The legs, while kicking, must work simultaneously and always under the water. But at least part of the head must at all times be 'above the general level' of the water, except at the start and at the turns, when one stroke of the arms and one leg kick are allowed while the swimmer is wholly submerged. The 'head up' rule was introduced after swimmers found they could go faster under the water, but it is notoriously difficult to enforce really accurately.

SKILLS & TACTICS

The best swimmers always look as though a motor is driving them. Their rhythm is regular and their progress steady, whatever the stroke. This comes from unbelievably long hours of practice, polishing technique and increasing their stamina.

In a sport where a hundredth of a second may be vital, starts and turns are particularly important. Most swimmers on the starting blocks coil the body in a tense, spring-like posture, grabbing the front of the block with both hands. When the starting pistol fires, they release the tension and drive upwards and outwards with all their force. Backstrokers start in the water, hands tightly gripping the edge of the pool and legs coiled ready to drive the body away, clear of the water.

To watch a front crawler executing a tumble turn well is an excitement in itself. Freestyle swimmers are the only ones who do not have to touch the end of the pool with their hands, so they somersault just before they get to it, trying to maintain their forward momentum and judging the distance so that they get a strong push-off with their feet. The fact that short-course – 25m – times are invariably faster than long-course times over the same distance is proof that freestyle turns actually increase the swimming speed of the competitors.

WATER BABY

The youngest swimming Olympic gold medallist was Krisztina Egerszegi of Hungary, who won the 200m backstroke at the 1988 Olympics aged 14 years, one month. She then went on to win two further titles at the World Championships and three more golds in the 1992 Olympics in the 100m, 200m backstroke and also the 400m individual medley.

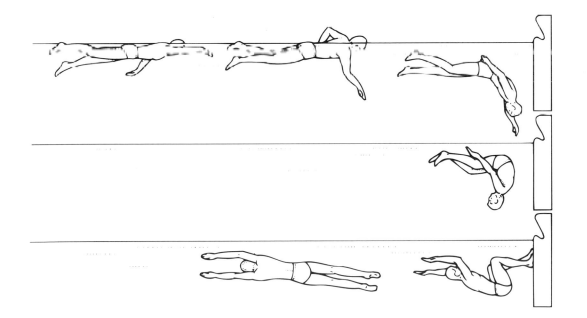

The freestyle tumble turn, that can add fractions of a second to a swimmer's speed.

Synchronized Swimming

Synchronized swimming was virtually unknown across the sporting world when the Americans first introduced it as an event at the Los Angeles Olympic Games in 1984. To nobody's great surprise, United States girls won the solo and the duet gold medals; Canadians won both the silvers and Japan both the bronze medals. At Seoul in 1988, Canada won both golds, the US both silvers, Japan both bronze medals. No change again at Barcelona in 1992: two golds for America, two silvers for Canada and two bronzes for Japan.

From the beginning, outsiders wondered how a soloist could perform a synchronized exercise. The official answer was that it is synchronized to music; though in fact we might never have seen a solo synchronized swimmer but for the Soviet bloc boycott at Los Angeles. The hosts had intended to include a duet competition in the swimming programme, but two months before the Games found that the swimming schedule was under-filled.

Some find it difficult to take this sport seriously, with its hair lacquer and waterproof mascara. But there is no question at all that extraordinary stamina and muscular control are necessary to go through such demanding, slow-motion routines with your head virtually always under the water.

The time synchronized swimmers spend beneath the surface is unbelievable. And all the while they are active, using up their oxygen intake by turning head over heels, raising an arm, a leg, two legs, one leg and one arm. And at the end of it all they come to the surface with gentle grace, not even gasping for breath. As for the uncomfortably high degree of artistic posing that is involved, there is probably just as much to be seen as with the performers on the ice rink.

As in figure skating, each competition comprises compulsory exercises and a free routine. The seven judges mark the compulsories out of 10, looking for movements that are clearly defined and always smoothly controlled. In the free routines there are two types of scores given, one for technical merit and the other for artistic impression.

Sisters have played a notable part in the short history of the duet competition of this sport: the Muellner sisters of Austria, the Vilagos sisters of Canada, and above all the Josephson sisters of the USA. They won the Olympic silver in 1988, the first World Championship in 1991 and the Olympic gold in 1992. They are not just sisters, but identical twins; and there is nothing that becomes a synchronized swimming duet competition as much as two swimmers so alike you cannot tell which one is under the water and which one is not. They are precisely the same height and weight and have the same colouring, eyes, teeth, costume and believe it or not – nose clips!

The best competitors look like two peas in a pod.

Few sports have been more ridiculed – and less understood – than synchronized swimming. The discipline and body control required are truly extraordinary as competitors (always women) have to hold their breath for an inordinate length of time. Nose bleeds and fainting are very common in training as the swimmers push themselves to the limit, testing not only their lung capacity but also their muscle control. And all the time, in a sport where presentation is as important as ability, the athletes keep smiling, never showing just how demanding each move, above and below the water, really is.

Water Polo

More than a century of water polo, begun in Britain, has sent it over the whole swimming world, and this rough and tough game is now played by women as well as men. Swimming speed and strength of arm are important attributes, but most necessary for the sport is the stamina to survive constant dunking under water.

THE POOL

The playing area should be 30m (33yd) long and 20m (22yd) wide, with water at least 1.8m deep (6ft). There are lines on the pool 2 and 4m (about 6 and 13ft) from each goal line. The goals are 3m (10ft) wide and less than 1m (3ft) high.

EQUIPMENT

Coloured caps identify the teams, white for one side, dark blue for the other, each one numbered. Goalkeepers wear red caps. The referee on the side of the pool has a stick with a white flag on one end and a blue one on the other, which he uses to indicate (with a blast on his whistle) which side has committed a foul.

Goalkeepers need strength as well as anticipation to block the short-range shots in this hard-hitting sport.

WINNING

Goals are scored by throwing the ball into the opponents' net. The ball can then be passed and also dribbled, which involves swimming with it between the arms of a front crawl stroke.

RULES

Seven players and four substitutes are allowed to compete in the game. It has four seven-minute periods of actual play, and the team in possession must attempt a shot at goal within 35 seconds. Only the goalkeeper can use two hands on the ball or touch the bottom of the pool. No player may advance beyond the opposing 2m (6ft) line unless the ball goes into that area before he does.

Minor offences are penalized by a free throw, but it is the major fouls that often decide the outcome of the game. They may result in penalty throws (taken from the 4m line, against only the goalkeeper) or in the offending player being banished out of play for 45 seconds.

The most common major fouls are holding or sinking an opponent who does not have the ball, and kicking or striking an opponent. Worst offence of all, and not a common one, is 'causing an act of brutality', for which the player is out for the rest of the game and may not be replaced. The same fate befalls any player who commits three major fouls.

SKILLS & TACTICS

Successful teams are constantly changing position until one player eventually manages to elude his marker. Quick acceleration in the water is vital, as is the ability to keep the upper body out of the water for passing and shooting shots. Equally important, though not appearing in the coaching manuals, seems to be the ability to persuade the referee that you have been fouled.

Diving

There are two competitions for each sex in this most graceful of sports, springboard and highboard, and ever since China returned to international competition, theirs have been the divers the rest of the world need to beat. They don't often manage it. In the 1988 Olympics China won six of the available 12 medals (two gold, three silver and one bronze), and in 1992 they won five, three of them gold.

Competitive diving was started in Britain in 1895, when the Royal Life Saving Society held the first National Graceful Diving Competition, open to the world, at Highgate Ponds in north London.

THE POOL

Special diving pools are used for major competitions, in which the water must be at least 5m deep (16ft 5in). The highboard for platform diving is 10m (33ft) above the water. The springboard, 3m (10ft) above the water, is made of a flexible aluminium alloy, the springing length of which the diver is able to adjust.

EQUIPMENT

A costume with strong shoulder straps, or trunks with secure fastening. (A body enters the water from a highboard at the speed of about 52kmph, more than 32mph.)

WINNING & RULES

As in gymnastics, a panel of judges mark each dive and the highest and lowest marks are discarded. The remainder are added together and then multiplied by the tariff value of the dive, based on its difficulty.

First a series of set dives must be performed, which test the competitor on forward and backward take-offs; rotating both forwards and backwards from each of them; twisting dives, which must show rotation as well as twist; and, for platform dives only, handstand take-offs.

Then the diver performs a series of voluntary dives, which can be as difficult to achieve as he wants them to be. The judges are looking for height from take-off, crisp execution and the smoothest possible entry to the water.

SKILLS & TACTICS

Confidence, style and perfect control denote the good diver. Entry to the water should produce hardly any splash, with the body perfectly straight so that the feet go in at exactly the same spot as the hands. In the voluntaries, the diver must first decide whether to use a relatively simple dive and hope to execute it perfectly and smoothly, or to go for a riskier one which obviously carries a higher tariff.

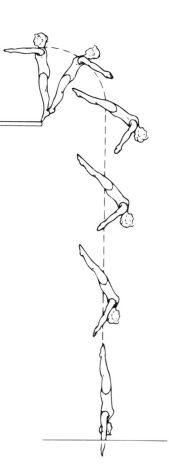

A straight back dive from the 10m board.

WORDS

Break-out: changing position in mid-air
Hurdle: the jump at the end of the springboard
Inward dive: rotating forwards from backward take-off
Pike: touching toes in mid-air

Reverse dive: rotating backwards from forward take-off
Swallow: forward dive with arms spread wide
Tariff: degree of difficulty, from 1.1 to 3.0
Tuck: knees to chest in mid-air

Table tennis was dominated by central Europeans in its early days. From the 1950s, Japan and China vied for world supremacy, but in recent years Sweden's men have broken the Far Eastern stranglehold.

TABLE TENNIS

THE MANY THOUSANDS OF SERIOUS PLAYERS OF THIS GAME DO NOT LIKE IT
BEING REFERRED TO AS 'PING-PONG', THE NAME BY WHICH THE INVENTION
WAS OFFICIALLY REGISTERED IN BRITAIN MORE THAN A CENTURY AGO

While it remains an admirable leisure activity that can be played on the dining table across a row of books, table tennis has become a huge international sport and another in which the Chinese threaten to dominate the world. The game was accepted into the Olympic Games programme of 1988 and four years later Chinese players won three of four Olympic gold medals.

In Europe, and particularly in Germany, professional leagues thrive. Many international players, some of them British, are signed up to represent German clubs, in the same way that foreigners play in the Football League.

Controversy has arisen in recent years over the type of surface that may be permitted on a bat, and the type of glue that may be used with which to stick it on. It was discovered that using an impact adhesive just before play began gave extra punch to the bat. Apart from the morality of the practice, over which there was much argument, the practical effect of the fumes on courtside officials was particularly unwelcome.

THE TABLE

For competition the table is 9ft (2.74m) long and 5ft (1.53m) wide. The increasing ability of top players to return the ball from extraordinary distances means that a minimum space of 40ft by 20 (12m by 6) is needed for each table. The surface is usually dark green, with a white line around the edges and down the middle of the table (to provide service courts for doubles). The net is 6in (15cm) high .

EQUIPMENT

As the ball is white and only about 1¹/₂in in diameter (3.8cm), dark clothing is always worn. There is no limit to the weight, size or shape of the bats, which tend to weigh between 4 and 7oz (115–200g). The blade must be of wood, and its surface dark in colour, but the precise surface varies according to the degree of speed or spin that the player likes to impart. The two sides of the blade will usually be finished with different surfaces, so that by twisting the bat in his hand he may deceive his opponent and exert more or less spin to the ball than is expected. A sponge rubber outer surface is banned, but a sandwich is often used with pimpled rubber stuck to a layer of sponge.

WINNING

The winner of a game is the first to score 21 points. If the score reaches 20–20, play goes on until one player has a two-point lead. Matches are usually the best of three, or five, games. Players change ends after each game, and as soon as one player has reached 10 in the deciding game.

RULES

Service must start with the ball on the open palm of the server's hand. It must be projected upwards without spin before being hit, and the umpire must be able to see this clearly. Each player has five services in turn, the ball bouncing on both sides of the net before being returned. If the score reaches 20–20, service changes with every point.

There is a unique system to prevent an ultra-defensive match dragging on too long. If a game is not finished within 15 minutes, the umpire calls for 'expedite'. The server is then given 13 strokes to win each point, which otherwise is given to the receiver. Service alternates with every point.

In doubles, service must be from the right-hand half of the court to the receiver's right-hand half. Thereafter, the ball must be struck in turn by all four players, wherever it lands. If players A and B are playing against players X and Y, and A serves first and X returns, the next shot must be by B and the next by Y, and so on strictly in that order.

SKILLS & TACTICS

At its highest level, table tennis has become a game of agility, athleticism and stamina, as well as being one to test coordination and reflexes. The half-ounce (15g) ball is hit with tremendous force and yet can be returned, often in a teasing lob, by a player with swift footwork and a cool head. Though a clever defensive strategy can be very frustrating against a player who likes all-out attack, it is usually the first player to launch an attack who wins the point.

There are two basic ways to hold a bat. They are so different they divide the table tennis world into two styles. The Western grip is similar to that of a tennis player – a 'shake hands' style; the so-called 'penholder' grip, in which the handle of the bat nestles almost upright between the thumb and forefinger, which grasp it at its juncture with the blade, has always been the sign of a player from the Far East.

The obvious advantages of the Western grip are the greater ease by which the reach can be extended, the facility to chop in defence and the fact that both sides of the

Few well-known sports can match the actual speed of top-class doubles in table tennis.

blade can be used. The penholder grip never changes, so the player is ready for any shot fractionally earlier; on the other hand, it is more difficult for him to reach far to the backhand wing, and even more difficult to counter the fast, heavily top-spun drive, particularly to the backhand. This shot, known in table tennis as the loop, is the most common attacking shot used throughout the game. It is produced from behind the baseline with a really exaggerated action of wrist, arm and body, and can often only be effectively countered by blocking tactics from the opponent.

WORDS

Backhand: played in front of the body, the back of the hand towards the opponent

Chop: defensive stroke that chops down on the ball, imparting backspin and returning the ball low

Counter-attack: returning attack with attack instead of defence

Drive: attacking shot with extra topspin

Forehand: played wide of the body, the palm of the hand facing the opponent

Loop: fast drive with heavy topspin, often hit when the ball is dropping low

Paddle: slang term for the table tennis bat

Penholder grip: Oriental style of gripping the bat as if it were merely a pen or a chopstick

Push: simple return without spin

Sidespin: by drawing the bat across the ball, it then bounces sideways when it lands on the table

Smash: hard attacking shot, hit flat

Topspin: ball spins towards the opponent, dips suddenly, and then shoots through on landing

Western grip: conventional 'shake hands' holding style of the bat

Tennis is played on different surfaces, each demanding slight adjustments to classic strokes such as (top left) a running backhand, (top right) a serve, (bottom left) a forehand volley and (bottom right) a low volley at the net.

TENNIS

FEW SPORTS OFFER THE FAN SUCH SATISFYING VIEWING AS A GLADIATORIAL
BATTLE BETWEEN TWO TALENTED TENNIS PLAYERS

Power and stamina, speed, subtlety and sheer character are clearly on display in tennis, and it is no wonder that the annual Wimbledon bonanza draws so many of us to our screens. The dramas are often enhanced by the glamour of the participants, names as well known as any in sport who seem to spend most of their lives jetting round the world earning enormous sums of money.

The All-England Championships at Wimbledon are one of the Grand Slam tournaments, the highest prizes in the game. The others are the Open Championships of Australia, France and the United States, and Wimbledon is the only one still played on grass. It is hard to imagine it any other way, but most professionals would rather see almost any other kind of surface there.

For some, it is their only grass tournament of the year. The rest of their time is spent on a variety of surfaces – wood, carpeted concrete, artificial turf, the hard composition courts of New York and the slow clay courts of Paris. Each has a different effect on the ball and the play, but the effect is constant and predictable. Grass is the most beautiful of surfaces to look at, but the speed of the surface (the ball tends to shoot on and keep low) favours the powerful player and demands a very high level of skill; constant and predictable it certainly is not.

THE COURT

A tennis court is 78ft long and 36ft wide (23.77m by 10.97), with 'tramlines' at each side reducing the width for singles play by 9ft (2.74m). The net is 3ft 6in (1.06m) high at the posts but sags to 3ft (91cm) in the middle – the bit you see the net judge measuring before every match.

On each side of the net, a white line across the court divides it almost in half, and another from that line to the net produces two equal rectangles into which the services must fall. Whatever surface is used, it should be absolutely flat, clearly marked and free of any imperfection.

EQUIPMENT

There is no restriction on the size, shape or weight of a tennis racket, and some heads are now much bigger than they used to be. Metal or graphite frames are used by most leading players, who carry a number of different rackets on to court. The tension of the stringing of some of the rackets may differ from others.

A powerful serve-and-volley player is more likely to use a tightly-strung racket that provides a rebound at maximum speed; the 'touch' player who uses greater subtlety needs less tension so that the ball stays longer on the strings. Natural gut, nylon or a combination of the two is the material used for the strings.

Tennis balls are controlled for size, weight and the air pressure within them. Greater pressure is used for slower courts, to provide a harder and faster ball for the players. New balls are often kept in a cool box at the courtside so that the bounce remains consistent.

White remains the predominant colour for clothing, though there is now a greater freedom than there used to be for players to introduce some colour and individuality into the clothing they wear.

WINNING

The strange terms used in keeping the score were inherited from the ancient game of real (royal) tennis, and were probably based on the quarters of a clock: the first point is 15, the second 30 and the third 40 (abbreviated from 45). A fourth point wins the game unless the score reaches 40–40, at which the umpire calls 'deuce'. This is possibly a corruption of the French 'à deux', indicating that two consecutive points must be won before the game is over.

After the first of these, the umpire calls 'advantage' to the server or the receiver. If the same player, or pair, also wins the next point, the game is won; if not, it is deuce again. A similar system applies to the number of games that must be won to secure a set: the first to six wins, unless the score reaches 5–5. Then a lead of two games must be established to take the set at 7–5.

If the score reaches 6–6, however, a 'tie break' game is usually played. The player due to serve, serves first, and thereafter the players serve alternately for two points each. Ordinary numerical scoring is used for this modern means of bringing a set to a conclusion, and the first to score seven points wins the game (and therefore the set). But again, if the score reaches 6–6, play goes on until a two-point lead is established.

Before the tie-break system was introduced Britain's Roger Taylor once played a King's Cup match in which the first two sets alone contained 116 games.

RULES

The server stands behind the right-hand half of the baseline and hits the ball over the net so that it bounces within the receiver's right-hand service court. That is the only time during a point that the ball has to be allowed to bounce. If a service fails to land within the proper service court (on the line is in court), 'fault' is called and the server tries again.

For many years women's tennis was regarded as a pleasant sideshow compared with the men's game. However, the establishment of a women's circuit 20 years ago soon began drawing crowds, first in the USA, and now all over the world. Standards of play, players, fitness and entertainment have risen dramatically thanks to women of the calibre of Chris Evert, Steffi Graf, Monica Seles and, most of all, Martina Navratilova.

Two faults loses the point. If a service touches the net and lands in the court, it is a 'let' and is taken again.

With each point the service changes between the right-hand and left-hand sides of the court until the game is won and service passes to the opponent. In doubles, all four players serve a game in turn.

The ball can be taken on the volley at any time other than a service. However, it must never bounce twice, nor can it be hit twice on the same side of the net; and a player loses the point if he, or his racket, touches the net.

All decisions rest with the umpire, but at major tournaments he is assisted by a number of linesmen whose job is to watch the boundary lines and signal if the ball is out. Such judgement may be critical – it may even decide the outcome of a match – but with the ball often travelling at 100mph (161kmph), it can be very difficult to make with certainty. An 'electronic eye' is sometimes used on the service line, which then emits a loud bleep if the ball is served out.

SKILLS

The greater the variety of strokes at a player's command, the greater is his chance of winning – as long as that variety is shrewdly used and soundly executed. At the heart of any player's game lie his service and his ground strokes, from which weaknesses must be eradicated.

The player with the ability to serve fast and accurately possesses an immediate attacking weapon, particularly on grass and other fast surfaces. When such a serve hits the receiver's service court deep and wide, it is likely to produce a weak return. The server races up from the baseline the instant he has hit it in the hope that he will be near enough the net to put the return away out of reach. This is known as the serve-and-volley game. It may not make fascinating viewing, but must be very satisfying to execute.

By slicing the face of the racket across the ball as he hits it, the server can impart spin. This can cause the ball to swerve in flight and to bounce erratically, and is often used by players who do not have a powerful

WORDS

Ace: a service the opponent cannot touch

Approach shot: deep drive that justifies an approach to the net

Break point: when the player receiving service is within a point of winning the game

Choke: a player is said to choke when his stroke is inhibited by nervous tension

Drop shot: gentle, under-spun shot that just clears the net

Let: any point that has to be replayed

Lob: shot designed to pass over an opponent at the net and drop down near the baseline

Match point: when one player is within a point of winning the match

Passing shot: one that passes an opponent who is at the net

Poach: in doubles, taking a shot that would normally be the partner's

Rally: the exchange of shots during a point

Retriever: player who specialises in returning the ball rather than hitting winners

Set point: when one player is within a point of winning the set

serve, or as a second serve by those who do. Many a match is lost by a player whose second service is not good enough to trouble his opponent.

Ground strokes are those played after the ball has hit the ground and are the inevitable ingredient of baseline rallies. Forehand and backhand must be equally strong, for a weakness on one side or the other will soon be exploited by the opponent. Many players, and particularly women, have developed double-handed ground strokes, used more often on the backhand. These can be very effective, giving more power, control and disguise; but the reach is slightly shortened and the player may be fractionally slower in getting into position for the shot.

To those basic strokes the winning tennis player must bring subtleties such as the sliced backhand, cutting under the ball on the drive, and the top-spun forehand, rolling over it so that it shoots on when it hits the ground. He must develop aggressive weapons like the volley and the smash, and delicate deceivers like the drop-shot, which falls just over the net, and the lob that soars above the reach of the opponent at the net and drops on the baseline in attack.

TACTICS

The serve-and-volley game is most effective on fast surfaces. Baseline players come into their own on slow courts, wearing down their opponents with consistently accurate deep shots, waiting patiently for an error to come, pulling them from side to side and occasionally testing them with a surprise drop shot.

The all-court player, able to play up or back, tries to create court space for a winning shot. He must decide which stroke is the one to follow to the net and must never be trapped half-way in. Varying the direction and the pace of the game, sometimes taking the ball early and sometimes taking it late, all upset an opponent's rhythm and may lead to error.

ANDRE AGASSI

The most flamboyant tennis player in the game today. His aggressive style and unconventional dress have made him hugely popular among the younger followers of the game. He grew up in Las Vegas, turned professional in 1986 and won his first title the following year. Despite a style more suited to the slower courts, he then surprised the tennis world in 1992 by winning on grass at the Wimbledon tournament, upsetting the big-serving player, Goran Ivanisevic. This was his first victory in a Grand Slam tournament following surprising and disappointing defeats in the finals of the French Open and US Open, which had given rise to doubts about his ability.

TRIATHLON

FOR MOST OF US, RUNNING A MARATHON WOULD BE THE CEILING OF OUR
AMBITION. FOR A FEW, THIS WAS NOT ENOUGH, SO THE
TRIATHLON WAS BORN

This desperate test of athletic stamina, a contest in long distance swimming, cycling and running completed in the one day, was first established in the United States in 1974. A world governing body and the first world championships were created in France 15 years later.

The internationally-regulated distances for the event are a swim of 1500m (1640yd), a cycle ride of 40km (25 miles) and a 10,000m run (6 miles) – now called the Olympic triathlon distance. But predating the first World Championships the annual Hawaii Ironman triathlon was instituted, an event demanding almost superhuman powers. The swim is of 3800m (2 miles), the cycling covers 180km (112 miles), and finally there is a marathon course of 42.195km (26 miles 385yd). The champions complete the event in about eight hours.

VOLLEYBALL

AN ESSENTIALLY SIMPLE GAME, VOLLEYBALL CAN BE PLAYED ALMOST
ANYWHERE, INDOORS OR OUT, BY PEOPLE OF ANY AGE AND LITTLE SKILL

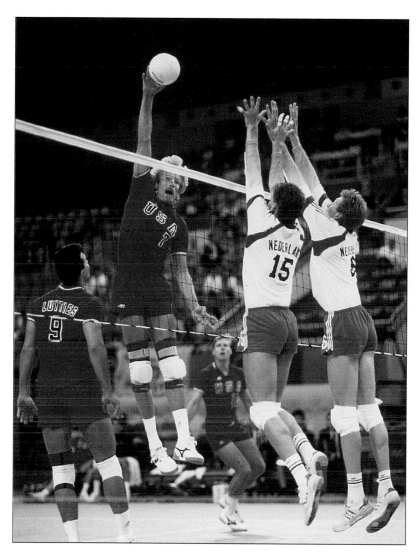

At its highest level, volleyball is one of the most exciting spectator sports in the world, with competitive matches always taking place on an indoor court.

The game began in America and has now spread to Europe and South America. It was devised in the last decade of the 19th century in a Californian YMCA, for the benefit of middle-aged men who found basketball too vigorous and wanted a game they could enjoy. Such players are not likely to have been inclined to hurl themselves across the floor as top players of both sexes do today.

Beach volleyball, with two players a side instead of six, will be a new Olympic event.

THE COURT

A rectangle measuring 18m by 9 (59ft by 29ft 6in), it is divided by a net 2.43m (8ft) high for men and 2.24m (7ft 4in) high for women. On each side, a line across the court divides it into the main attack zone and the back of the court.

EQUIPMENT

The ball is about the same size as a football but very much lighter. Players need lightweight shoes with a good grip, and most wear protective pads on elbows and knees.

WINNING

Points can only be won by the team that are serving, and the same player continues to serve – using his hand as a racket – as long as his team continues to win the rallies. As soon as they lose one, service passes to the other side. A rally is lost by hitting the ball into the net or out of court, or allowing the ball to hit the floor of the court; or by breaking the three-touch rule.

The first team to reach a score of 15 points win the set (it is called a set, not a game) and a match is usually decided by the best of five sets.

RULES

The server puts the ball in play by hitting it from behind his baseline into the opponents' court. On each side, three players are in the attacking zone and three in the back court. When play has begun they can move into any formation they choose, but the three designated defenders may not take part in blocking the ball at the net nor in attacking the ball above the level of the net.

A rotational order is given to the referee before the game, which determines the players' positions on the court at the start of play. Every time the service changes ends, everyone on each team moves clockwise one place in the order. Thus one of the attackers drops back and one defender moves forward. This order is strictly enforced throughout the match.

A team may touch the ball a maximum of three times before it is returned over the net. There is one exception: a fumbled block at the net, when the ball squirts off a front man back into his own defence, does not count as a touch. The same player must not touch the ball twice in succession, but he can make the first and third touches.

Players must never touch the net. The ball must never be held, nor must it touch a player below the belt, but it can rebound from any part of a player above the belt. As in tennis, the server's feet must be behind the baseline; but he is only allowed one attempt at a good service.

In any one set, the coach may use up to six substitute players and call two 30-second time-outs.

SKILLS

Good serving is vital and is likely to be overarm. Some services are hit very hard, the player leaping in the air as he smashes it; some float with a deceptive wobble, dropping suddenly. The usual way to receive service is with both forearms extended and close together (a dig), taking the speed out of the ball and directing it up and towards a player in the attack zone.

The second touch is the set, when a player tries to make contact with the ball at about head height and with the fingers of both hands, setting it up delicately and precisely across court ready for a smash (spike). If properly played, the set should enable the third player to leap as high as possible above the net and to smash the ball hard downwards.

The front court players of the opposing team will try to block a smash by forming a wall of hands where the ball is likely to cross the net. If successful, this will send the ball rebounding straight back to the other court. Receiving players will go to any lengths to keep the ball in play, diving and rolling over the floor in the hope that it can be set up for another attack.

TACTICS

Though dig-set-smash is the basic format, deception and surprise are important elements in a volleyball attack. The setter may spot an opening and send the ball there himself. When the set ball loops up for the smash, one player may make a dummy attack and another come behind him to hit it. Alternatively, the smasher himself may just tip the ball over the net.

A good setter is a specialist, and whatever his position in the rotation he is likely to penetrate quickly to take up his centre court, play-making role.

The setter is the key player in volleyball, like a quarterback in American football or fly half in rugby.

WORDS

Block: wall of hands created to prevent a smash from getting through to score a point

Dig: pass made with the forearms

Double-touch: when the ball has not been played cleanly

Dump: fake smash that tips the ball just over the net or the block

Penetrate: a back court player moving to the front to set

Rotation: clockwise movement of players when service changes

Setter: player who volleys the ball up for his attackers to smash

Shoot set: a fast volley pass which has a very low trajectory

Volley: playing the ball with the fingertips of both hands in an overhead shot

Waterskiers, like their snow-based cousins, need the perfect balance to achieve distance. The competitor stands relatively upright, with skis angled and the tow handle kept low.

WATERSKIING

TOURNAMENT WATERSKIING IS THE VERSION OF THE SPORT MOST USUALLY
SEEN BY THE PUBLIC, WITH ITS SPECTACULAR DISCIPLINES OF SLALOM,
JUMP AND TRICKS

Though skills cannot be developed without the support of a club and expert coaching, many have come to the sport from the simplest seaside-holiday beginnings.

There are two other distinct forms of the sport, less well known but each with its own world championships. Barefoot waterskiing follows the three-event tournament pattern but without the skis, the general principle being that as long as the body is being towed fast enough, it will not sink. The spectators' eyes may water a bit when it comes to the jump, for although the ramp is only 45.5cm (18in) high, distances of more than 26m (85ft) have been recorded. Surprisingly enough, competitors do not seem to suffer.

Waterski racing, at which Britain has been very successful, is usually an against-the-clock competition in which the skier is towed at the fastest speed at which he thinks he can remain upright. Major competitions are held on three different types of water – lake, river and open sea – with the aggregate points producing the winner. Training is a problem for many competitors, not only because of the rarity of suitable venues, but because of the high cost of the boats and their fuel. In the following section, all information that is given should be presumed to refer only to tournament skiing.

THE COURSE

Tricks: a rehearsed programme is performed during two 20-second passes in front of the judges, between two sets of buoys 175m (191yd) apart .

Slalom: the course is 259m (283yd) long and 23m (75ft) wide. The towing boat proceeds at a set speed straight down the middle. The skier tries to round six buoys, staggered three on each side at the extremities of the width.

Jump: a ramp 7.3m (24ft) long and 3.9m (13ft) wide can be varied in height to accommodate competitions for men or women. The boat motors straight down the course past the ramp at a set speed. The skier must time the speed and direction at which he approaches it.

EQUIPMENT

A skier can increase his overall speed dramatically by cutting back across the competition course.

Different skis are used for each event, but the specifications are a matter of individual preference. The single trick ski is comparatively short and wide, with a binding for only one foot. The single slalom ski has bindings for both feet. The pair of jump skis are longest and widest of all. A flotation garment is worn for slalom and jump events, and a helmet for the latter.

WINNING

Tricks: each trick has a pre-determined points value. Skiers perform turns of 180 and 360 degrees, step over the tow rope, hold it behind the neck, and at least once must hold it with one foot. A top-class performer will hope to execute 30 different tricks within the 40-second time limit.

Slalom: half a point is scored as soon as the outside of a buoy is rounded, and another half when the skier returns to the centre of the course. With each successful pass down the course, the length of the tow rope is reduced and thus the speed increases at which the skier has to travel to keep up with the boat. The score is given as the number of buoys rounded followed by the length of the rope when the run ended, e.g. three at 10.25m (11yd).

Jump: the skier is allowed three attempts. The distance is then calculated mathematically, by taking the angle to the point of landing from three different stations. The longest one scores, provided the skier passes through the gate at the end of the course. The best jumpers may reach as much as 60m (200ft).

A winner is declared in each event, but those skiers who compete in all three may become overall champion on the aggregate score they achieve.

RULES

Tricks: no trick can be repeated, and a movement not executed to the satisfaction of the judges does not receive any points. Boat speed is at the discretion of the skier, but must remain constant. The usual tow line is about 20m long (65ft).

Slalom: boats must keep a constant speed of 58kmph (36mph) for men and 55kmph (34mph) for women. The tow rope starts at a length of 16m (52ft 6in) and shortens by about 1m (1⅛yd) after each successful pass. Both the boat and the skier must start and

When they do tricks, skiers seem to defy gravity itself by balancing precariously on the end of the tow rope.

finish by passing between pairs of buoys which form a series of gates at each end of the course.

Jump: for women, the top of the ramp is 1.5m (5ft) from the water and the boat runs at a speed of 51kmph (32mph); for men the height goes up to 1.8m (6ft) and the speed increases to 57kmph (35.4mph). If the boat speed falls below that, the skier has the option of going again; if the speed goes up above the set figure, he must jump again.

WORDS

Balk: when a skier has mistimed his approach and has to abandon the jump

Binding: rubber shoe that is attached to the ski

Cutting: the act of a skier pulling away from the boat with his skis on an edge

Gates: the buoys at the beginning and end of a course

Pass: successful run in any discipline

Quick release: an attachment that releases the tow rope if a skier falls

Wake: disruption of the water caused by a moving boat

SKILLS & TACTICS

Tricks: agility and coordination are the keys to this nerve-racking event. An early fall during the immensely complicated series of leaps and twists means instant disaster.

Slalom: long arms and legs are a help, as they have the effect of lengthening the tow rope (the world record rope length, 10.25m, or 34ft, is less than the distance from the boat to the buoy). Strength of thigh and shoulder, timing and balance are vital to achieve success.

Jump: pinpoint accuracy, strength and tremendous courage are needed to compete in jumping. Much of its art is in the run-up to the ramp, for the faster you hit it the further you can travel. The boat's speed is the same for every participant, but the skier can greatly exceed that speed by his style of approach. From his start immediately behind the boat, he will swing first to the jump side of the run, then as far out on the other side as he can, sometimes even drawing level with the boat. There he 'hangs out' for a while, staying almost stationary, before suddenly hurtling back across the wash to hit the jump ramp at frightening speeds that can be up to 130kmph (80mph).

When it comes to drug testing, no sport is more in the spotlight than weightlifting. With stricter controls, it was noticeable that only one Olympic record was broken at the last Games in Barcelona.

WEIGHTLIFTING

More than in any other sport, the competitor is exposed to public view. Centre stage, his hopes and fears, his agony and his ecstasy, are clear for all to see.

There are few complexities to understand. Can he or can he not pick up that terrible weight and hold it still over his head? To enable the small as well as the large lifters to compete and to succeed, there are 10 weight categories for lifters, comparable to those for boxers. They range from flyweight to super-heavyweight and in any category it is common for the best performers to raise twice their own bodyweight in a single lift.

The quite separate but very similar sport of powerlifting developed during the 1960s and held its first official world championships in 1973. Though technical skill as well as strength figure in both branches of lifting, the methods used in powerlifting emphasize the brute strength that is necessary. The former Olympic weightlifting champion Paul Anderson raised 544kg (1200lb) in a single powerlift squat; and Britain's Precious Mackenzie, in an aggregate of three lifts, raised 11 times his own bodyweight.

THE ARENA

The competition area consists of a wooden platform 4m (13ft) square. The barbell is placed in the centre of the platform and the competitor must not step off it while lifting.

EQUIPMENT

The barbell, 2.2m long (7ft 2$\frac{1}{2}$in), is loaded with the requisite pairs of heavy discs to reach the competitor's target weight. There are eight discs available, in metal or heavy rubber, weighing between 50kg (110lb) and 1kg (2lb). When in position, they are locked on to the ends of the barbell.

Lifters usually wear a leotard over a pair of trunks, sometimes a T-shirt as well, and a strong pair of sports boots. Bandage supports for wrists and knees are common, as is a body belt.

WINNING

There are two competition lifts: the snatch, and the clean and jerk, both made with two hands. Every competitor is allowed three lifts in each category, working up to the greatest weight he thinks he can manage.

Every lifter must declare before the competition at what weight he wants to start lifting, and the event begins at the lowest requested weight. As the weights are gradually added to the bar, so the stronger competitors come in for their three attempts. If a competitor succeeds with his first lift, he must attempt at least 5kg (11lb) more with his second; if he fails on the first or second attempt, he may either try the same weight again or risk increasing it.

The snatch is contested first. This is a one-movement lift in which the barbell is taken directly from the floor to above the head. The whole three-attempt process is repeated for the clean and jerk, in which much heavier weights are invariably lifted. In its first part, the bar must be lifted cleanly to the upper chest, followed by the jerk taking it aloft. The winner of the competition is the lifter whose best effort in each category produces the highest aggregate weight. If there is a tie, the prize goes to the lifter with the lighter body weight.

The clean and jerk requires two movements. Here the competitor, having lifted the barbell off the floor, must now hold it aloft.

RULES

Three referees watch each lift to see that no fault is committed (there are 11 listed for the snatch and 15 for the clean and jerk). When the lifter is standing motionless with the bar fixed at arms' length overhead, he can replace it on the platform. Each referee then switches on a white light to indicate that the lift was good, or a red light if a fault has been committed. A majority verdict prevails.

When a lifter is called to the platform by the announcer, a timekeeper starts his clock. The lifter has one minute to prepare himself mentally, chalk his hands and start the lift. If the bar has not left the floor by then, the attempt is disqualified. A lifter who is taking two lifts in succession on his own is given two minutes for the second attempt.

The basic requirement for the snatch is that the bar must pass along the body in a continuous movement until it is fully extended above the head. In the process, the feet may be moved. Most lifters, their feet apart, will drop into a squat while the bar moves up. When it is extended, they have unlimited time in which to recover the upright position, after which they must stand motionless, in order that the judges approve the lift.

In the first part of the clean and jerk, the bar must reach the shoulders in a single movement, without touching the trunk on the way. The lifter then has unlimited time to stand upright, get his feet in line and even adjust his grip on the bar before the final jerk movement that takes the bar motionless up above his head.

SKILLS

Probably the most frequent cause of 'no lift' is failure to get the body precisely under the bar when it is in the extended position. A fraction too far forward or back and the bar comes crashing down. In the snatch, the lifter will pull the bar close to his body so that the lift is as near vertical as possible. Halfway through, he will drop into the squat to get right under the bar and support it with straight, locked arms. The second part of the clean and jerk, in which the bar must rise from its rest on the collar bone to the extended position above the head, is usually accomplished with a split jump. One leg goes forward and one back, again with the purpose of keeping the body right under the bar. When it is there, with the arms locked, the lifter recovers to his upright position, feet in line.

WORDS

Bodyweight: weight divisions in men's and women's weightlifting

Clean: the smooth but swift lifting of the bar from the ground to the shoulders

Clean and press: now no longer recognized as a competition lift

Collar: locking nut on the end of barbell

Dumb bell: a one-hand weight, not used competitively

Jerk: the explosive move needed to lift bar from shoulders to the arms-straight position above the head; after the clean

Press: to straighten the arms

Split: to move the legs simultaneously, one forward and one back

Snatch: the single, rapid move lifting the bar from the ground to a straight, locked arm position above the head; the legs move into a squat or split to support the weight

Squat: deep knees bend

POWERLIFTING

WHERE WEIGHTLIFTING REQUIRES EXCELLENT TECHNIQUE ALLIED TO
STRENGTH, POWERLIFTING GAUGES OUT-AND-OUT STRENGTH ALONE

The same bar is used as in weightlifting. The same circular weights are used in the same colours – 50kg (110lb) green, 25kg (55lb) red and 20kg (44lb) blue – but powerlifting also uses a 45kg (99lb) weight (gold). The competition weight categories are the same, but with an extra class – where weightlifting puts all men over 108kg (242lb) together, powerlifting has another division at 125kg (275lb). Similarly, there is an extra class for women of over 90kg (198lb).

There are three different lifts: the squat, bench press and deadlift. The competitor has three attempts at each and his result is the aggregate weight of his best in each category. In the case of a tie, the lifter with the lighter bodyweight wins.

SQUAT

The bar rests on a stand at a height convenient to the lifter, who then takes the weight across his shoulders, behind his head. With his feet set slightly wider than his hips, he lowers himself into the squat position. His head is up, his back straight and his knees pointing outwards.

He must not squat completely, with his bottom on his heels, but must start his recovery at once by standing up again. This is the toughest part of the lift, as the strong muscles on the inside of the thigh tend to pull the knees inwards, throwing the lifter off balance and straining the lower back.

BENCH PRESS

The competitor lies on a small, solid bench 45cm (18in) high. Buttocks, shoulders and head are braced against the bench, but the knees are bent and the feet flat on the floor. When he is in position with his forearms vertical, the bar is put in his hands and he lowers it comfortably to his chest. On the referee's signal, he pushes upwards as hard as possible, testing first the pectoral and then the triceps muscles. When the arms are straight and the bar steady, the attendants remove it.

Britain's greatest-ever powerlifter, Ronald Collins (eight times World Champion in the 1970s), developed a way of arching the back for the bench press that now bears his name – the Collins Arch – and is used by all leading lifters. For maximum effect, the arch must be high and has to be maintained throughout the lift.

DEADLIFT

This may not be dramatic, but as a sheer test of brute strength there is nothing to beat the two-hands deadlift. The bar is on the ground. The competitor has to bend down, pick it up and in one continuous smooth movement lift it to his thighs.

The grip used is called hooking, with the fingers wrapped tightly over the thumb. Because the sudden violence of the pull tends to make the bar roll in the hands, lifters use an alternate gripping method: one hand faces forward, the other backward.

With the feet comfortably under the bar and the hands well apart, the lifter needs a pull that is inclined inwards, as a vertical one would pull his body forward and off balance. The most difficult part comes when the bar is knee-high and the pressure is on the fulcrum of the hips and the muscles of the back. The body then wants to lay back, but this is not allowed. The back must be absolutely straight, with the head up, the chest high, shoulders braced and the knees locked.

Powerlifting is a specialist sport, yet many people are familiar with it through weight training in the gym. Some ex-shot putters are now successful powerlifters, particularly in the USA.

PUMPING IRON

Powerlifting's living legend is Paul Anderson. After winning the heavyweight weightlifting title at the 1956 Olympic Games, the 24-year-old American hoisted nearly three tons using a back lift. The 165kg (26st) giant raised 2844kg (447st) . . . that's 17 times his own bodyweight. As a professional powerlifter he notched up 1200kg (188st) with three lifts – 544kg (85st) squat, 284kg (45st) press and 371kg (58st) dead lift. He was nicknamed 'The Dixie Derrick'.

WORDS

Barbell: steel bar to which heavy discs (weights) are added

Bench press: lift executed by competition, lying on the bench

Deadlift: lifting barbell from ground to thigh level

Hooking: grip where thumb is under fingers

Lift: often means a good, clean, successful lift

No lift: an illegal attempt

Power set: the three powerlifting lifts; bench press, dead lift and squat

Weigh-in: all lifters are weighed naked before a competition to ensure that they are in the correct weight division

Professional wrestling has had a new lease of life on television in Europe with the arrival of American show-biz style competitions, complete with make-up and costumes.

WRESTLING

WRESTLING IS ONE OF THE OLDEST, MOST BASIC
AND MOST NATURAL OF SPORTS

Many nations, and regions within nations, have maintained their traditional form of wrestling – sumo in Japan, kushti in Iran, glima in Iceland, Cumberland and Westmoreland in England – but only three are recognized by the international governing body and have world championships. Of these, sambo is a Russian form of jacket-wrestling with similarities to judo, and does not appear in the Olympic Games. The other two do. In the Greco-Roman style (almost unknown in Britain), wrestlers may not seize the opponent below the hips nor grip with the legs. In most other respects, the rules are exactly the same as for the more popular freestyle, and they both have the same 10 weight categories.

The fighting area is a circle 9m (10yd) in diameter, inside which is a broad red strip that shows wrestlers when they are near the limit. Competitors wear either a red or a blue leotard, which leaves most of the upper chest and shoulders bare, and lightweight boots.

Ideally, a bout is won when a wrestler pins his opponent's shoulders squarely on the mat for one second. Known as a fall, this is the equivalent of a knockout in boxing and the bout ends. Usually, a bout goes the distance (three rounds of three minutes' actual fighting each) and the decision is on points.

FACT FILE

Although Olympic wrestling is limited to two styles – freestyle and Greco-Roman – the sport is one of the oldest and most traditional in the world. Wall paintings depict special grips and holds in Ancient Egypt in 2350BC. In Iran, kushti wrestlers wear leather trousers, while in Iceland, where glima is practised, the competitors wear a special harness. Russia's sambo wrestlers are akin to judo players in skill, wearing jackets while yagli wrestlers in Turkey grease their upper bodies and wear tight leather trousers. By contrast, Swiss Schwingen wrestlers have short leather trousers which have to be gripped at the back and leg as competitors, as in all wrestling, attempt to throw opponents to the ground.

It's all a matter of timing – converting an opponent's energy into his downfall.

Amateur

Amateur wrestling is a very clean sport, with no hair pulling, ear twisting or bending an opponent's arm behind his back more than 45 degrees. Points are immediately subtracted for unfair or dangerous tactics, even to the extent that a competitor must drop to one knee when throwing an opponent to lessen the impact and the chance of injury.

There is a good deal of valuable cross-fertilization between wrestling and judo despite their obvious differences. There are no strangleholds or armlocks allowed in wrestling, for instance, and throws are seldom as decisive because it is difficult to maintain a firm grip on an unclothed body.

Greco-Roman wrestling tends to be more static than freestyle, as only the top part of the body can be grasped and there is no diving at the legs, nor tripping sweeps with the feet.

Professional

Television has made millions of professional wrestling fans around the world. Compared with the strict rules of amateur wrestling, professional wrestling has all the elements of show-business – paid performers, glamorous stage names, flamboyant attire, and spectacular acrobatics. All forms of wrestling are based on physical strength with both men in the same weight category, so each tries to overpower the other by seeking out his weaknesses. The first move is to engage the wrestler's hold when the two link up by putting one arm around the opponent's neck and grabbing the other arm. They then try to pull each other down to the canvas or try to throw each other by using a variety of throws such as a standing cross buttock. This is the throw that many children use naturally in the playground, using a hold round the neck and the hip as a pivot. A standing flying mare is executed by throwing an opponent over the shoulder after grabbing an arm as a lever. A neck mare involves a hold around the neck and a throw over the shoulder. More spectacular is the drop kick. As an opponent moves into attack, the wrestler throws his feet up into the air, trying to plant them flat on the attacker's face or body. Also effective is the monkey climb. Clasping his hands behind his opponent's neck (facing him), the wrestler jumps up and puts his feet on the outside of the groin. By pulling backwards, the opponent shoots into the air!

All wrestlers have favourite holds and some prefer to grapple on the floor. The single leg Boston crab can be a very painful hold putting pressure on the knee as well as the base of the spine. To carry out the standing full Nelson a wrestler has to slip round to the back of his opponent where he puts his hands under the opponent's arms and then grips them together at the back of the man's neck, clasped in an unbreakable butcher's grip, with the fingers interlocked.

The winning wrestler is the first to achieve two falls, two submissions or a knockout. A fall is given when both shoulder blades are held down on the canvas for a three-second count. A submission occurs when one wrestler secures his opponent in a hold that is not only unbreakable but also painful. To stop suffering the wrestler taps the canvas to acknowledge defeat. However, a referee may have to intervene to prevent a stubborn wrestler being injured. A knockout is awarded if a wrestler, like a boxer, does not recover in 10 seconds. If he is thrown out of the ring at any time, he has to climb back before the 10-second count is over in order to continue.

The referee must not allow any choke holds, which cut off the air supply in any way. European wrestling is not too keen on sleeper holds, although they are allowed in North America. These are executed by putting pressure on the side of the temple which cuts off the blood supply to the head and renders a wrestler unconscious quite quickly. Eyes must not be gouged, but ears tend to take a pounding. Forearm smashes to the head cause cauliflower (swollen) ears with the bone at the point of the elbow causing the damage. As long as breathing is not hampered, no-one worries too much about noses!

While forearm smashes to the chest or head are allowed, punches with the fist are not. Chops or blows with the side or the flat of the hand are common.

The most lethal move is the piledriver, which requires tremendous strength as a wrestler picks up his opponent, turning him upside down, with one hand holding the crotch, the other the shoulder in the bodyslam position – with the feet pointing at the lights and the head down at the canvas. Trapping the unfortunate opponent's head between his knees, the wrestler then drops to his knees, thus hitting the head on the canvas, like a piledriver. Not surprisingly, this vicious type of move usually produces a knockout.

However much the pro wrestlers choreograph their matches, they still hit the deck hard.

ACKNOWLEDGEMENTS

Additional research: David Hunn, Simon Mann, Matthew Carter, Nicola Fairbrother
Photographs: Allsport, Canon Renault, Tom Arnold.